The Saints
From A to Z

An Inspirational Dictionary

CYNTHIA CAVNAR

CH*A*RIS

SERVANT PUBLICATIONS
ANN ARBOR, MICHIGAN

Charis Books is an imprint of Servant Publications especially designed to serve Roman Catholics.

This book does not intend to anticipate the judgment of the church regarding the sanctity and ultimate canonization of the individuals herein. Such decisions remain under the jurisdiction of the church.

Servant Publications
P.O. Box 8617
Ann Arbor, MI 48107

Cover design by Paz Design Group, Salem, Oregon

00 01 02 03 10 9 8 7 6 5 4 3 2 1

Printed in the United States of America
ISBN 1-56955-190-1

LIBRARY OF CONGRESS CATALOGING-IN-PUBLICATION DATA

Cavnar, Cindy.
    The saints from A to Z / Cynthia Cavnar.
        p.   cm.
    Includes bibliographical references and index.
    ISBN 1-56955-190-1 (alk. paper)
    1. Christian saints—Biography—Dictionaries.   I. Title.

BX4655.8.C38 2000
282'.092'2—dc21
    [B]   00-060263

Acknowledgments

I would like to thank James C.G. Conniff for his excellent editorial advice and Fr. Leo Cooper, archivist for the Catholic Archdiocese of Kansas City in Kansas, for use of the archdiocesan library. Many thanks also to Nick, Tim, Matt, and Anna for their support and for patiently listening to endless stories about the saints.

Contents

A Note to the Reader

This book is a dictionary not only of saints but also of those on the way to sainthood. These are known by the successive titles of Servant of God, Venerable, and Blessed, the three stages preceding canonization. With canonization comes the designation as Saint.

The Vatican confers the title Servant of God when it decides that it has no objections to a candidate's cause for sainthood moving forward (Dorothy Day, for example, falls in this category). Once the cause has been thoroughly investigated and it has been determined that the individual lived a life of heroic virtue, he or she receives the title "Venerable" (Pierre Toussaint, for example).

At this point, a miracle—usually a physical healing—must take place through the intercession of the candidate. Once a miracle has been accepted by a panel of doctors (Vatican standards are extremely exacting), the candidate is beatified and is named "Blessed." No miracle is required for the beatification of martyrs. With beatification, the Vatican permits the public veneration of the Blessed but almost always restricts such veneration to a particular diocese or country or religious order. (Acknowledging that, the feast days of Blesseds are included in this book to better serve Catholics worldwide).

Another miracle is required for canonization. When the Vatican approves that final miracle, the candidate is declared a saint and venerated throughout the universal church.

1. Servant of God
2. Venerable
3. Blessed
4. Saint

A

Alacoque, St. Margaret Mary

(1647-1690. B. at Janot, France; d. at Paray-le-Monial.) Margaret Mary's teenage years took place in an atmosphere that can best be described as abusive. Her father died when she was eight and Margaret Mary, sent away to school, soon fell ill with rheumatic fever. "For four years I was unable to walk, my bones piercing my skin," she said. She recovered and returned home to discover that her mother had ceded control of the house to relatives. "She and I were reduced to a state of captivity ... Everything was kept under lock and key [and] I was ... even obliged to borrow both hat and coat." She endured the "continual martyrdom," as she called it, heroically, developed a strong interior life, and resisted her family's attempts to marry her off. Instead, she became a nun of the Visitation Convent at Paray-le-Monial in 1671. Here, she soon experienced visions of Christ.

In December 1673 she received the first of a series of revelations in which Christ told her to spread the love of his Sacred Heart throughout the world. This devotion was to include receiving communion on the first Friday of every month and spending an hour in prayer each Thursday in remembrance of Christ's suffering at Gethsemane. Also, Margaret Mary was to help establish a feast day honoring the Sacred Heart. "This divine heart is an ocean full of all good things wherein poor souls can cast all their needs," she wrote.

Margaret Mary encountered opposition to her task from her superior, theologians, and fellow nuns. Ultimately, she received the necessary support, and before her death, the devotion began to spread through France. It was helpful in countering the religious indifference common at the time as well as the severity dominating the French church due to the Jansenist heresy. Feast: October 16.

Albert the Great, St.

(1206-1280. B. at Lauingen, Swabia; d. at Cologne.) One of the greatest intellects of the medieval church, Albert the Great spent his last years a victim of what today might be diagnosed as a type of dementia. The illness progressed rapidly following a brilliant career in the academic world.

Albert entered the Dominican order in 1222, and for the next twenty years taught in Germany and then Paris, where he also earned a master's degree in 1248. He served as director of studies at the Dominican house in Cologne, where he recognized and championed the brilliance of his student St. Thomas Aquinas. Albert worked for the Dominicans in a number of capacities, organizing the studies for the whole order, serving as provincial in Germany, defending the Dominicans in Rome against unfounded accusations, and participating in the general council of the church at Lyons. He was appointed bishop of Regensburg in 1260 but was allowed to resign after two years and resume teaching.

Albert's contemporaries called him the "Universal Doctor," and "the Great," and said he was "no less than godlike" because of his powerful intellect and encyclopedic knowledge. He wrote extensively on biblical and theological topics as well as the natural sciences, and his wide-ranging interests took him into biology, physics, geography, geology, and botany. He applied Aristotelian philosophy to Christian thought, thus pioneering the Scholastic method developed by Aquinas and central to much of Catholic theology.

In 1278, Albert's memory suddenly failed him while he was giving a lecture. Within two years, his memory loss was virtually complete and he died peacefully in Cologne. He is a Doctor of the Church. Feast: November 15.

Al-Hardini, Bd. Nimatullah Youssef Kassab

(1808-1859. B. at Hardin, Lebanon; d. at Kfifan.) The monk Al-Hardini was strict with himself but so indulgent toward his fellow monks that he supported their right to smoke. When his monastery attempted to prohibit the pastime, he objected. Al-Hardini was ordained a priest of the Lebanese Maronite Order and served as a professor and director of their school at Kfifan (the Maronite church is one of the eastern churches in communion with Rome). He had a great love for Mary and was particularly devoted to the Blessed Sacrament. Often, he could be found in the chapel on his knees, arms raised in the form of a cross as he gazed at the tabernacle.

Al-Hardini resisted the temptation to become a hermit because "those who struggle for virtue in community life will have greater merit," he said. Within the community, he was known as an especially devout, gentle, and kind man who believed that "a monk's first concern ... should be not to hurt or trouble his confreres." He was appointed general assistant of the order in 1845. Numerous miracles have been attributed to his intercession both before and after his death, including the healing of a Lebanese man terminally ill with leukemia.

Alipius, St.

(c. 360-430. B./d. at Tagaste, Africa.)
Most of what we know of Alipius
comes from the writings of his close
friend, St. Augustine. Alipius studied
under Augustine, who was about six
years his senior, at Tagaste and
Carthage. "I was fond of him,"
Augustine said, "because ... he had
much natural disposition to goodness."
Unfortunately, Alipius became addicted
to the bloodthirsty gladiatorial games,
an obsession that threatened "to ruin a
future that promised so well." Learning
of Augustine's disapproval, Alipius managed through sheer self-control to overcome the habit. Some time later, however, he allowed friends to lure him to
the games and succumbed again,
"drunk with the fascination." Augustine
credited God with helping his friend
conquer his addiction: "You taught him
to trust in you, not in himself."

Alipius went to Rome, studied law,
and eventually was appointed to a judi-
cial office. Augustine joined him there
and they moved to Milan in 384.
Alipius was with his friend when
Augustine decided to become a
Christian and Alipius converted, too, a
decision that "very well suited his moral
character, which had long been far, far
better than my own," Augustine wrote.
The men moved back to Africa, lived a
devout community life with others, and
were ordained priests.

Alipius became bishop of Tagaste in
about 393, and remained Augustine's
close friend and confidant. He died in
430, probably not long after Augustine.
Feast: August 15.

Ambrose, St.

(c. 340-397. B. at Trier; d. at Milan.)
Ambrose was the governor of the
province of Emilia-Liguria, which he
ruled from Milan, seat of the Imperial
government in the west. The Arian
heresy divided the church at Milan as
elsewhere. On the death of the city's
Arian bishop, Ambrose went to the
church—where both Arian and
Catholic believers had gathered—to
exhort the crowd to remain peaceful.
To his surprise, both sides took up the
chant, "Ambrose, bishop." Though he
was still a catechumen and unbaptized,
the emperor ordered the well-loved but
reluctant Ambrose to take up the post.
He was baptized and a week later consecrated bishop on December 7, 374.

He immediately gave everything he
owned to the poor and devoted himself
to theological study and pastoral work.
He himself prepared catechumens for
baptism, and it is said that when he
heard confessions, he wept with the
penitent. He cleansed his diocese of the
Arian heresy even when his stand
brought him into conflict with the
authorities. He preached regularly and
effectively (he impressed Augustine, his

most famous convert) and kept open hours at his house during which anyone could come and speak to him.

Ambrose's position in the imperial city necessarily involved him in politics. He didn't hesitate to rebuke emperors as when, for example, he demanded that Theodosius I do public penance for ordering a massacre of some seven thousand men, women, and children. On two occasions, he refused to hand over churches for the use of Arians and once, in a dispute with the Arian Empress Justina, occupied a church with his congregation to make his point. During the occupation, he led them in singing psalms and hymns and also preached, enunciating his famous principle: "The Emperor is within the church, not above it." Ambrose also thwarted an imperial effort to reinstate the cult of the goddess of victory.

He wrote numerous moral, exegetical, and dogmatic works as well as sermons, letters, and hymns. He was "a faithful leader of the church," Augustine said, "...even at peril of life itself." Feast: December 7.

Anchieta, Bd. Joseph de

(1534-1597. B. at Tenerife, Canary Islands; d. in Brazil.) Anchieta joined the Jesuits as a teenager and went to Brazil in 1553 as a missionary. It was hoped that the mild climate would improve the chronic back pain he suf-

fered as a result of an accident. Despite the fact that there was no improvement, Anchieta ministered effectively in Brazil for forty-four years.

He worked among the rain forest people, to whom he became deeply attached. He learned various native languages and wrote plays for the Indians, having noted their interest in drama. He also wrote a popular catechism. Once, when taken hostage by a tribe, Anchieta spent his five months of detainment composing a poem in honor of the Blessed Mother. Lacking pen or paper, he composed in wet sand, committed the four thousand lines to memory, and wrote them down when freed.

Anchieta defended the Indians from Portuguese commercial interests and traveled extensively throughout Brazil without concern for danger or comfort. To those interested in similar work, he said that enthusiasm was not enough for success: "You must come with a bag-full of virtues." Feast: June 9.

Andrew, Bd.

(c. 1625-1644. B. at RanRan, Vietnam; d. at Ke Cham.) Andrew was educated by a Jesuit missionary, Fr. De Rhodes. Baptized when he was fifteen, he became a catechist, made a public, formal vow to serve the church by spreading the gospel, then threw himself into his apostolate. A year later, in

1644, authorities attempted to halt the growth of Christianity in Vietnam by first directing their attention to the Vietnamese catechists. Soldiers arrested Andrew, who was about nineteen, on July 25, and brought him before the governor. They reported that from the time of his arrest, he "had continually spoken of the law of Christ, with exhortations to accept this law." The governor, unable to shake the catechist's faith, sent him to prison where he encouraged others, saying: "Let us give love for love to our God ... life for life."

The next day, the governor sentenced him to death. At five in the afternoon, tightly surrounded by soldiers, Andrew walked through the streets to a field outside the city. Fr. De Rhodes received permission to spread a mat under Andrew to collect his blood, as was customary, but Andrew preferred his blood fall to the ground in imitation of Christ. He asked the Christians present to pray for him and encouraged them to remain faithful. Soldiers pierced his left side repeatedly with a lance. As one beheaded him, Andrew said "Jesus" and died. Feast: July 26.

Andrew, St.

(first century) Andrew was a disciple of John the Baptist, one of the twelve apostles, and the brother of St. Peter. He was a fisherman, lived at Capernaum, and is always one of the first four in the lists of the twelve apostles. According to tradition, he preached in northeastern Greece, although completely unreliable accounts place him in Ethiopia. He was said to have been crucified on an X-shaped cross in Patras, Greece, although the description of the cross can be traced back no farther than the fourteenth century. Similarly, all accounts of his later life and death are unreliable. He is the patron saint of Russia because he was said to have preached there. He is the patron saint of Scotland because, according to legend, a disciple in the fourth century took his relics there at the direction of an angel and built a church where the angel told him to stop. Over the centuries, various parts of his supposed relics traveled to Greece, Constantinople, Scotland, and Italy, his head remaining in Rome for six centuries. It was returned to Constantinople in 1972. Feast: November 30.

Angelico, Bd. Fra

(c. 1400-1455. B. at Vicchio di Mugello, Italy; d. at Rome.) Named as patron of Catholic artists by Pope John Paul II, Fra Angelico—born Guido di Piero—grew up near Florence, Italy. He was a painter prior to entering the Dominican order around 1420. His religious name was Fra Giovanni but he earned the soubriquet "Angelico," perhaps due to the religious feeling of his work or to his use of angels. He continued to pursue his art after ordination in about 1429.

His works include a crucifixion and other studies he painted on the walls of the monastery at San Marco; The Last Judgment; The Descent from the Cross; Coronation of the Virgin; and scenes from the lives of St. Stephen and St. Lawrence that he painted for a chapel in the Vatican. Michelangelo said of him: "One has to believe that this good monk has visited paradise and been allowed to choose his models there."

Fra Angelico was active in the administration of his order, serving as prior for two years, but refused an appointment to serve as archbishop of Florence. A contemporary wrote that he was "a magnificent brother, a master painter, famous above all the painters of Italy." His genius is evident in his many surviving works, revealing his spiritual sensitivity as well as his grasp of color, perspective, and light. Feast: February 18.

Anthony of Egypt, St.

(c. 251-356. B. near Memphis, Egypt; d. at Mount Kolzim.) Anthony is regarded as one of the founders of monasticism even though he lived most of his 105 years as a hermit in the deserts of Egypt. He was born to well-to-do Christian parents who died when he was about twenty. Several months later, he gave away his inheritance and retired to the desert when he heard the Gospel passage: "If you wish to be perfect, go, sell what you have and give to the poor.... Then come, follow me" (Mt 19:21). For the next thirty years, he lived a solitary life of prayer and penance, struggling with violent temptations and, it is said, demonic assaults. Around the year 306, he emerged from solitude and organized the disciples who had gathered in the area around him into a loose monastic community under a rule.

In 311, during an outbreak of persecution, Anthony went to Alexandria to encourage the martyrs there. He himself "burned with the desire for martyrdom," wrote St. Athanasius, Anthony's friend and biographer, "but he did not think it right actually to give himself up." The judge failed to arrest him, even when, having been banished from court, Anthony showed up there to support the martyrs. When the persecution ended, he returned to the desert in about 313, founded another monastic community, and then retreated to a cave on Mount Kolzim where he lived for the rest of his life. He returned to Alexandria briefly in his eighties to help Athanasius refute the supporters of the Arian heresy.

Anthony was known for his wisdom, holiness, and insight into human nature, and many came to the desert for his advice. He is a leading example of the "Desert Fathers," those men of the fourth century who, following the end of widespread persecution, went to the wilderness in search of a more dedicated Christian life. Feast: January 17.

Anthony of Padua, St.

(c. 1193-1231. B. at Lisbon, Portugal; d. near Padua, Italy.) Anthony joined the Canons Regular of St. Augustine when he was fifteen and over the next eight years of study developed an extraordinary knowledge of Scripture, the foundation for his future ministry.

When he was about twenty-five, he met some Franciscans who were martyred shortly after in Morocco. Moved by their sacrifice and wanting to imitate them, Anthony transferred to the Franciscan order in 1220. He became ill on his first missionary trip to Morocco and returned to Europe, where the Franciscans assigned him to a hermitage near Forli. He divided his time between prayer and menial chores. One day at an ordination, his superior asked him to preach extemporaneously since no one else had come prepared to speak. His years of prayer and study converged at this moment and his words impressed his audience. He was immediately assigned to preach throughout the area, and St. Francis himself approved his appointment as theology teacher to his fellow Franciscans.

Anthony's learning, eloquence, and zeal drew many back to the faith, and he often preached in the open air, since no building was large enough to accommodate the huge crowds. He had enormous moral courage that empowered him to preach against the oppression of the poor, the immorality of the clergy, and the many heresies flourishing at the time. He was known as the Hammer of the Heretics and the Repository of Scripture.

Anthony's reputation as the saint who intercedes for the return of lost or stolen items possibly dates to an incident in his own life. A novice quit the order and left, secretly taking Anthony's psalter with him. Anthony prayed for the book's return and the novice came back, rejoined the community, and restored the psalter to Anthony. The core of this story seems to be true although it was later embellished with fantasy.

The church honors Anthony for his biblical scholarship rooted in deep piety and love for the poor. He died at the age of thirty-six. He was declared a Doctor of the Church in 1946. Feast: June 13.

Apor, Bd. Vilmos

(1892-1945. B. at Segesvar, Transylvania; d. at Gyor.) Apor was a Hungarian bishop whose courageous defense of Jews and other minorities led to his death during World War II. He was ordained a priest in 1915 and earned an immediate reputation for caring about the poor and for social justice. Once, a visitor found him barefoot because he had given away his shoes to a poverty-stricken father of seven. He also established himself as an ecumenist, and over a twenty-five-year period "created and maintained a golden age of denominational peace," according to the dean of Guyla's Reformed Church.

Apor was appointed bishop of Gyor in 1940 and during World War II was outspoken in his defense of the Jews. He assisted Jewish refugees, tried to visit those in the camps but was refused permission, and went to German headquarters to try to block their deportation. "One cannot tolerate anti-Semitism," he wrote to another bishop. "It must be condemned.... One must state openly that nobody may be punished for the blood in his veins."

In 1945, fighting began in Gyor between Russians and Germans. The bishop was sheltering about four hundred people in the massive cellars of his residence when Russian soldiers threatened to harm one of the women. Vilmos came to her defense, and when he told the soldiers to leave, one of them shot him. He died several days later. Feast: April 1.

Athanasius, St.

(295-373. B./d. at Alexandria, Egypt.) Athanasius was a pivotal figure during the doctrinal controversies of the early church. For nearly fifty years he fought to establish the doctrine that Jesus is truly God and truly man in opposition to the well-entrenched Arian heresy that denied the full divinity of Christ. He endured exile, slander, and the political whims of emperors and for a time was a hunted man with a price on his head.

As deacon and secretary to the bishop of Alexandria, Athanasius attended the Council of Nicaea with him in 325. The Council condemned Arianism, stating in a crucial formula that the Son is "of one substance" with the Father. Shortly after, on the death of the bishop, Athanasius was elected to the office and spent the first seven years overseeing his diocese while the Arian party intrigued against him for his refusal to compromise with them. A campaign of harassment entangled him in civil charges—all proved false—involving taxes, sacrilege, and the murder of an Arian bishop. In fact, the Arian bishop was alive, his cohorts having bribed him to go into hiding.

Nevertheless, Athanasius was summoned to appear before a council at Tyre, where the pro-Arian forces managed to secure his exile. Two years later the emperor recalled him, but

Athanasius endured four more exiles over the course of his life, including a six-year stretch he spent hiding in the desert. He continued to direct his diocese from there. The church in Alexandria suffered too, at one time living under an Arian bishop imposed by force, at other times enduring persecution that included the sacking of the cathedral.

The people were deeply devoted to Athanasius and on his return from exile in 346 they streamed out to meet him "like a second Nile," cheering as they accompanied him into the city. That return was followed by ten years of peace and widespread spiritual revival. These were Athanasius' most productive years, not only in terms of the spiritual life of his diocese but also in his output of writings that refuted the Arians theologically and exposed their political machinations. He spent his last seven years peacefully in Alexandria, working for reconciliation in the church.

Athanasius is one of the most important figures in Christian history for having steadfastly defended the faith against overwhelming odds at a crucial moment of doctrinal development. Athanasius also assisted the monks who spearheaded the ascetic movement in the deserts of Egypt and was a friend of Sts. Pachomius and Anthony. His well-known biography of Anthony introduced monasticism to the West. He is a Greek Doctor of the Church. Feast: May 2.

Augustine of Canterbury, St.

(D. c. 604 at England.) Pope St. Gregory the Great sent the monk Augustine and about thirty fellow monks to evangelize England in 596. At Provence, fear of the unknown troubled the party and they petitioned the pope to turn back. "It is better never to undertake any high enterprise than to abandon it when once begun," Gregory wrote them, and refused permission. Gregory made Augustine a bishop (later an archbishop) and the group arrived in Kent in 597. Within a few years, they converted the king of Kent and many of his subjects. According to St. Bede, the historian, their success was due in large measure to the simplicity of their life. "They were constantly at prayer; they fasted and kept vigils, they preached the word ... they regarded worldly things as of little importance...." Gregory guided the enterprise by letter, Augustine submitting even the smallest concern to him. Augustine successfully established two dioceses beyond his own, one at London and one at Rochester. He was the first archbishop of Canterbury. Feast: May 27.

Augustine of Hippo, St.

(354-430. B. at Tagaste, Africa; d. at
Hippo.) Augustine was born to
Patricius, a pagan who became a
Christian shortly before his death, and
Monica, a Christian and model of
virtue. Monica raised him in the faith
but he was not baptized (at the time
baptism was frequently reserved for
adulthood). When he was sixteen,
Augustine went to school in Carthage,
where he quickly shed any vestiges of
Christianity and indulged in a profligate
lifestyle. He took a mistress when he
was eighteen, and they remained
together for about fifteen years,
producing a son, Adeodatus.

Augustine studied rhetoric, developed an interest in philosophy, and
became a member of the Manichaean
sect. He remained a member for nine
years, but finally became disillusioned
when a celebrated Manichaean leader
was unable to answer Augustine's prob-
ing questions about their faith. He
taught rhetoric and grammar at
Carthage but in 383 went to Rome to
open a school there. "I had heard that
the behavior of young students at
Rome was quieter," he said.
Unfortunately, the students had a habit
of switching masters frequently to avoid
paying tuition, and after a year of this,
Augustine moved to Milan. There,
attracted by Neoplatonic works and by
the preaching and insight of Ambrose,
the bishop of Milan, he gradually drew
nearer to Christianity.

Augustine's mother moved to Milan
and renewed her influence over her son.
He sent his mistress away, torn between
his attraction to the world on the one
hand and his desire to live for God on
the other. He was particularly troubled
by the thought of living a chaste life.
Unable to make up his mind, he went
to the garden of a friend and there, in
an agony of indecision, threw himself
down beneath a tree. As he wept, he
heard the voice of a child playing in a
nearby house, chanting, "Take it and
read, take it and read." Augustine saw
this as a sign, picked up the Bible, and
read the first passage his eye came
upon: "Let us conduct ourselves
properly as in the day, not in orgies
and drunkenness, not in promiscuity
and licentiousness.... But put on the
Lord Jesus Christ and make no
provision for the desires of the flesh"
(Rom 13:13-14). The incident
completed Augustine's conversion.
He and his son, Adeodatus, to whom
he was devoted, were baptized and
returned to Africa but the son died not
long after. Augustine lived a kind of
monastic life with some friends and was
ordained a priest in 391. In 396 he was
named bishop of Hippo, an office he
held until his death.

Augustine told his life story down
through his conversion in his autobiography, *Confessions*, one of the greatest
explorations of human psychology and

religious motivation in all literature. He wrote *The City of God*, another great work, in response to pagan accusations blaming Christians for various calamities. Augustine was a prolific writer: over 113 of his books and treatises survive as well as 200 letters and 500 sermons. His writings include polemical works that reflect his battles with various heresies; philosophical, moral, pastoral, and dogmatic works; and writings on Scripture. His contemporaries recognized his genius: "Hail to thee," St. Jerome wrote. "The world resounds with thy praise. The Catholics admire thee as the restorer of the ancient faith."

Augustine ranks as one of the greatest theologians of all time, providing tremendous impetus to the development of Christian thought on such topics as the Trinity, grace, the sacraments, and the church. Not all of his conclusions are congenial to modern religious understanding, but his intelligence, piety, and pastoral sensibility have had a fundamental influence on Catholic theology. His warm personality coupled with his unparalleled intellect continues to influence readers through the ages. Augustine died of a fever at the age of seventy-six, during the siege of Hippo by the Vandals. He is a Doctor of the Church. Feast: August 28.

B

Bakanja, Bd. Isidore

(c. 1887-1909. B. at Ikengo, Democratic Republic of Congo; d. at Busira.) Isidore, born to pagan parents, worked as a bricklayer for a Belgian company in Mbandaka. There he first learned about Catholicism, became a zealous catechumen, and was baptized in 1906. Later, he took a job as servant to a director of a Belgian mining company. While visiting the company's mines, Bakanja met a local manager, Van Cauter, who hated Catholicism and feared that the faith undermined European authority over the Africans.

Van Cauter insisted Isidore stop catechizing the other Africans and ordered him to remove the scapular of the Blessed Virgin from around his neck. When Isidore refused, Van Cauter ripped the scapular off and had Isidore beaten with an elephant hide whip studded with nails. Isidore was then chained to a single spot and left alone in a filthy room, his wounds unattended. Van Cauter attempted to hide the incident from the visiting camp director and forced Isidore into the forest.

But Isidore emerged and came before the director. "I saw a man come from the forest with his back torn apart by deep, festering, malodorous wounds, covered with filth, assaulted by flies,"

the director wrote. "He leaned on two sticks in order to get near me—he wasn't walking, he was dragging himself." The director dressed his wounds and sent him to safety in Busira, where after six months of suffering, Isidore died. "I am dying because I'm a Christian," he said. "The white man didn't like Christians.... He yelled at me when I said my prayers." He had publicly forgiven Van Cauter, who was tried and sent to prison. Feast: August 15.

Bakhita, Bd. Josephine

(1868-1947. B. near Nyala, Sudan; d. at Schio, Italy.) Slave traders kidnapped Bakhita when she was nine years old and sold her into slavery, where a series of owners treated her badly. One beat her senseless for breaking a vase. Another, wanting a fashionable-looking slave, had her tattooed, a process that involved pouring salt into sixty incisions on her torso. "I thought I would die," Bakhita wrote of the experience.

Eventually the Italian vice-consul bought her, took her to Italy, and gave her to a Signora Michieli. Bakhita served as companion to the Signora's daughter, and together they boarded at the Venice convent of the Daughters of Charity of Canossa. There, Bakhita became a Christian: "I had asked who could be the master of the sun, moon, and stars. Now at last I knew him." She refused to leave when the Signora came for her. Slavery was illegal in Italy, and the authorities sided with Bakhita, who then became a Canossian sister and remained one for fifty years. She was known for her outstanding holiness, charity toward all, and good humor. Feast: February 8.

Barberi, Bd. Dominic (of the Mother of God)

(1792-1849. B. near Viterbo, Italy; d. at Reading, England.) Barberi was a Passionist priest who, for twenty-six years, nurtured the hope that he would serve as a missionary in England (the Passionists had no houses in that country, which was still suffering from centuries of anti-Catholic discrimination). In 1814, still only a novice, he had a revelation while at prayer. He saw "the date when, as an ordained priest, I would begin my ministry and where among dissident Christians I would work: in northwestern Europe, and England in particular." He served as provincial of the order, established a Passionist presence in Belgium, and in 1840, founded a house in England at Staffordshire.

Dominic lived in complete poverty there, and his shabby appearance combined with his heavily accented English initially made him an object of scorn.

However, his humility and voluntary poverty soon won many over, and miracles were attributed to him. He is best known for receiving John Henry Newman into the church at Littlemore in 1845. "All that I have suffered since I left Italy has been well-compensated by this event," Barberi wrote. Newman's conversion rocked the Anglican world, and many assumed Barberi had somehow lured him into the church. However, Newman later wrote that he had encountered him only briefly once before: "[Fr. Dominic] is a simple, holy man and withal gifted with remarkable powers. He does not know of my intention but I mean to ask of him admission into the One Fold of Christ...." Feast: August 27.

Barbieri, St. Clelia

(1847-1870. B./d. at Le Budrie, Italy.) At Barbieri's beatification in 1968, the pope called attention to her "interior innocence." She had a ready smile and an unaffected goodness, and she asked, at her confirmation, how a person goes about becoming a saint. In answer to her own question, she decided to devote herself to God within the context of her own parish. She taught religious education and cared for the sick and elderly, and in this, she is a model for Catholic parishioners today.

Soon several women joined her, and in 1868, Barbieri and three of her followers moved into a house next to the church. This was the beginning of the Little Sisters of Our Lady of Sorrows, dedicated to parish work, the needy, and education. The parish priest, Gaetano Guidi, guided the women and, in the anticlerical atmosphere of the times, suffered much persecution on their behalf. (He was arrested twice while the state launched an investigation against the institute. The inquiry cleared both the priest and the congregation.) Barbieri experienced mystical graces in prayer, including ecstasies and levitation, but died at the age of twenty-three of tuberculosis. Her order merged with the Servants of Mary in 1951. Feast: July 13.

Bartholomew, St.

(first century) The synoptic Gospels and the Book of Acts name Bartholomew as one of the twelve apostles. Some scholars also identify him as the apostle named Nathanael in John's Gospel. That Gospel says of Nathanael that Jesus hailed him as "a true Israelite. There is no duplicity in him" (Jn 1:47). Apart from references in Scripture, nothing certain is known of him. According to Eusebius' *History of the Church* (c. 323), he traveled to India, where he left behind a copy of the Gospel of Matthew. *The Roman Martyrology* says he preached in Armenia, where he was flayed alive

before being beheaded. His body was said to have been taken to Rome and buried at the site of the present Church of St. Bartholomew. Feast: August 24.

Basil, St.

(329-379. B./d. at Caesarea, Cappadocia.) Basil's wealthy, pious family produced seven saints, including Basil, three of his siblings, his parents, and his grandmother. Basil was well educated and taught rhetoric but abandoned his promising career to live as a monk. He is considered the father of communal monasticism in the Eastern church. After five years with the community and another five years as a hermit in the company of his good friend St. Gregory Nazianzen, he was ordained.

In 365, the bishop of Caesarea summoned him to combat the Arian heresy then threatening to overwhelm orthodoxy. When the bishop died in 370, Basil was appointed in his place and continued to fight Arianism while also reforming clerical life. Among other works, he gave away his inheritance to the poor, opened a soup kitchen, and promoted the rehabilitation of thieves and prostitutes. He built the Basiliad, a huge complex that included a hospital and a hospice for travelers, and was one of the greatest social relief works in the ancient church. To those who remained tightfisted in the face of human need he said: "...When you have buried your fortune, you will find you have buried your heart with it."

Basil experienced a rift in his friendship with Gregory, conflict with the church in the West, and ill health and died while Arianism was still relatively strong. "For my sins, I seem to fail at everything," he said. Nevertheless, he played a key role in defeating the heresy, and his funeral was attended by weeping crowds, a testimony to his enormous popularity. He is a Greek Doctor of the Church. Feast: January 2.

Becket, St. Thomas

(1118-1170. B. at London, England; d. at Canterbury.) Until his ordination to the priesthood in 1162, Thomas was not notably devout, much less ascetic. Nor was he particularly humble, a virtue he may never have practiced to any great degree.

Ordained a deacon, he became archdeacon of Canterbury in 1154. In that capacity, he worked from time to time with the Crown, and King Henry II chose him as his chancellor in 1155. He lived nearly as sumptuously as the king, who was his great friend. Once, sent to France to arrange a royal marriage, Thomas brought along a retinue of several hundred men—soldiers, clerics, servants—as well as musicians, hawks, hounds, and monkeys. He carried out delicate diplomatic missions on the one hand and on the other led troops into battle, spearheading assaults and engaging in hand-to-hand combat.

In 1162, the king named him archbishop of Canterbury, which required his ordination to the priesthood. Thomas resisted, certain that in this position he would feel compelled to defend the interests of the church against the aggressive policies of the state. "I should soon lose Your Majesty's favor," he said, "and the affection with which you honor me would be changed into hatred." This need not have been the case, given the tenor of Thomas' life to that point. However, his manner of life changed dramatically from the time of his ordination prior to becoming archbishop. He wore a hair shirt, dressed in a simple black cassock, rose early to read Scripture, and attended or celebrated daily Mass. He visited the sick, ran his household on monastic lines, and personally examined candidates to the priesthood to winnow out the unsuitable. He also resigned his chancellorship, to the anger of the king, but remained a man of action, determined, stubborn, and outspoken.

The conflicts Thomas anticipated came soon enough and culminated in a disagreement over the right of church courts versus the right of secular courts to discipline clerics accused of crimes (a moot point today but a real issue in the religious Middle Ages). In the face of the king's wrath, Thomas fled England rather than capitulate. His exile in France lasted six years, during which he prayed, did penance, and never wavered in his convictions.

After negotiating a settlement with the king, Thomas returned to England in 1170. Before his arrival, he sent ahead letters excommunicating certain bishops who had infringed on his rights in an ecclesiastical-political matter. These bishops complained to Henry who, in Normandy at the time, fell into a rage and spoke words that some present interpreted as a call for the death of the archbishop.

Four knights crossed the channel and accosted the archbishop at his residence, demanding, among other things, that he reinstate the bishops. The knights left, threatening and cursing, but returned almost immediately. They found Thomas in his church, abandoned by all but one of his monks. "Where, where is the traitor?" they cried, peering through the dim evening light. "Here I am," Thomas said, "the servant of Christ whom you seek." They seized him and attempted to pull him outside, but he wrenched free and threw one man to the ground. They then attacked with their swords, and Thomas fell to his knees, wounded, saying, "I am ready to accept death for the name of Jesus and the defense of the church." He collapsed and the knights finished the job, smashing his skull.

He was immediately hailed as a martyr and his cult spread quickly throughout Europe. There has since been much discussion of his character, for he was in some ways difficult—headstrong and demanding and not in the usual cast of saints. But he was courageous and devout and died in defense of religious freedom, a cause that continues to claim martyrs into the present century. Feast: December 29.

Bede the Venerable, St.

(673-735. B. near Sunderland, England; d. at Jarrow.) Bede entered the monastery at Jarrow for his education at the age of seven and stayed the remaining fifty-five years of his life. "It has ever been my delight to learn or teach or write," he said, but he was also a priest, known for his humility ("marvelously learned and not at all proud," according to a contemporary). He was sensitive to the needs of the laity and thought some lived such holy lives that they should receive communion weekly, even daily—unheard of at the time.

Bede is best known for his writings, particularly *The Ecclesiastical History of the English People,* considered one of the great historical works of all time and still widely read. He also translated Scripture and wrote commentaries, poetry, lives of the saints, and other works. Bede died after a brief illness while singing the doxology, sitting on the floor of his cell where he had asked his fellow monks to place him. St. Boniface, hearing of his death, said: "The candle of the church, lit by the Holy Spirit, is extinguished." Feast: May 25.

Bellarmine, St. Robert

(1542-1621. B. at Montepulciano, Italy; d. at Rome.) Pope Clement VIII said that Bellarmine had no "equal for learning" and on that basis made him a cardinal in 1598. He was undoubtedly the man for the hour, bending his formidable intellect to the controversies surrounding the Protestant Reformation and Catholic Counter Reformation. His learning, far from isolating him from the human condition, was lit from within by a deep faith, simplicity, and pastoral sensibility. At a time when cardinals lived princely lives, he limited household expenses to the essentials, subsisted primarily on bread and garlic, and used the tapestries hanging on the walls of his room for clothing for the poor. "The walls won't catch cold," he said.

He was a Jesuit, recognized early on for his brilliance and holiness ("the best of our school and not far from the kingdom of God," the rector of the Jesuit college said). For seven years, Bellarmine was a professor at Louvain, Belgium, where he became involved in controversies stemming from the Reformation. He also learned Hebrew, wrote a Hebrew grammar, and was an enormously popular preacher.

Bellarmine went to Rome in 1576, to teach and to serve as chair of "controversial theology" at the Roman (now Gregorian) College. There he crafted his magnum opus, *Disputations on the Controversies of the Christian Faith Against the Heretics of This Age.*

This book—the bedrock for Catholic response to the Reformation—was banned in Elizabethan England. That didn't stop the English from somehow getting hold of it and circulating it widely. The work was so monumental that Bellarmine's opponents were convinced it was the work of a team, not one man. As in all his dealings with his adversaries, Bellarmine was moderate and fair, avoided vituperative attacks, and carefully presented the reformers' views in the best light, even defending them at times from unjust interpretations of their thought. Never one to argue simply for the sake of argument, he also prayed daily for those he opposed.

Bellarmine ministered briefly as archbishop of Capua, but was recalled to Rome by the pope in 1605. He remained there the rest of his life, serving as a spokesman for and defender of the church. He was a champion of the papacy but held that the pope's power was primarily spiritual, not temporal. He was part of the team that produced the revised edition of the Vulgate Bible. He also wrote two catechisms that remained popular for several centuries, inspiring the Baltimore Catechism of recent memory. As a friend of Galileo, he urged the astronomer to present as hypothesis rather than fact his theory that the sun, not the earth, was the center of the universe. He was not involved in the condemnation of Galileo, which took place eleven years after Bellarmine's death.

Bellarmine spent the last years of his life writing spiritual works such as *The Mind's Ascent to God* and *The Art of Dying Well*. He is a Doctor of the Church. Feast: September 17.

Benedict, St.

(c. 480-c. 547. B. at Nursia, Italy; d. at Monte Casino.) Most of what we know of Benedict comes from the *Dialogues* of Gregory the Great (c. 540-604), who is long on tales of Benedict as wonder-worker and short on fact. Although little is known of his life, it seems Benedict was born to a distinguished Italian family and went to Rome as a teenager to study. Disgusted by the licentiousness of the city, he fled and lived for three years as a hermit in a cave at Subiaco. A group of monks asked him to be their abbot but then, when he reluctantly agreed, resisted his attempts to impose a stricter monastic observance. When they attempted to poison him, he returned to Subiaco and organized his growing band of followers into twelve small monasteries. In about 529, he took some of these to Monte Cassino, where he established another monastery. Here, he composed his Rule, a well-balanced, compassionate guide outlining the principles and practical details of monastic life.

The *Rule of St. Benedict* had a profound impact on Western civilization, particularly during the Middle Ages. Its flexibility and reasonableness allowed monasteries to become centers of learning and culture as well as of piety. The *Rule* insists on single-minded devotion to God but respects the needs of the individual. "Laying aside your own will," Benedict says, "take up the all-powerful and righteous arms of obedience to fight under the true King, the Lord Jesus Christ." He adds: "In this school for God's service ... we hope nothing harsh or oppressive will be directed." Benedict became ill with a fever, received communion, and died while standing in his chapel, supported by his disciples. His *Rule* is still used in monasteries throughout the world. Feast: July 11.

Benedict the Moor, St.

(c. 1526-1589. B. at San Fratello, Italy; d. at Palermo.) Benedict's parents were

African slaves, and Benedict, though freed, endured taunts from others due to the color of his skin and his heritage. A man named Lanza, the head of a group of Franciscan hermits, noted Benedict's patience and dignity when insulted. Impressed, he invited him to join the group. Benedict did and was elected superior when Lanza died.

In 1562, the pope dispersed bands of hermits, and Benedict entered the Friars Minor of the Observance near Palermo. He served as cook, enjoying the solitary nature of this position but unable to hide his extraordinary goodness from others. Against his will, he was appointed guardian of the house. He could neither read nor write but he was an excellent leader, wise and tactful, with a reputation for sanctity and miracles. He successfully implemented a stricter interpretation of the Franciscan rule.

Benedict served in other positions, including novice master, but eventually was allowed to return to cooking. His holiness continued to draw many, including the poor, the sick, and those seeking advice and spiritual direction. He died after a short illness, having led a life of simplicity, prayer, penance, and fasting. Feast: April 4.

Benildus, St.

(Peter Romancon) (1805-1862. B. at Thuret, France; d. at Saugues.) Benildus achieved sanctity by enduring "the terrible daily grind," Pope Pius XII said, in this case as a teacher for over forty years with the Brothers of Christian Schools. He was at heart a catechist. "I live for the apostolate," he wrote. "If through my fault these children don't grow in goodness, what is the use of my life?" He reinforced his effective classroom presence with a holiness that permeated all he did. "Brother Benildus did not worship God like an angel only when he was in church," a priest noted, "...but always and everywhere—even among his cabbages in the garden."

His impact was so profound and his love for the congregation so evident that at the time of his death, there were more than two hundred brothers and a large number of priests who had been his students. He died at Saugues, an isolated village in southern France where he had served for twenty years as director of a school and as a teacher. Feast: August 13.

Bernard of Clairvaux, St.

(1090-1153. B. near Dijon, France; d. at Clairvaux.) Bernard was above all a monk, although he so completely dominated the twelfth century that he defies traditional notions of a sequestered

monastic life. His charismatic personality had evidently asserted itself by the
time he entered the monastery at
Citeaux, for he brought with him
thirty-one of his fellow noblemen,
including four of his own brothers. The
monks at Citeaux—Cistercians—sought
to restore the Benedictine Rule to its
original austerity, and Bernard soon
took the lead. In 1115, three years after
his arrival, he was ordained and made
abbot of a new foundation at Clairvaux,
where he nearly died as a result of fasts,
vigils, ill health, and poverty. Over the
next ten years, he carried on extensive
correspondence with many who sought
his advice. He became known as a mystic and miracle worker and started three
foundations from Clairvaux.

Bernard complained of being "over-
run in all quarters with anxieties ... the
troubles and cares of business" and of
having little time for prayer. His reputation spread quickly, and he was soon
drawn into public affairs. He helped
resolve the disputed papal election of
1130 when he championed Innocent II
and won the whole church to his side.
At the request of Pope Eugenius III, a
former monk of Clairvaux, he stirred
enthusiasm for a crusade (it proved disastrous, due in part to the thuggish
nature of the crusaders). Again at the
pope's request, he preached a campaign
designed to win Albigensian heretics
back to the church (it, too, was ulti-

mately unsuccessful). During this time,
he wrote prodigiously and brilliantly,
and many of his works are read today,
such as *On the Love of God, On the Song
of Songs*, and his lively letters. Calling
himself "Our Lady's Faithful Chaplain,"
he promoted devotion to her by writing
sermons in her honor that are among
his most beautiful works. Throughout
all this, he guided his monks and helped
establish numerous foundations (there
were seven hundred monks at Clairvaux
when he died, and over four hundred
Cistercian houses).

Bernard had enemies, some among
those clergy he criticized for extravagant
living ("The poor, the naked, the starv-
ing ... cry: 'Your luxury devours our
lives! Your vanity steals our necessi-
ties!'") He vehemently opposed the
persecution of Jews, calling them "the
living words of Scripture." Exhausted
by the demands placed upon him, his
health undermined by his austerities, he
died at Clairvaux after reconciling two
warring factions at Metz. He is a
Doctor of the Church, known as
"Doctor Mellifluous," the "Doctor
whose teaching is as sweet as honey."
Feast: August 20.

Bernard the Penitent, St.

(D. 1182 at St. Omer, France.) Bernard
spent his adult life as a penitent in
reparation for what his bishop called
"horrible crimes." We know nothing of

his criminal activity beyond the fact that Bernard participated in an uprising during which an unpopular governor was murdered. The certificate of penance his bishop issued survives, however, and its severity is a measure of serious wrongdoing on Bernard's part.

For seven years he was to go barefoot, and he was forbidden to wear a shirt for the rest of his life. The severe fasting imposed on him included a full Lenten fast for the forty days preceding Christmas, no meat on Wednesdays and Saturdays and nothing but bread and a little wine on Fridays. Bernard set out as a pilgrim loaded with heavy iron fetters, and after much traveling and hardship he settled at St. Omer in a house next to the monastery of St. Bertin. He prayed with the monks, who regarded him as a saint, continued his penances, and eventually joined the monastery. Miracles were attributed to him, and his funeral was attended by such vast crowds that the monks had a hard time proceeding with the ceremony. Feast: April 19.

Bessette, Bd. André

(1845-1937. B. at St. Gregoire d'Iberville, Canada; d. at Montreal.) "People who suffer have something to offer the good God," Bessette often said, although he was known specifically for the healing ministry he carried out under the auspices of St. Joseph. In spite of his own poor health, he was admitted to the Holy Cross Brothers at Montreal in 1870. "I am sending you a saint," his pastor told the congregation.

For forty years, Bessette served as porter at the order's college. His devotion to St. Joseph, intense spiritual life, and commitment to the suffering led him to visit and pray for the sick, many of whom recovered. Nevertheless, he said: "We shouldn't always pray for miseries to be removed. Sometimes we should pray for strength to bear them better." He attributed all healings to the intercession of St. Joseph—he called himself "St. Joseph's little dog"—but soon thousands were flocking to him, disturbing the life of the college. He proposed building an oratory to St. Joseph on nearby Mount Royal where he could receive the sick. He helped raise the necessary funds and built a small wooden structure, since replaced by the Basilica of St. Joseph. Today the shrine attracts two million visitors a year. Feast: January 6.

Biernacka, Bd. Marianna

(c. 1888-1943. D. in Naumowicze, near Grodno, Poland.) Polish freedom fighters during World War II often hid in the woods and, from there, fought the Germans. The Gestapo retaliated for the resulting deaths of German soldiers by executing Polish civilians. Mrs. Biernacka was about fifty-five years old, devout but illiterate, and completely taken by surprise one day when German soldiers came to her door. They demanded her pregnant daughter-in-law as a reprisal for the deaths of some of their soldiers. Mrs. Biernacka, intent on saving the expectant mother and unborn child, begged the commander to take her instead. He did. During her imprisonment, she asked only for a rosary. It is not known whether the Nazis granted this request. Two weeks after her arrest, she was shot to death.

Billiart, St. Julie

(1751-1816. B. at Cuvilly, Picardy, France; d. at Namur.) In her teens, Julie worked as a farm laborer to help support her family and taught religion to her fellow field hands during breaks. For reasons unknown, someone shot at her father through a window as they sat together in their house. The attempted murder so shocked Julie, by then in her early twenties, that she gradually became paralyzed and remained so for over twenty years. But she kept on teaching from her bed, and many—attracted by her holiness and cheerfulness—came to her for advice. During the French Revolution, she sheltered priests, carried on her apostolate, and became a target of revolutionaries. She was forced to flee five times in three years, once barely escaping a mob by hiding in a cart under some hay.

Together with her friend, Frances Blin Bourdon, Julie founded the Institute of Notre Dame (Sisters of Notre Dame de Namur) at Amiens in 1804. The sisters were and still are dedicated to Christian education, particularly of the poor, and to teacher training. In the same year, Julie was healed of her paralysis after a priest organized a novena to the Sacred Heart on her behalf but unbeknownst to her. For the next sixteen years she devoted herself to her rapidly expanding order, traveling incessantly, establishing schools, and encouraging her sisters. "She was happy and liked to see us happy too," said one. "… She used to make us laugh." Julie combined intelligence, quick wit, and a well-balanced personality with ready compliance to the will of God. She was able to do more for the church "in a few years," her bishop said, "than others can do in a century." Feast: April 8.

Blandina, St.

(D. 177 at Lyons.) Blandina was one of the martyrs of Lyon whose passion was included by Eusebius in his *History of the Church* (c. 323). Christians who survived the persecution wrote the account, determined to preserve the details.

Blandina was a young slave, apparently slight in appearance. She endured extensive torture, to the amazement of her torturers, who "confessed themselves beaten—they could think of nothing else to do to her." Throughout her ordeal, carried out before a mob in the amphitheater, she repeated "I am a Christian. We do nothing to be ashamed of." She was finally hung on a post for the wild beasts, but they refused to touch her. Returned to prison, she was brought out on the last day of the games along with Ponticus, a fifteen-year-old boy. She encouraged him, "urging him on and stiffening his resistance," until he died, and then she was tortured again, dropped into a basket, and tossed to a bull that gored her to death. Blandina, her fellow Christians wrote, was "a woman ... who had put on Christ and in bout after bout had defeated her adversary ... and won the crown of immortality." Feast: June 2.

Bobola, St. Andrew

(1591-1657. B. at Sandomira, Poland; d. at Janov.) Pope Pius XII, on canonizing Bobola, said he was "Christ's unconquered athlete." This was a reference both to his zealous pastoral work and the extreme sufferings of his martyrdom. Bobola was a Jesuit priest and pastor in Lithuania, where he was known as an outstanding preacher. He organized parishioners to visit the poor and prisoners, to serve as catechists, and during two outbreaks of plague, to care for the sick. In his missionary work, he brought many Orthodox, some of whom were former Catholics, into communion with Rome (for this, he earned the nickname "hunter of souls").

Meanwhile, relations between Orthodox Christians and Catholics in the region were deteriorating, and Cossack gangs succeeded in forcing many Catholics out. They drove the Jesuits from their churches, but Prince Radziwill, in Pinsk, offered the priests refuge at his home. Andrew joined them and had great success in encouraging and strengthening Polish Catholics. He was captured in 1657 and subjected to horrific torture that included whipping, being dragged by horses, having the skin torn off much of his body and holes cut in his hands. He was finally beheaded. His body was examined in 1923, the signs of his torture still evident. He is considered the apostle of Lithuania and patron of Poland. Feast: May 16.

Boniface, St.

(c. 675-754. B. probably at Crediton, England; d. in Friesland.) Boniface was baptized Winfrid, but he so impressed Pope St. Gregory II that, on sending him as a missionary to Germany, he renamed him Boniface: "he who performs good works." Boniface then went on to minister for forty years in Europe and had a fundamental impact on culture and religion there.

Prior to this, Boniface taught at his monastery in Nursling and wrote the first Latin grammar produced in England. He was ordained when he was thirty but resisted the lure of a comfortable academic career in order to work as a missionary. After an initial, unsuccessful foray into Friesland (now in the Netherlands), Boniface left England forever in 718 and, with the approval of the pope, began to evangelize Germany. He was a powerful preacher, an effective teacher, a good pastor and administrator, and his work prospered. He boldly cut down the oak of Thor, a sacred pagan tree, and when the gods failed to avenge the sacrilege, many conversions followed. He appealed to England for monks and nuns, and they came in great numbers, staffing the monasteries that became centers of religion, education, and culture.

Boniface traveled to Rome three times, was named archbishop to Germany in about 732, and convened numerous synods in his reordering of the German church. He then moved on to the reform of the church in France. He was nearly eighty when he stepped down from his leadership role and went again as a missionary to Friesland, the site of his first missionary efforts. While he was awaiting the arrival of candidates for confirmation, a band of pagans attacked his camp on the banks of the Borne River. Boniface, in his tent read-ing the Gospels, instinctively held up his book to protect himself, and a sword dented its wooden cover. He and his companions were slaughtered. Boniface's tomb is at his monastery at Fulda, as is the book he held at his death, stained with what is believed to be the martyr's blood. Feast: June 5.

Boscardin, St. Mary Bertilla

(1888-1922. B. at Brendola, Italy; d. at Treviso.) Bertilla's father was an alcoholic whose violent, drunken bouts occasionally forced his family to flee for safety. Bertilla's education was minimal—she was nicknamed "the goose" because of her apparently limited ability—but she was devout and entered the Sisters of St. Dorothy at Vicenza when she was sixteen. Assigned to menial chores, she quietly took on the least desirable work. "I can't do anything," she told her superior. "...Teach me. I want to become a saint."

The sisters trained her as a nurse and in 1907 assigned her to the children's diphtheria ward at their hospital. Proving to be especially skilled at caring for the most seriously ill, she flourished in her new vocation. The hospital served the military during World War I and in 1917 was in the middle of some of the bloodiest conflicts of the war. During air raids, Bertilla—in spite of her own fear—stuck by those patients too sick to be moved to safety, praying while the bombs fell. Bertilla continued to serve the sick after the war in spite of intense suffering from a painful tumor. She died after unsuccessful surgery to relieve the problem. A plaque at the hospital at Treviso honors her as "a chosen soul of heroic goodness—an angelic alleviator of human suffering." Feast: October 20.

Bosco, St. John

(1815-1888. B. at Becchi, Italy; d. at Turin.) John grew up in poverty, the son of Francisco (who died when John was two) and Margaret, who later helped her son in his ministry. John had a dream when he was nine that set the course for his life. He saw himself changing children from wild animals into lambs, a foreshadowing of his work with abandoned boys. Characteristically, he immediately prepared to win souls for Christ by learning to juggle, walk a tightrope, and do acrobatics, having observed the ease with which traveling performers captured the attention of a crowd. John mixed his highly successful performances with brief catechism lessons and prayer.

Ordained a priest in 1841, Bosco dedicated himself to the care and education of the army of neglected boys who roamed the streets of the newly industrialized city of Turin. The boys flourished under his regimen of picnics, hikes, singing, games, theater, and jokes—intermingled with Mass, confession, prayer, and religious instruction. "Enjoy yourselves as much as you like," he said, "if only you don't sin."

John expanded his work, housing many of the boys with the help of his mother and providing instruction in various trades. He never used formal punishment, winning over his charges—they eventually numbered eight hundred—through "reason, religion and love." In the politically volatile, anticlerical atmosphere of nineteenth-century Italy, some feared he was a revolutionary, and numerous attempts were made on his life. Once, someone shot at him through a window while he was teaching a class, but the bullet passed through the sleeve of his cassock. He always escaped harm and for a period of time was protected by a mysterious dog that came to his aid and then disappeared.

Don Bosco began the Society of St. Francis de Sales (the Salesians) in 1859 to work with boys. In 1872, with Mary Mazzarello, he founded the Daughters of Our Lady Help of Christians (Salesian Sisters) to work with girls. Feast: January 31.

Bossilkov, Bd. Eugene

(1900-1952. B. at Belene, Bulgaria; d. at Sofia.) Bossilkov was a victim of Stalin's persecution of the church in

Eastern Europe, martyred at the age of fifty-two. He was a Passionist priest and secretary to the bishop of his diocese when, a pastor at heart, he requested and received a position as a parish priest.

After the Russian invasion of Bulgaria following World War II, Bossilkov was appointed bishop of Nikopol. He knew that it was the intention of the communists to crush the church and was not surprised when severe persecution began in 1950. He refused exile, saying that he could not abandon his flock. "The shedding of our blood will open the way to a glorious future," he wrote. "...Others will harvest what we've sown through our suffering."

The secret police arrested the bishop while he was on vacation near Sophia. He was tortured and during a sham trial was accused, among other crimes, of being a spy for the Vatican. His alleged subversive activities included a series of popular missions during which the bishop, a powerful preacher, delivered a basic presentation of the faith.

Bossilkov was executed by firing squad and buried in an unmarked grave. "Don't worry about me," he told friends. "I am already clothed with God's grace and have remained faithful to Christ and the church." Feast: November 11.

Bourgeoys, St. Marguerite

(1620-1700. B. at Troyes, France; d. at Montreal, Canada.) Bourgeoys arrived in Montreal when it was nothing more than a small fort and spent nearly fifty years there, living a life of heroic deprivation as a pioneer and missionary. She had attempted to join the Carmelites and Poor Clares in France but had inexplicably been turned down. She then met the governor of Montreal, who was in France looking for teachers for his colony. He recruited her to establish a school there. Bourgeoys arrived in Canada in 1653, opened the first school at Montreal in 1658, and returned to France to bring back more helpers. She founded the Congregation of Notre Dame of Montreal in 1676. She soon accepted two Iroquois women into the order, a testimony to her unwillingness—unusual at the time—to distinguish between races.

Marguerite persevered through terrible poverty, ongoing violence between the settlers and Iroquois, and a fire that destroyed the convent and killed two sisters. She herself lived simply, giving away her bed and blankets to the needy and sleeping on the floor even in the frigid Canadian winters. She died shortly after praying that she might offer her life for the life of the novice mistress, a younger woman who was seriously ill. The novice mistress recovered. Feast: January 12.

Brandsma, Bd. Titus

(1881-1942. B. at Friesland, the Netherlands; d. in Dachau concentration camp.) Brandsma was a Carmelite priest known for his intellectual brilliance. For nineteen years, he was a professor of philosophy at the Catholic University of Nijmegen and a prolific writer, an expert on mystical theology and a friend to the needy who often came to him for help. Among many quiet acts of generosity, he celebrated Mass weekly, without a stipend, at a home for the elderly that couldn't afford to hire a chaplain.

Even before the German occupation of the Netherlands, he was a vigorous critic of Nazism, calling it "a black lie" and frequently writing and speaking against it. He was the spiritual advisor to journalists writing for Dutch Catholic newspapers, a position that brought him into direct conflict with the German occupiers. Titus delivered a mandate from the Dutch hierarchy to the journalists forbidding them to print any Nazi advertisements, press releases, or other propaganda. He was arrested and sent to Dachau concentration camp, where he was a steady source of consolation to other prisoners, although brutally treated himself. "Those who want to win the world for Christ," he said, "must have the courage to come into conflict with it."

Titus' health collapsed and he was placed in the dreaded camp hospital, where doctors conducted barbaric experiments on him. He repeated aloud, "Not my will but Thy will be done." Too sick for further tests, he was killed by lethal injection. Feast: July 26.

Brébeuf, St. Jean de

(1593-1649. B. at Conde-sur-Vire, Normandy, France; d. at St. Ignace, Ontario, Canada.) Brébeuf's life among the Huron Indians of Canada ended with one of the more gruesome martyrdoms in Christian history. When he arrived in Quebec in 1625 as a Jesuit missionary, he adapted quickly to the rugged life of the Indians and learned the Huron language. That enabled him to write a Huron dictionary and catechism. With fellow Jesuit missionaries, he conducted a ministry that was, for several years, almost entirely unsuccessful. "Anyone who comes here to seek anything but God will be sadly disappointed," he wrote.

He and his coworkers left for France when the English took control of Quebec in 1629. When Canada reverted to the French in 1633, they returned. Brébeuf spent most of his remaining years with the Hurons, overcame opposition from hostile members of the tribe, and saw the tide turn as many requested baptism. However, the Iroquois, enemies of the Hurons, intensified hostilities against the tribe.

On March 16, 1649, they took Brébeuf and Fr. Gabriel Lalemant in a raid. The Iroquois tied the men to stakes, cut off their flesh and ate it before their eyes, and tortured them with fire. When Brébeuf preached to the onlookers in spite of his suffering, the Indians cut off his lips and nose. Both priests were "baptized" with boiling water. According to witnesses, Brébeuf never uttered a cry. He suffered "like a rock," a fellow missionary wrote, "...keeping a profound silence, which astonished his executioners themselves." He died after four hours, Lalemant after seventeen. Feast (of the North American Martyrs): October 19.

Brendan, St.

(c. 460-578. B. at Kerry, Ireland; d. at Annaghdown.) Brendan was a monk and founder of numerous monasteries, most notably that of Clonfert at Galway. He is remembered chiefly for his seven-year voyage over the Atlantic Ocean with some fellow monks in search of the Land of Promise. The story of this adventure has come down to us in *The Voyage of Brendan,* written in the mid-ninth century by an expatriate Irish monk. It combines elements of folk tale and mythology as well as Christian notions of pilgrimage, exile, and self-conquest.

While it is certain that Brendan did in fact make a journey, scholars long disputed the claim that the land he reached was actually North America. However, an expedition in 1976-77 followed the instructions in *The Voyage,* built a coracle such as Brendan used, sailed from Ireland to Newfoundland, and demonstrated that such a landfall was possible. Little is known of Brendan personally but *The Voyage* says that "he lived a very ascetical life, was renowned for his powers as a miracle worker and was spiritual father to almost three thousand monks." Feast: May 16.

Brigid, St.

(c. 452-524. B., according to tradition, at Faughart, Ireland; d. at Kildare.) We know little with any certainty of Brigid, whose name is also rendered as Bride and Briege. There are many accounts of her life from the centuries following her death, but these are mostly legends and miracle stories with strong elements of Irish pagan mythology. Nevertheless, it is known that she founded and was abbess of the first convent of nuns in Ireland. This monastery, at Kildare, developed into a center of spirituality, and Brigid herself had a strong influence on the growth of the Irish church. She was widely admired for her charity and is revered for her role in establishing the religious life for women in Ireland. She is the patron of Ireland together with Sts. Patrick and Columba. Feast: February 1.

Britto, St. John de

(1647-1693. B. at Lisbon, Portugal; d. at Oriur, India.) John was born into the Portuguese aristocracy and entered the Jesuits when he was fifteen, determined to be a missionary. In 1673, he left for India, where he spent the remaining twenty years of his life, except for a brief return to Portugal.

John was superior of the Madura mission and enjoyed great success, due in part to his adapting to local custom. He dressed and ate like the local people and followed the life of a sannyasi, an ascetic of the Brahmin caste. As such, he could freely associate with those of high or low caste in the rigidly stratified Indian society. He won so many to Christianity that he aroused the anger of Hindus who, in 1686, attacked and tortured him along with some of his catechists.

He converted a rajah to Christianity, and the man agreed to give up all but one of his wives so that he might be baptized. One of the displaced wives complained and John was imprisoned. He was beheaded at Oriur, near Ramuad, for teachings opposed to the Hindu gods. Feast: February 4.

Buonaccorsi, Bd. Bonaventure

(D. 1315 at Orvieto, Italy.) The conversion of Buonaccorsi at the age of thirty-six made a deep impression on his fellow citizens. He was a nobleman, a leader of the antipapist Ghibelline party and notorious for fomenting rebellion. He caused much misery among the people, but one day he heard St. Philip Benizi preach and repented on the spot. He wanted to join the Servite Order, of which Philip was a member, but the saint was uncertain of the depth of his conversion. He tested Buonaccorsi by imposing a public penance. Benizi insisted he make restitution for all his wrongdoing and personally repent and ask forgiveness of all he had harmed. Buonaccorsi did this so thoroughly that he was admitted to the order and ordained. He spent much of the rest of his life preaching on behalf of peace. His ministry was extremely effective during a time of civil war and general unrest. He served several times as prior for the Servites and as director of an order of Dominican nuns he helped found. In his lifetime, he was called "il Beato," and miracles took place through his intercession both before and after his death. Feast: December 14.

Bus, Bd. Caesar de

(1544-1607. B. at Cavillon, France; d. at Avignon.) Caesar was a poet, painter, writer of plays, and a soldier. He took part in the French Wars of Religion and led a dissipated life in Paris for three years. He then fell seriously ill, had a change of heart, and decided to become a priest. He was ordained in 1582 and quickly settled on what would become the main task of his life, the religious education of ordinary men, women, and children. His work anticipated the catechetical insights of modern times by devising a system of religious education that targeted the whole family, not just children. Through such education, Caesar hoped to counter the scandalous ignorance of the laity which, he thought, seriously weakened the church. With his cousin, Jean-Baptiste Romillon, he cofounded the Fathers of Christian Doctrine to further this work. Feast: April 15.

C

Cabrini, St. Frances Xavier

(1850-1917. B. at Sant' Angelo Lodigiano, Italy; d. at Chicago, Illinois.) As a young teacher, Cabrini attempted to join several religious orders but these turned her away because of her poor health. At the request of her bishop, she took over the direction of a mismanaged orphanage. The founder of the institution, who seems to have been mentally ill, obstructed Frances' work to such a degree that the bishop eventually closed the orphanage but invited Cabrini to found a missionary order. There were many obstacles to overcome, particularly the objection of some Catholics to missionary work by women (it was seen as inappropriate). Nevertheless, in 1887 Pope Leo XIII approved the Missionary Sisters of the Sacred Heart. He told Frances not to look to China, where from childhood she had wanted to serve, but "to the West."

For nearly thirty years, under extremely difficult conditions, Cabrini traveled throughout the United States and to Central and South America, England, France, and, repeatedly, Italy, establishing convents, schools, hospitals, and other institutions. When people pointed out the difficulty of her work, she asked: "Are we doing this—or is our Lord?" Her nuns loved Frances and she had excellent business sense, but her limited education sometimes showed. In the early days, she was sharp-tongued regarding Protestants and sometimes rigid, as when she refused to allow children born outside of marriage in her schools.

She died in Chicago at the age of sixty-seven, her health undermined by long-standing malaria. She had founded nearly seventy institutions devoted to health, education, and needy children and her congregation numbered fifteen hundred nuns. She became an American citizen in 1909 and is the first American citizen to be canonized. Feast: December 22.

Cafasso, St. Joseph

(1811-1860. B. at Castelnuovo d'Asti, Piedmont, Italy; d. at Turin.) Cafasso influenced a generation of priests, most notably St. John Bosco, who chose him as his mentor and became his close friend. Cafasso was a small man who stooped due to a twisted spine, but he had a spirit of "undisturbed tranquillity," Bosco said. He was known for his good humor and kindness.

Cafasso was a priest, teacher, and then rector at Convitto Ecclesiastico seminary in Turin. He helped restore a sense of God's mercy to Catholics, many of whom were demoralized by the then-prevalent Jansenist heresy with its extreme emphasis on humanity's sinfulness. When hearing confessions, he told priests and seminarians, "our Lord wants us to be loving ... to be fatherly to all who come to us, without reference to who they are or what they have done. If we repel anybody, if any soul is lost through our fault, we shall be held to account." He urged priests to maintain a simple lifestyle, saying that worldliness was their greatest enemy. In a time of anti-Catholic persecution, he encouraged the clergy to resist compromise with a government intent on crippling the church.

Cafasso also worked in the prisons and accompanied over sixty men to execution, all of whom died repentant: "My hanged saints," he called them. Besides John Bosco, he helped numerous other individuals establish works of charity before his death, at the age of forty-nine, from pneumonia. Feast: June 23.

Calasanz, St. Joseph

(1556-1648. B. at Aragon, Spain; d. at Rome.) Calasanz suffered terribly at the hands of his own religious order and the church. He was ordained in 1583 and was so successful in his pastoral duties that the bishop appointed him vicar general of the diocese. He resigned in 1592 to pursue his primary interest, the education of the urban poor, particularly homeless and abandoned children. He went to Rome and started the first free school there in 1597. By 1611, his school had twelve hundred pupils and Calasanz had founded and was superior of a religious congregation dedicated to this ministry, the Clerks Regular of the Christian Schools (Piarists).

In 1621, Joseph experienced a betrayal that would trouble the remaining twenty-five of his ninety years. Mario Sozzi, one of his priests, obtained a position of authority in the order and viciously attacked Joseph's character. Sozzi's accusations—all of them false, including the assertion that the founder was senile—prompted the Vatican to arrest Calasanz, parade him through the streets, and suspend him from his office. Rome then appointed an apostolic visitor who colluded with Sozzi and refused to investigate the situation.

In 1646, after Sozzi's death and in spite of the fact that a committee had recommended Joseph's reinstatement, the order was reduced to nothing more than a society of priests under the local bishops. Calasanz endured with heroic patience. "The Lord gives and the Lord taketh away," he said, quoting Job 1:21. "Blessed be the name of the Lord." His order was not fully restored until 1669, twenty-one years after his death.

Cardinal Lambertini (later Pope Benedict XIV) said of Joseph that he "was a perpetual miracle of fortitude and another Job." Feast: August 25.

Callo, Bd. Marcel

(1921-1945. B. at Rennes, France; d. at Mauthausen concentration camp.) Callo was a devout Catholic but not an outstanding student. He became an apprentice to a printer when he was thirteen, and at fourteen joined the Young Christian Workers. Through that organization, he devoted himself to bringing his fellow workers to Christ. A natural leader, he became president of the group and his zeal and good humor transformed the association into a center of intense evangelical life. He became engaged to Marguerite, a fellow member, when he was twenty-one.

During the German occupation of France, the Nazis assigned Marcel to forced labor in Germany. Rather than go into hiding, which would have exposed his family to reprisals, he viewed the circumstance as a missionary opportunity. En route to the Walther armaments factory in Germany, however, Marcel's spirit and health broke. He arrived depressed but after two months, "Christ made me snap out of it," he wrote in a letter. "...He told me to get on and see my comrades. Then my *joie de vivre* returned."

Marcel organized spiritual and recreational activities for the deportees, and in April 1944 the Gestapo, who said he was "too much of a Catholic," arrested him. In October, he was sent to Mauthausen concentration camp where brutal treatment and malnutrition destroyed his health. He died after five months. In his last letter to his family, he wrote: "Happily, I have a Friend who does not leave me for a moment and can support me when things are difficult.... With him, all can be borne." Feast: March 19.

Calungsod, Bd. Pedro

(c. 1654-1672. B. in the Phillipines; d. at Tumon, Guam.) Calungsod was eighteen years old, a lay catechist and native of the Phillipines, when martyred for his faith in Guam. He was about fourteen when he accompanied Jesuit missionaries there along with sixteen other Filipino assistants, many of them teenage boys. The group lived in community, received no pay, and participated fully in the missionary effort by teaching, helping construct chapels, serving as sacristans, and living devout lives.

On the morning of April 2, Calungsod and Bd. Diego Luis de San Vittores gathered children and adults together on the beach to teach them about the faith. Matapang, a local chief and lapsed Catholic, was angry with San Vittores for baptizing his infant daughter, brought to the priest by Matapang's wife. He persuaded his friend Hirao to join him, and together they attacked the men, killing Calungsod first when he came to the defense of the priest. The assailants speared the men, split their skulls with machetes, tied their bodies together, and threw them into the sea. Feast: April 2.

Camillus of Lellis, St.

(1550-1614. B. at Bocchianico, Italy; d. at Rome.) Camillus was a soldier who led a dissolute life dominated by a hot temper and an addiction to gambling. He developed an incurable disease of the leg, gambled away everything, and in a moment of remorse, vowed to become a Franciscan. His health prevented that but his conversion was genuine. He began to care for the sick at a hospital in Rome, eventually becoming bursar. Camillus decided to become a priest in order to better serve the spiritual needs of his patients and started a religious order, the Ministers of the Sick (Camellians).

The order grew steadily, its members caring for the poor, for galley slaves, for plague victims, and for wounded soldiers during war in Hungary and Croatia. There, they deployed the first medical field unit on record. Camillus himself practiced extreme generosity to the poorest of the poor. He visited prisons where he shaved and washed the convicts, sent food and clothing anonymously to needy widows and orphans, and even cared for animals. Once, he took in a dog with a broken leg. "I, too, have had a bad leg," he said, "and I know the misery of not being able to walk."

Camillus continued to serve the sick in spite of a series of painful afflictions and died having established fifteen houses for his order and eight hospitals. Feast: July 14.

Campion, St. Edmund

(1540-1581. B. at London, England; d. at London.) A born leader and skilled orator, Campion was a student at Oxford University when he delivered the official welcoming address to the visiting Queen Elizabeth I. He won the patronage of the queen and was ordained a deacon in the Church of England but found himself drawn to Catholicism, then outlawed. He fled to France, where he was received into the Catholic Church at Douai in 1571. He was ordained a Jesuit priest in Rome in 1578 and left for the first Jesuit mission to England in 1580.

The assignment meant almost certain martyrdom, which Campion acknowledged in the famous *Brag* he wrote to state his case in the event of his capture. Jesuits will continue to come to England, he said, "while we have a man left ... to be racked by your torments or consumed with your prisons. The expense is reckoned, the enterprise is begun; it is of God, it cannot be withstood. So the faith was planted, so it must be restored." He ministered in secret, wrote and published the *Decem Rationes*, a defense of the Catholic position, and was betrayed in 1581. He was tortured repeatedly on the rack and condemned to be hanged, drawn, and quartered. At his execution, some of his blood splattered on a witness, the easy-going Henry Walpole. He was reconciled to the church, became a Jesuit priest, and thirteen years later met the same fate as Campion. Feast: December 1.

Cantarero, Bd. María Sagrario

(1881-1936. B. at Lillo, Spain; d. at Madrid.) Maria was one of the first women in Spain to receive a degree in pharmacy. She worked at her profession for a number of years, supporting her young brother after the death of their father. In her early thirties, her family obligations fulfilled, she joined the Carmel of St. Anne and St. Joseph in Madrid. She served as prioress and novice mistress. She often spoke of her desire for martyrdom. She was serving a second term as prioress when the Spanish Civil War broke out.

On July 20, rebel forces attacked the convent, but Maria managed to get the nuns to safety. She stayed with another nun at the home of that sister's parents and was arrested there on August 14. The secret police questioned her, attempting to learn the locations of the other nuns as well as some priests. When she remained silent, they shot her. At her beatification, Pope John Paul II praised her integrity in choosing death over betrayal in order to save others.

Casey, Ven. Solanus

(1870-1957. B. at Prescott, Wisconsin; d. at Detroit, Michigan.) From his roots in the Wisconsin prairie, the all-American Casey farmed with his pioneer family and went on to hold numerous jobs before finally becoming a priest. One of these jobs brought him into contact with Jesse James' gang. While moonlighting at Stillwater Penitentiary in nearby Minnesota, Casey's kindness so impressed prisoners Jim and Cole Younger—James' accomplices—that Cole gave him a clothing trunk. Casey used it for years, hauling it with him when he went to the seminary.

Casey failed in his first attempt to study for the priesthood because he could master neither Latin nor the German required in the seminary of the region. He succeeded at the Capuchin Franciscan monastery of

St. Bonaventure in Detroit and was ordained in 1904. Because of his academic limitations—he was not a gifted student although he was a natural leader with a strong personality—he couldn't hear confessions or give formal sermons.

For many of his nearly fifty years as a priest, Casey held the post of door-keeper at various Capuchin parishes from Harlem to Detroit. He welcomed and counseled the poor and the homeless as well as the affluent, and soon gained a reputation as a healer. Not just Catholics but Protestants, Jews, and atheists sought him out by the thousands. The demands of this ministry exhausted him. Often, after a grueling day of counseling, he fell asleep on the floor of his office or in the church. Sometimes, at one or two in the morning, he would unwind by playing his fiddle in front of the Blessed Sacrament.

He suffered from a painful skin condition toward the end of his life—his colleagues described his flesh as "raw meat." He died in bed on July 31, 1957, after stretching out his arms and saying, "I give my soul to Jesus Christ."

Catherine of Genoa, St.

(1447-1510. B./d. at Genoa, Italy.) Catherine wanted to be a nun but her relatives insisted she marry when she was sixteen. She was a member of the powerful Fieschi family, and the groom chosen for her was the dissolute Guiliano of the rival Adorno family. The match was meant to cement a truce of sorts. Guiliano was a gambler, an adulterer—one of his affairs produced a daughter—and had a hot temper. Catherine was sensitive and intelligent. She fell into depression as the years with Guiliano dragged on. She gave herself up to prayer and penance but after five years reentered society in an effort to alleviate her sadness. Her charm and intelligent conversation made her an instant success, but after another five years, still depressed, she begged God to intervene in her life. One day, while kneeling for the blessing of a priest, she was so overcome by God's love that she was transformed on the spot. She gave away all her fine clothing and retired into an austere life.

Not long after, Giulano's lifestyle brought them to the verge of bankruptcy. Impressed by his wife's evident holiness, he reformed his life and became a Third Order Franciscan. The couple agreed to live as brother and sister and together devoted themselves to nursing the sick at the Pammetone hospital. They moved there in 1479, and the energetic, capable Catherine became the hospital director in 1490. Guiliano died in 1497, but Catherine continued her service to the sick even though, for the last nine years of her life, she suffered from an agonizing undiagnosed illness. Her prayer life from the moment of conversion was intense and marked by mystical experiences. Her *Dialogue Between the Soul and the Body* and *Treatise on Purgatory* are considered classics of mystical literature. Feast: September 15.

Catherine of Siena, St.

(1347-1380. B. at Siena, Italy; d. at Rome.) Catherine, one of the church's great mystics, would have preferred to remain "alone with the Alone," as she said, but spent herself in active service to the church. At an early age she dedicated her life to God, to the dismay of her parents. Her voluble mother was particularly disapproving, and shadowed her daughter, heaped chores upon her, and in every way attempted to distract her from her intention. Catherine remained immovable, and her parents finally gave up. They assigned her a small private room in their house where she spent several years in fasting, silence, and prayer, leaving only to attend Mass. At the age of twenty-one, she emerged to begin serving the needy, maintaining a strict asceticism that resulted in her barely eating anything the rest of her life.

As a Third Order Dominican (she joined the lay association as a teenager), Catherine nursed the poor in hospitals. Soon her extraordinary holiness won her many followers. These she called her "family" and as their "mother" she taught them and prayed for them and formed with them a notably cheerful band, dedicated to works of charity and spiritual growth.

Spectacular and numerous conversions took place through her ministry. One of the best known cases was that of Niccolo di Toldo, a prisoner who had assaulted the priest who tried to prepare him for death. Catherine went to the prison, and Niccolo was so transformed by the encounter that he confessed, received communion, and asked Catherine to be at his side at his execution. At the scaffold, she wrote, he was "like a meek lamb and, seeing me, he laughed." She knelt by his side, heard his last words—"Jesus, Catherine"—and received his head into her hands.

In 1375, Catherine attempted to persuade the pope to leave Avignon, seat of the papacy for nearly seventy years, and return to Rome. She badgered him—"Be a man," she said—and addressed him with amazing familiarity, calling him "Dear little Babbo." Encouraged by Catherine and others, he returned to Rome but died shortly after. Following the election of his successor, the papacy fell into the Great Schism in which two and, later, three men claimed the papal throne. She went to Rome to work for the reunification of the church but died there at the age of thirty-three, shattered by grief over the situation.

Catherine was involved in wider public affairs for the last five years of her life, but it is chiefly for her faith and holiness that she is remembered. She left behind a huge collection of letters, many directed at civil and religious authorities in her work to bring peace to the tumultuous times. Her book, *Dialogue,* presents her mystical insights and is written as a dialogue between God and the Christian soul. She is a Doctor of the Church. Feast: April 29.

Cebula, Bd. Jozef

(1902-1941. B. at Malnia, Poland; d. at Mauthausen concentration camp, Austria.) Cebula was sixteen when he recovered unexpectedly from incurable tuberculosis. Shortly after, he joined the Oblates of Mary Immaculate and was ordained in 1927. He served as superior of the Oblates at Lubiniec and as novice master at Markowice. Germany invaded Poland in 1939 and in May 1940 shipped Cebula's novices to Dachau concentration camp. Cebula remained behind, and although the Nazis forbade any priestly ministry, he defied the ban. He was arrested on April 2, 1941, and sent to Mauthausen.

Witnesses of his imprisonment and death testified that he was singled out for mistreatment because he was a priest. Assigned to the punishment company, he had to carry twenty to thirty-pound rocks on his shoulders to a camp nearly two miles away. Along the way, he and the other prisoners were forced to climb the Death Stairs—a staircase of 144 steps—while guards and soldiers taunted and beat them. Completely broken after two trips and unable to go on, Cebula chastised the guards for their cruelty and threatened them with God's punishment. The guards, slightly taken aback, ordered him to run with a rock on his back. He collapsed near a fence after a few yards, and a guard killed him with machine gun fire, listing him as having been shot "while trying to escape." He died on May 9, 1941. Feast: June 12.

Cerioli, Bd. Paula

(1816-1865; B. at Soncino, Italy; d. at Cormonte.) Paula's unusual second vocation—preparing orphaned children for agricultural careers—came late in her life. Her first, and possibly more arduous vocation, was her marriage at the age of nineteen to a sixty-year-old widower of difficult temperament, Gaetano Buzecchi-Tassis. As was the custom, her parents had arranged the marriage. Paula and Gaetano had three children, two of whom died in infancy, the third at sixteen. When Gaetano died in 1854, Paula took the fortune he left her and, inspired by her parish priest, devoted it to caring for the orphaned children of peasants and training them to work the land. In 1857, she founded the Sisters of the Holy Family for this work and, five years later, a brothers' branch devoted to male orphans.

Her bishop gave his full support but reported to her that some said she was "cracked." "So I am," she answered, "by the lunacy of the Cross." Paula had long been in delicate health and died peacefully in her sleep on Christmas Eve. Devout from childhood, she was known for her inner peace and her devotion to Jesus Christ and St. Joseph. Feast: December 24.

Chabanel, St. Noel

(1613-1649. B. at Saugues, France; d. along the Nottawasaga River, Ontario, Canada.) Chabanel might well be considered the patron saint of those who persevere in spite of personal inclination and apparent failure. He came to Canada as a Jesuit missionary to the Indians in 1643 and soon discovered he was completely unable to grasp the native languages. The situation never improved. "Even after ... five years," a coworker wrote, "he made such little progress that he could hardly be understood, even in the most ordinary conversation." This was no small mortification for a man who had previously been a successful college teacher in France. Further, he found the Indian way of life difficult and fought depression and a sense of abandonment by God.

He endured all this in the shadow of his far more successful fellow missionaries, compounding his sense of failure. In order, he said, to "cooperate with the designs" of the Holy Spirit, he took a private vow to remain in the missions for life. He served at a variety of Huron villages, assisting future martyrs such as Sts. John de Brébeuf and Charles Garnier, until Iroquois attacks decimated the Huron people. On December 5, 1649, Chabanel left the mission of St. Jean, as ordered by his superiors, for the comparative safety of Christian Island. He never arrived. Later, an apostate Christian Indian admitted killing Chabanel with a hatchet, out of hatred for the faith. Feast (of the North American Martyrs): October 19.

Chantal, St. Jane Frances de

(1572-1641. B. at Dijon, France; d. at Moulins.) Jane was born to the nobility and married the Baron Christophe de Chantal in 1592. They were an exceptionally happy couple and the parents of seven children, four of whom survived infancy. After nine years of marriage, Christophe died in a hunting accident, shot by a friend who mistook him for a deer. Jane, overwhelmed with grief, turned her attention to the care of her children and to prayer. At his insistence, she and her children lived for a time with her father-in-law, an unpleasant man who treated her shabbily.

In 1604, Jane met St. Francis de Sales, who became her spiritual director and devoted friend. "There could not be a greater intellect united with deeper humility," he said of her. "As soon as I came to know him," she said of him, "I called him a saint from the bottom of my heart." He tempered her penances and helped her balance her life in the world and as a mother with her inclination to the religious life. In 1610, they cooperated in founding the Order of the Visitation, designed to accommodate women who couldn't endure the austerities of religious orders of the time.

The order flourished in the face of much opposition. Jane, as superior, met each challenge with equanimity, sustained by her profound interior life, her friendship with Francis de Sales, and her strength of character. She also proved to be a gifted administrator. She endured the deaths of St. Francis, her son, and many close friends and, toward the end of her life, experienced terrible spiritual dryness, interior trials, and temptations. St. Vincent de Paul, who knew her well, said: "...I regard her as one of the holiest souls I have ever met on this earth." She died at the age of sixty-nine and is buried near St. Francis de Sales at her convent in Annecy. Feast: December 12.

Chrysostom, St. John.

(347-407. B. at Antioch; d. at Pontus.) John was dubbed Chrysostom, "Golden Mouth," in tribute to his eloquent preaching. His devout mother, widowed at the age of twenty, raised him in the faith and gave him an excellent education that built on his natural talent. The celebrated pagan orator Libanius, his teacher, when asked who should succeed him on his death, said he would have chosen John "if the Christians had not stolen him."

John lived for about seven years as a hermit, returned to Antioch to assist the bishop, and was ordained in 386. He was renowned as a preacher and in this capacity is remembered especially for a series of sermons that helped restore peace when riots broke out after the imposition of new taxes. John's first concern was the poor, however, and he not only took care of their needs but urged others to as well. He once warned a rich woman that at the final judgment, "Christ will make you pay the price for those pearls and bring the poor who have perished with hunger into our midst."

Against his wishes, John was named bishop of Constantinople in 398. He immediately began a thorough and necessary reform of the church there, but his zeal and blunt honesty won him highly placed enemies, most notably Eudoxia, wife of the emperor. The unworthy archbishop of Alexandria, Theophilus, coveted his position, despised him, and conspired against him. The emperor summoned a synod, known as the Synod of the Oak for the site where it met. There John's enemies, led by Theophilus, tried him on false charges and deposed him.

The emperor sent him into exile but recalled him almost at once. When he refused to temper his views, the emperor sentenced him to an exile so harsh it ensured his death. After three years of what he described as "indescribable solitude, daily death," he was moved to a more remote location. On the forced march there through terrible weather and with little rest, John died, sick and worn out.

His many homilies include highly regarded expositions of the Old and New Testament in which he captures the spiritual point of the authors and suggests practical application of their teaching. He also left behind moral and pastoral exhortations and letters that, like all his work, are direct, concrete, and relevant today. Feast: September 13.

Clare, St.

(c. 1193-1253. B./d. at Assisi, Italy.) Clare, born to the nobility, resisted family pressure to marry and instead felt drawn to the religious life. When she was eighteen, she sought the advice of St. Francis of Assisi, then transforming the countryside with his radical Christianity. He "exhorted her to contempt of the world, vividly showing her how vain was earthly hope" (*The Legend of St. Clare*). On the night of Palm Sunday, 1212, she ran away from home to the Portiuncula, Francis' headquarters. He cut off her hair, gave her a sackcloth habit, and placed her in a nearby convent, later moving her to a house at San Damiano on the edge of Assisi. Her sister Agnes soon joined her, both successfully defying family efforts to force their return.

An order of women, eventually known as the Poor Clares, grew up around them. Francis gave them a "way of life" to follow and in 1215 appointed Clare the abbess, a position she filled for the remaining forty years of her life.

Clare's independence and strength of character are revealed not only in her determination to become a nun but also in her lifelong fight to retain for her order the "privilege of poverty." This included the freedom to live on alms without owning property. Clare told Pope Gregory IX, who offered to absolve her from the vow of strict poverty: "I crave absolution from my sins but not from the obligation of following Jesus Christ." Eventually, she wrote her own rule, becoming the first woman to write a rule for female religious in the history of the church. It was approved two days before her death, and she died with it in her hands.

Clare, who outlived Francis by twenty-seven years, expressed his ideals to perfection and through her order did much to promote a spirituality based on complete abandonment to God. Feast: August 11.

Claver, St. Peter

(1580-1654. B. at Verdu, Spain; d. at Cartagena, Colombia.) Claver joined the Jesuits in his native Spain and attended college in Majorica. There, he was deeply influenced by fellow-Jesuit St. Alphonsus Rodriguez, the doorkeeper of the college, who encouraged Claver's interest in the missions. In 1610, Claver left for Cartegena, Colombia, a center for the slave trade, where he ministered to slaves for nearly forty years ("the slave of the slaves forever," he said of himself). He brought food and medicine to the docks when the ships pulled in and cared for the slaves both there and on the plantations, often under unspeakable conditions and with limited assistance. He instructed, baptized, and offered spiritual support to the Africans and attempted to alleviate their suffering by demanding better treatment from ship owners and masters. Claver's unbounded solicitude for the slaves drew the ire of civil authorities and the criticism of some clergy who felt his enthusiasm was indiscreet.

Claver also served the general population, visiting hospitals weekly, ministering to sailors and prisoners, and preaching in the town square. In 1650, he fell victim to the plague and recovered but remained in pain and incapacitated, neglected by all. The town remembered him again only as he lay on his deathbed and heaped upon him the honor and attention formerly withheld. Feast: September 9.

Clement of Rome, Pope St.

(first century) Clement was one of the earliest bishops of Rome, generally accepted as third after St. Peter's successors, Sts. Linus and Cletus. He is occasionally identified as St. Paul's colleague (see Phil 4:3), but this is unlikely although not impossible. According to St. Iraneaus, writing some fifty years after Clement's death, Clement knew and was a student of the apostles. The tradition that he died as a martyr dates from the fourth century and is not mentioned by the earliest writers.

Clement is remembered, however, for his extremely important "Letter to the Corinthians," sent to admonish unruly church members who had driven out their leaders. Written about A.D. 96, it is the earliest example of the intervention of the Roman church in the affairs of another church.

Clement is solicitous but firm and

clear-sighted: "Let us have a little humility; let us forget our self-assertion and braggadocio and stupid quarreling." He urges repentance and a reinstatement of the leadership and, along the way, gives valuable insight into questions of early church ministry and the history of the Roman church. He is considered the first of the Apostolic Fathers. Feast: November 23.

Clitherow, St. Margaret

(c. 1555-1586. B./d. at York, England.) Margaret was witty, attractive, and kind, the wife of the wealthy John Clitherow, a butcher. Both were Protestant but she converted to Catholicism, which was forbidden by law, three years after their marriage. She refused to attend Protestant services as legally required. Her husband, who claimed that "she is the best wife in all England," paid the fines for nonattendance. He turned a blind eye to her other religious activities, allowing her to provide for the Catholic education of their children and harbor priests who celebrated Mass in their home.

A raid on their house led to the discovery of vestments and missals, and Margaret was arrested. When brought before the judges, she refused to plead guilty and go to trial, knowing that if she did so her children and servants would be compelled to testify against her. She defended herself with poise and intelligence. When the court condemned her—she would be pressed to death beneath eight hundred pounds of weight—she accepted her sentence calmly. Before her death, she was not allowed to see her four children (three of whom later entered the religious life). She saw her husband only once.

When told that she died for treason, she replied, "No, no ... I die for the love of my Lord Jesus." At her execution, a sharp stone was placed under her back and her arms were stretched out in the form of a cross, her hands tied to stakes. A door was laid upon her, loaded with weights. She cried out, "Jesus, Jesus, Jesus, have mercy on me!" and died about fifteen minutes later. Margaret is one of the forty martyrs of England and Wales whose feast is commemorated on October 25. She also has a separate feast on March 25.

Compiegne, Martyrs of

(D. 1794) Early in the French Revolution, religious orders not engaged in teaching or nursing were suppressed. In 1790, the Carmelites of Compiegne were evicted from their convent but attempted to follow their religious life as much as possible. They subscribed to the revolutionary oath to support the nation but later retracted their statement, the oath having been condemned by prominent Catholics. In 1794, they were arrested and accused of continuing their former way of life and of plotting against the Republic.

Their trial was a sham and they were denied legal help. When the prosecutor accused them of fanaticism, Sister Mary Henrietta demanded he explain the term. "I mean by it your attachment to your childish beliefs and your silly religious practices," he said. "You see," she said to her sisters, "we are condemned for clinging to our holy religion. We have the happiness to die for God."

They were executed by guillotine at what is now the Place de la Nation. As they rode to their deaths through the streets of Paris, they sang the *Miserere, Salve Regina,* and *Te Deum* and prayed the prayers of the dying. The sixteen victims met their deaths in the reverse order of seniority, the prioress having requested permission to die last. They knelt, renewed their religious vows, and pardoned their executioners. The crowd, contrary to custom, maintained absolute silence throughout the ordeal.

Sixteen sisters died as well as a layman, Mulot de la Menardiere, who had assisted them. Julia Louisa, a widow who had entered the convent after an exceptionally happy marriage, said that as victims of the age, "we ought to sacrifice ourselves to obtain its return to God." Feast: July 17.

Cordero-Munoz, St. Miguel Febres

(1854-1910. B. at Cuenca, Ecuador; d. at Premia, Spain.) Cordero joined the Christian Brothers, a teaching order, when only fourteen. Before he turned twenty, he was an accomplished teacher and the author of a Spanish grammar used in all Ecuadoran schools. Scholarly and literary fame came fast, but he was a teacher at heart. When another Christian Brother commented on his extensive preparation for class even though he'd been at the job for years, Cordero replied: "If I should teach the same material for twenty years, I would prepare each time with the same attention because every time I find a better way of teaching these same things."

Cordero overcame family resistance to his vocation as well as frail health and the handicap of deformed feet, which left him in pain and barely able to walk. He lived through periods of revolution in Ecuador but remained unafraid even when the brothers' school came under direct attack. "Brother Miguel ... continued working ... in his office ... merely raising his eyes from time to time and whispering a prayer," a coworker commented. Cordero spent the last years of his life in France, Belgium, and Spain, where he developed and translated textbooks for the Spanish-speaking world. Over his lifetime he produced more than fifty books. He was elected to the

Ecuadoran Academy of Language, the Spanish and Venezuelan Academies, and was awarded a diploma from the French Academy. He died from pneumonia at the age of fifty-six. Feast: February 9.

Cottolengo, St. Joseph

(1786-1842. B. at Bra, Piedmont, Italy; d. at Chieri.) With no money or investments but with absolute reliance on God, Cottolengo launched an extraordinarily effective ministry to the sick and needy poor in Turin. He called his work the Little House of Divine Providence although it grew to resemble more of a town with schools, workshops, and houses for the orphaned, the sick, the elderly, the mentally ill, the homeless, and destitute girls.

An incident in 1827 propelled Cottolengo, a priest at the Turin basilica, into his work. A French family passing through town couldn't find medical help for their seriously ill mother who was pregnant and had tuberculosis. She ended up in a room provided by the city for the sick destitute. Cottolengo, known for his work with the poor, came to administer last rites and stayed with the woman until she died. The incident opened his eyes to the need for accessible health care for the poor, and shortly after, he began his Little House with two rented rooms and no plan: "Providence," he said, "can do everything and will decide what is to happen."

He chose as his motto, "The love of Christ propels us forward." "All the poor are our patrons," he said, "but those who seem outwardly to be the most disgusting and repellent are our dearest patrons, indeed are our jewels." He founded a number of religious communities for the work including the Brothers of St. Vincent, Priests of the Holy Trinity, and the Sisters of St. Vincent. He himself lived a life of poverty and prayer and died at the age of fifty-six of typhoid fever. Feast: April 30.

Czartoryski, Ven. Augustus

(1858-1893. B. at Paris, France; d. at Turin, Italy.) A Polish prince as well as the grandson of the queen of Spain, Czartoryski grew up in exile due to the Russian occupation of Poland. His father had chosen a military career for him, but he rejected it in order to join St. John Bosco's Salesian priests. Before he met Czartoryski, Bosco had a vision that the prince would join the order but, to test his constancy, he rejected the young man's appeals for four years.

To the dismay of Czartoryski's wealthy family, Bosco admitted him to the novitiate in 1887. He was ordained in 1892 and died on April 2, 1893, of tuberculosis. In her book *Modern Saints, Their Lives and Faces,* Ann Ball points out that by the time of Czartoryski's death, his example had inspired over one hundred Polish-speaking young men to join the order. Bosco had predicted that the Salesians would eventually work in Poland, and in 1898 they established their first house at Oswiecim—Auschwitz, in German. Pope John Paul II studied with the Salesians in an underground seminary near Cracow. He declared Czartoryski "venerable" in 1979.

Damien De Veuster, Bd.

(1840-1889. B. at Tremelo, Belgium; d. at Molokai, Hawaii.) Damien, a native of Belgium, died on an island in Hawaii, "decorated," he said, "with the cross of ... leprosy." He was a priest of the congregation of the Sacred Hearts of Jesus and Mary and a volunteer in their Hawaiian missions from 1863 until his death.

For nine years he worked in two mission stations and then volunteered for the work that brought him to the attention of the world, the care of lepers restricted by law to the island of Molokai. There he found drunkenness and squalor and about eight hundred lepers with nothing to do. "I make myself a leper to the lepers to gain all to Christ," he said. Among other activities, he repaired houses, introduced better hygiene, administered medicine, enlarged the hospital, built an orphanage, visited those too sick to leave their huts, played with the children, shared his meals, counseled the troubled, prayed with the needy, and administered the sacraments. He was also an effective fund-raiser, sending out appeals worldwide.

Damien suffered from critics who questioned his motives and ministry and who accused him, when he con-

tracted leprosy, of breaking his vow of celibacy (many assumed the disease was contracted primarily through sexual contact). His intense interior life sustained him, and he saw in each leper "a soul redeemed by the adorable blood of our divine savior." After his death from the disease, attacks on his way of life continued, and in response to this controversy, Robert Louis Stevenson wrote a defense of the man and his work. Feast: April 15.

Daniel, St. Anthony

(1601-1648. B. at Dieppe, Normandy, France; d. at Teanaustaye, Ontario, Canada.) Daniel arrived in Canada in 1632 to serve as a Jesuit missionary and died there as a martyr sixteen years later. After working for a time with St. Jean de Brébeuf, he took charge of the mission to the Huron Indians at Teanaustaye. On July 4, 1648, the Iroquois, bitter enemies of the Hurons, attacked the village just as Fr. Daniel finished celebrating Mass. Panic erupted but Daniel calmly took care of the Hurons, baptizing as many of his catechumens as he could and ignoring their advice to escape. He went through the cabins encouraging and baptizing the elderly and sick and returned to the church, where he urged the Christians gathered there to flee. He then went out alone to plead with the Iroquois. They shot him with arrows, stripped him, and threw his body into the church, which they then burned. Feast (of the Martyrs of North America): October 19.

David, Bd. Vicente Vilar

(1889-1937. B. at Manises, Spain; d. at Valencia.) David was married and an industrial engineer with his family's ceramics business. He was a devout Catholic, active in his parish, with a special commitment to the poor and to the rights and needs of workers. During the Spanish Civil War, he assisted priests and made no attempt to hide his faith in spite of the fierce persecution of the church. He was arrested on February 14, 1937. As he was led away, his wife said to him, "See you tomorrow!" "Until tomorrow or in heaven," he answered. Moments later, she heard gunfire and knew her husband had been shot. Had he not been martyred, the cause for his canonization could have proceeded solely on the basis of his heroic virtue in everyday life.

Day, Dorothy, Servant of God

(1897-1980. B./d. at New York City.) For fifty years, Day fed the hungry, housed the homeless, organized boycotts, walked on picket lines, fought prejudice, and as a pacifist, opposed all war. Day converted to Catholicism in 1927 following several love affairs, an abortion, a brief marriage, and a common-law marriage that produced her only child. A writer and activist with many friends among bohemians and intellectuals in New York City, Day said: "I did not convert with my eyes closed. I knew the Catholic Church had plenty of sin within it. How could there not be sin within a church made up of men and women?" However, "[I] wanted to be part of it, obey it and in return, receive ... the mercy and love of Jesus."

Together with Peter Maurin, a social activist, she founded the Catholic Worker Movement and produced a newspaper, the *Catholic Worker,* to bring a Christian perspective to issues of social justice. In the early 1930s they founded Houses of Hospitality to feed, clothe, and shelter the poor, an outreach that soon spread across the United States. Day guided the Movement, which was never formally tied to the church although she herself lived a life of prayer, chastity, radical poverty, and obedience to church teaching.

Day's pacifism cost her many supporters during World War II and led her to oppose the Korean and Vietnamese wars, and to actively support conscientious objectors. She fought racism and, for her commitment to civil rights, found herself shadowed by the FBI, shot at, and verbally abused. Day was jailed numerous times, the last at the age of seventy-five for her protest with the United Farm Workers against the Teamsters Union. She wrote a column for the *Catholic Worker* for nearly fifty years as well as several books, including her autobiography, *The Long Loneliness*, and *Loaves and Fishes*, the story of the Catholic Worker Movement. She helped to found Pax Christi, the Catholic peace movement, and attended the last session of the Vatican Council as a Pax delegate, hoping to influence the bishops to make a clear statement supporting nonviolence. The Council eventually published *The Church in the Modern World*, which reflected some of her concerns. Day opened Maryhouse for homeless women in New York City when she was seventy-eight. She died there on November 29, 1980, her daughter by her side.

Del Bufalo, St. Caspar

(1786-1837. B./d. at Rome, Italy.) Del Bufalo was ordained at Rome in 1808. Shortly after, Napoleon occupied the city and exiled most of the clergy when they refused to swear allegiance to him. Del Bufalo returned after five years to a morally bankrupt countryside ripe for the sort of missionary activity at which he excelled. In 1815, with the encouragement of the pope, he founded the Missionaries of the Most Precious Blood, dedicated to preaching missions to ordinary people and encouraging repentance and conversion.

He and his missionaries carried on this ministry with great success in the face of extreme hardship and opposition. "I was sent into a forest infested by wild beasts rather than ... intelligent beings," one priest wrote of his audience, "a mob of wretches without manners and without any discipline." Before the missionaries arrived in one town, the opposition plastered the walls with posters blaspheming the Eucharist. On another occasion, an assassin pulled a knife on del Bufalo but dropped it when the priest quietly asked if he wanted to go to confession. It was said that del Bufalo's preaching was like "a spiritual earthquake," and he exhorted his priests to "be ready for anything. [Missioners] ... must never surrender."

Del Buffalo was in bad health when he preached what proved to be his final mission at Chiesa Nuova in Rome. He went on to care for victims of a cholera epidemic and succumbed himself. Feast: January 2.

Diego, Bd. Juan

(c. 1474-c. 1548. B. probably at Cuautitlan, Mexico; d. at Tepayac, now Mexico City.) Diego, born during the time of the Aztec Empire, was a farmer who also wove mats. He and his wife,

Maria, were childless. Following the Spanish conquest of Mexico, both converted to Christianity, and when Maria died in 1529, Diego moved in with his uncle. This uncle, also a Christian, had raised him from childhood after the death of Diego's parents.

Each weekend, Diego walked eighteen miles to church. On the morning of December 9, 1531, as he crossed the hill called Tepayac, he heard music and saw a bright light. He heard a woman call, "Juanito ... Juan Dieguito," an affectionate diminutive of his name, and found himself face-to-face with a vision of the Blessed Virgin. She greeted him warmly and announced that she wanted a church built on that spot where she would show her love and protection to the people. She asked him to convey that message to the bishop of Mexico City.

Diego's first visit to the bishop proved fruitless, but when he returned, at the request of the Blessed Virgin, the bishop suggested he ask Mary for a sign as proof of the apparition. He did so and the Virgin told Diego to climb Tepayac, where he found his sign— fragrant roses growing out of season in the rocky soil. He gathered them in his *tilma,* or mantle, and when he presented them to the bishop, discovered that an image of the Virgin as she had appeared to him was imprinted on the inner section of the mantle. The bishop,

convinced, immediately set about fulfilling her request and constructed a small chapel on the site that has since been replaced with a massive basilica. Diego became caretaker of the chapel and died there in about 1548. Following the apparitions of Our Lady of Guadalupe, as she is known, conversions among the Indians, which had been few, increased dramatically. Feast: May 30.

Diez y Bustos de Molína, Bd. Victoria

(1903-1936. B. at Seville, Spain; d. at Hornachuelos.) A teacher and art student, Victoria was an only child of devout parents whose example inspired her to develop an intense spiritual life. She joined the Teresian Association, an organization founded on Carmelite ideals to promote apostolic activity through the teaching profession. She was involved in Catholic Action and religious education, helped the needy, and cultivated a deep prayer life. "Praying before the Blessed Sacrament I find strength, courage, light, and all the love I need to help those entrusted to me," she said. She was working in Hornachuelos at the start of the Spanish Civil War. During the persecution of the church that followed, Victoria was arrested and taken to a house converted into a prison. On August 12, she and seventeen others were taken to the abandoned mine shaft of Rincon and thrown in. Victoria encouraged her fellow victims, saying: "Come on, our reward is waiting for us!" Her final words were, "Long live Christ the King!"

Dominic, St.

(1170-1221. B. at Calaruega, Spain; d. at Bologna, Italy.) Founder of the Order of Friars Preachers (Dominicans), Dominic was ordained an Augustinian priest. In about 1206, he accompanied his bishop, Diego, on a preaching mission to the heretical Albigensians in southern France. Diego and Dominic lived in radical poverty and persuasively presented their carefully prepared arguments to the heretics. The work was slow-going, but Dominic persevered after the death of Diego in 1207 and throughout five years of a bloody crusade against the Albigensians. Dominic repudiated the violent tactics of the crusaders, saying to one that enemies of the faith would be defeated not with swords but with prayer and humility.

Three times Dominic refused appointment as a bishop, concentrating instead on his work of preaching to heretics, educating the laity, and developing an order of men who would combine prayer, study, and pastoral work, especially preaching. The Order of Preachers was formally approved in 1216.

Known for his emphasis on study,

Dominic was equally attentive to the human condition and the inner life. A contemporary said of him: "Nothing disturbed his equanimity except a lively sympathy with any suffering. A person's face shows whether he or she is really happy. Dominic's was friendly and joyful. You could see that he was at peace inwardly." Feast: August 8.

Drexel, St. Katherine

(1858-1955. B. at Philadelphia, Pennsylvania; d. at Bensalem.) Drexel carried on a unique apostolate on behalf of native and African Americans during a period of intense racial bigotry in the United States. One of the wealthiest women in America—she inherited more than twenty million dollars—she was born to a leading international banking family. Her socially prominent parents attended daily Mass with their three children and gave much of their wealth to the poor, even running a dispensary out of their home to provide medicine for the needy.

Katherine had been interested in the plight of Native Americans since childhood. When approached by missionaries for financial assistance, she visited the western United States herself and met the great chief Red Cloud, with whom she formed a close relationship. Soon after, Drexel, who had long been interested in the religious life, decided to start an order devoted to missionary work among people of color. In 1891, she founded and was the first member of the Sisters of the Blessed Sacrament and poured her enormous wealth into the work.

In her efforts to help African Americans, Katherine endured years of harassment from white people who opposed her efforts. She started Xavier University in New Orleans, the only Catholic university in the United States specifically for blacks. Drexel herself founded 145 missions, twelve schools for native Americans, and fifty-five for African Americans. "If someone was different from her in language, heritage, and race, she rejoiced in that," one of the nuns who knew her said after the pope announced Drexel's canonization (*New York Times*, March 11, 2000). Drexel spent the last twenty years of her life in semiretirement after suffering a severe heart attack. Feast: March 3.

Duchesne, St. Rose Philippine

(1769-1852. B. at Grenoble, France; d. at St. Charles, Missouri.) Duchesne entered the Visitation convent at Grenoble but returned home in 1791 when the French Revolution suppressed religious orders. Efforts to revive the convent following the revolution failed. In 1804, St. Madeleine Sophie Barat, founder of the Society of the Sacred Heart, established a house of her sisters at Grenoble and Rose joined them. She made her profession in 1805 and in 1818 went to America as a missionary, fulfilling an ambition she had formed at the age of eight when she heard stories of America from a Jesuit priest. She served there for nearly thirty-five years, much of that time as superior, founding convents and establishing schools, including the first free school west of the Mississippi River.

She and her sisters served an area that ranged from Missouri to Louisiana to Kansas, their ministry complicated by the challenges of pioneer life. They endured everything from inadequate housing to yellow fever to such bitterly cold weather that the milk in the pail froze between the barn and the house. At one point, slander from jealous outsiders nearly ruined a school: "They say everything about us except that we poison the children," Duchesne wrote. When she was seventy-one, she helped to set up a school for Native Americans in Kansas but after a year retired to her convent in St. Charles, Missouri. She died there at the age of eighty-three. A contemporary said that "everything in and about her was stamped with the seal of a crucified life.... She was the St. Francis of Assisi of the Society." Feast: November 18.

E

Elizabeth of Hungary, St.

(1207-1231. B. at Bratislava, Hungary; d. at Marburg, Germany.) The marriage of Elizabeth, daughter of King Andrew II of Hungary, and Ludwig, landgrave (count) of Thuringia, was arranged for political purposes but turned out to be exceptionally happy. She was devout and extraordinarily generous, building and working in a hospital close to their castle, feeding the poor and caring for orphans. When members of Ludwig's household, annoyed by Elizabeth's generosity, urged him to send her back to Hungary, he said that he wouldn't give her up for a mountain of gold.

The couple had three children, but in 1227 after six years of marriage Ludwig joined a crusade and died of the plague before reaching the Holy Land. Elizabeth, devastated, wept uncontrollably and cried, "The world is dead to me and all that was pleasant in it." The accounts are unclear, but she either was then turned out of the castle by her brother-in-law, who resented her generosity, or left voluntarily to pursue a life of poverty. She provided for her children, joined the Third Order Franciscans, and started a hospice. She died after a brief but generous life of serving the poor and practicing great personal austerities. Feast: November 17.

Elizabeth of Portugal, St.

(1271-1336. B. at Zaragoza, Spain; d. at Coimbra, Portugal.) Elizabeth was a queen known as a peacemaker, a reputation she earned at great personal cost. "What a life of bitterness I am leading!" she wrote. "On whom but God can I lean?" Daughter of the king of Aragon, she married King Denis of Portugal when she was twelve. He was an effective ruler but a bad husband, fathering numerous illegitimate children. Elizabeth prayed for his conversion and gave herself up to a life of prayer and charity. Among other works, she founded a hospital at Coimbra, a house for reformed prostitutes, and an orphanage, and provided lodging for pilgrims.

Elizabeth and Denis had two children, Alfonso and Constance. Twice, Elizabeth successfully intervened between father and son when Alfonso led an armed rebellion against his father. (His father, he felt, favored his illegitimate children at the expense of his legitimate heir.) For a time, however, the king banished Elizabeth from court because he thought she was a threat to his policies. He pardoned her in 1324 and died a year later, having repented of his sins in confession.

Elizabeth's other peacemaking ventures resulted in her averting war between Portugal and Castile and negotiating peace between several royal houses. Following the king's death, she spent the last eleven years of her life in a house near a Poor Clare convent she had founded at Coimbra. There she continued her works of mercy. Feast: July 4.

Elizabeth of the Trinity, Bd.

(1880-1906. B. at Camp D'Avor, Bourges, France; d. at Dijon.) Born to Joseph Catez, a French soldier, and his wife Marie, Elizabeth soon earned a reputation as a strong-willed child with a hot temper—"a real devil," her mother wrote in a letter to her husband. Her father died of a heart attack when Elizabeth was seven, an event that seems to have deepened her religious convictions and helped her to bridle her volcanic temper. She was an unusually gifted pianist with the potential for a career in music, but by the time she was fourteen, she was determined to enter the Carmelite cloister in Dijon. Her mother initially resisted but allowed her daughter to enter when she turned twenty-one.

Elizabeth had a profound devotion to the Blessed Trinity and a desire to suffer and to sacrifice herself as Christ did. "There are exchanges of love," she said, "that take place only on the cross." She developed an intense mystical life, was keenly aware of the pres-

ence of God, and practiced great charity. In 1903 she was diagnosed with Addison's Disease, a condition of the adrenal glands characterized by anemia, and at that time fatal. She endured her final agonizing decline heroically: "I go with Christ to my passion in order to participate in his work of redemption," she said. She died in 1906. Feast: November 8.

Escrivá de Balaguer, Bd. Josemaría

(1902-1975. B. at Barbastro, Spain; d. at Rome, Italy.) Escrivá was a priest in Madrid in 1928 when he founded an organization of lay spirituality known as Opus Dei (Work of God). The work was ahead of its time, emphasizing the holiness and active apostolate of the laity thirty-five years before similar conclusions emerged from Vatican Council II. Some accused Escrivá of being a dangerous progressive. After the Council, others accused him of being too conservative because of his support of traditional church teaching.

Ministering secretly during the violently anti-Catholic Spanish Civil War, Escrivá found himself a hunted man when authorities placed a bounty on him. Once, soldiers hanged a captive from a tree in front of Escrivá's mother's house, thinking the victim was the priest. After the war, Escrivá received a doctorate in theology, worked for several Vatican commissions, and traveled extensively to foster the growth of his movement.

Today, Opus Dei is a personal prelature—essentially a nonterritorial diocese. Critics charge that it is secretive and rigid, but Opus Dei has enjoyed substantial growth, now numbering about eighty thousand members. Membership includes married people (the majority), single, and clergy.

Pope John Paul II said at Escrivá's beatification that "[he] untiringly preached the universal call to holiness and apostolate.... Work, too, is a means of personal holiness ... done in union with Jesus Christ." Feast: June 26.

Eymard, St. Peter Julian

(1811-1868. B./d. at La Mure d'Isere, France.) The Blessed Sacrament was the center of Eymard's life both as a diocesan priest and later when he joined the Marist order. "Without it I should have been lost," he admitted. After he'd carried the host in one Corpus Christi procession, he said, "My soul was flooded with faith and love for Jesus in the Blessed Sacrament. Those two hours seemed but a moment. I laid at the feet of our Lord the church in France and throughout the world, everybody, myself."

He decided to found a religious order devoted to the Eucharist, and in 1856, released from his commitment to the Marists, he began the Priests of the Most Blessed Sacrament. They performed all the regular tasks of the clergy, but with the additional and chief responsibility of maintaining perpetual adoration before the Blessed Sacrament. Eymard also founded an order for women, the Servants of the Blessed Sacrament, as well as a number of organizations and societies devoted to the Eucharist. "If the love for the Eucharist dies out in a heart," he said, "faith vanishes [and] indifference holds sway...." St. John Vianney, who knew Eymard, said: "He is a great saint.... His work will do great things for God. Adoration by priests! How fine!" After Eymard's death from a stroke, miracles took place at his tomb. Feast: August 1.

F

Fabiola, St.

(D. c. 399 at Rome, Italy.) The lively, wealthy Fabiola was a member of the famous patrician family, Fabia, and a Christian. She divorced her first husband for his dissolute life and remarried, contrary to church law. On the death of her second husband, she performed public penance, was readmitted to the church, and led an austere life. She gave much of her wealth to the poor and in 395 went to Bethlehem to visit St. Jerome. She intended to settle there in a convent but found the life too confining (she preferred the stimulation of crowds and activity).

Fabiola returned to Rome and threw herself into charitable activities. With St. Pammachius, she started a hospice for poor and sick pilgrims, the first of its kind in the West. Jerome wrote that within a year it "became known from Parthia to Britain." The restless Fabiola was preparing for another journey when she died unexpectedly. Romans, grateful for her many charities, turned out en masse for her funeral. Feast: December 27.

Favre, Bd. Peter

(1506-1546. B. at Vilardet, France; d. at Rome.) Favre, one of the first companions of St. Ignatius Loyola, was perhaps the most ecumenical of the early Jesuits. He was so kindhearted and tolerant that, in an intolerant age, he prayed for Martin Luther as well as for the pope. A contemporary said that "...by his lovable and pleasing manner, he earned everyone's good will and affection" and won many to the love of God.

Favre was ordained as a priest in 1534. That same year he celebrated the Mass at Montmartre, where Loyola and six companions, including Favre, took their vows as Jesuits. In 1537, he accompanied Loyola to Rome, taught at a university there and, at the request of the pope, attended conferences in Germany in an unsuccessful attempt to heal the rift between Protestants and Catholics in that country. The state of the church in Germany so appalled him that he launched a ministry of preaching and spiritual direction aimed at reforming the lives of Catholic clergy and laity. He saw this approach—rather than conferences and discussions—as a more effective response to the Protestant Reformation. He enjoyed tremendous success in Germany, Spain, and Portugal and wrote guidelines for ecumenical contact in which he stressed personal conversion as essential to ecumenism.

In 1546, Pope Paul III asked Favre

to serve as his theologian at the Council of Trent, but he arrived in Rome sick and overwhelmed by the stifling heat. He died soon after, attended by Ignatius himself, who held him in his arms as he passed away. Feast: August 11.

Felix of Cantalice, St.

(1515-1587. B. at Cantalice, Italy; d. at Rome). This gentle, humble Capuchin brother was known as "Brother Deo Gratias" for his use of the phrase "Thanks be to God" in response to everything from greetings to insults. He was the questor—beggar—for the Capuchins at Rome for forty years, gathering food and alms to support the community. The post inevitably exposed him to humiliations and fatigue compounded by his insistence on going barefoot, fasting, and wearing a penitential shirt of iron links and barbs. Nevertheless, he was a particularly joyful individual, and his great friend, St. Philip Neri, also noted for his good humor, considered him a saint.

When St. Charles Borromeo sought Neri's help in writing constitutions for his new order, Neri recommended the illiterate Felix as the best possible ad-viser. Felix protested but Borromeo read him the rules, Felix made suggestions (primarily to mitigate certain overly strict regulations), and Borromeo accepted the advice. Felix was especially

popular with the children of Rome. He would gather them in a circle and sing songs that he had composed about the happiness to be found in a good life and the ugliness of sin. He died at the age of seventy-two after seeing a vision of Mary. Feast: May 18.

Ferrini, Bd. Contardo

(1859-1902. B. at Milan, Italy; d. at Suna.) Ferrini was a layman who never married (he took a private vow of celibacy when he was twenty-one). He devoted his life to God primarily through his brilliant scholarship and called his teaching and writing "a hymn of praise to the Lord of all learning." He was a precocious student as well as a devout Catholic who received daily communion, even as a teenager. He earned a law degree from Borromeo College at Pavia in 1880 and went on to study at the University of Berlin. There, he joined the local St. Vincent de Paul Society and became involved in serving the needy, a ministry he continued throughout his life.

Ferrini was fluent in German, Latin, and Greek, knew eight other languages well, and had some knowledge of Coptic and Sanskrit. He held various chairs in law, his last at the University of Pavia as Professor of Roman Law. His expertise in this field won him an international reputation. Although strict, Ferrini was kind, encouraging, and good-humored with his students. Many came to his classes not simply because of his outstanding reputation but because in an age of unbelief, he, a professor, still believed in God. He joined the Franciscan Third Order (for laity), served on the city council in Milan, and managed to write over two hundred monographs and several textbooks before his death at the age of forty-three of typhoid fever. He died at his father's vacation home on Lake Maggiore, his father by his side. Contardo pursued perfection, a friend said, "with serenity and simplicity of heart." Feast: October 27.

Foucauld, Ven. Charles de

(1858-1916. B. at Strasbourg, France; d. at Tamanrasset, Algeria.) Born to the aristocracy, Charles was left an orphan at age six and raised by his grandfather. He abandoned his Catholic faith as a teenager, entered military service, led an excessively dissipated life, and was suspended from active duty. De Foucauld had developed a passion for Africa during a tour of duty there and returned to explore and map Morocco in 1883-84. *Reconnaissance au Maroc,* his book recounting this journey, earned the gold medal of the Paris Geographical Society.

Impressed by the faith of Moslems and Jews in Africa and dissatisfied with his life, Charles moved to Paris and returned to Catholicism in 1886. "The moment I realized God existed, I knew I could not do otherwise than live for him alone," he said. He entered the Trappist order in 1890. In search of greater solitude, he left the Trappists in 1897, living in Nazareth for three years as a servant of the Poor Clares.

Ordained a priest in 1901, he moved to Algeria where he lived alone, at the service of all, seeking to emulate the hidden life of Christ at Nazareth. "I want everyone here, Christian, Moslem, Jew, pagan, to look on me as a brother, a universal brother," he wrote. He drew up plans for two religious orders—"Little Brothers of Jesus" and "Little Sisters of Jesus"—whose members would live among the poor, work for a living, and influence others through their presence rather than through preaching. Not a single candidate joined Charles' nor did he have any converts. From 1905, he lived among the Tuareg tribe at Tamanrassett, spending his time in prayer, penance, and works of charity and writing a Tuareg dictionary.

On the night of December 1, 1916, Charles answered a knock on his door. Members of the rebel Senussi tribe seized him, bound him, and ransacked his home, leaving him under the guard of a fifteen-year old boy with a rifle. Two soldiers, unaware of the raid, approached, and Charles made a gesture to warn them away. The boy panicked and shot De Foucauld through the head. He died instantly. Since his death, five religious congregations based on his plans carry on his work in small fraternities around the world. There are also associations of priests and laity inspired by the ideals of De Foucauld.

Fournet, St. Andrew

(1752-1834. B. at Maille, France; d. at La Puye.) As a boy, Fournet resisted his mother's attempts to steer him toward the priesthood. He said he was bored with religion and once wrote in an exercise book that he was "not going to become a priest or monk." His interest in pleasure and amusement seemed to support that conclusion. He studied law and philosophy at Poitiers, tried the army, and attempted secretarial work until his family, near despair, sent him to his uncle, a parish priest in a rural area.

Andrew flourished there, studied theology, and was ordained a priest in 1776. He served in several parishes, was generous to the poor, and gave away almost all his possessions when a beggar criticized his lifestyle. During the French Revolution, he refused to take the oath required of priests and was sent to Spain, out of danger. He returned and ministered in secret, once escaping the police by pretending to be a corpse surrounded by candles and praying women. During this time, he met St. Elizabeth Bichier and later helped her to found the Daughters of the Cross to care for the sick and to teach girls from the country. "There are ruins to be rebuilt, ignorance to be remedied," Andrew told her.

Suffering from poor health and fatigue, Fournier resigned his parish at the age of sixty-eight. He spent his final years assisting the new congregation, helping in neighboring parishes, and advising many, both clergy and laity. Feast: May 13.

Frackowiak, Bd. Gregory

(1911-1943. B. at Lowecice, Poland; d. at Dresden, Germany.) Frackowiak was a brother in the Society of the Divine Word (SVD) and worked at a printing press in Poland during the Nazi occupation. In 1942, the Germans began to arrest large numbers of people in response to a proliferation of anti-Nazi leaflets. Frackowiak had read the leaflets and passed them on to others, and so was among those targeted. His superiors urged him to hide. Instead, he asked if, as manager of the press, he could take the blame and offer himself in place of other workers, some of whom were husbands and fathers. With their permission he did so and was arrested. The other detainees were released, but Frackowiak was beheaded at a prison in Dresden.

Frances of Rome, St.

(1384-1440. B./d. at Rome.) Frances wanted to be a nun but when her wealthy, pious parents arranged a marriage for her, she agreed and lived happily with her husband, Lorenzo Ponziano, for forty years. With her like-minded sister-in-law, Vanozza, Frances ministered to the poor and the sick of her native Rome. Their mother-in-law, worried about their health, asked her sons to intervene but the men were devoted to their wives and refused to hinder them.

Frances and her husband had three children, two of whom died young. In spite of her many obligations (the extended Ponziano family all lived together and she was in charge of the household), she devoted herself to the care of her children. "It is most laudable in a married woman to be devout," she once said, "...but sometimes she must leave God at the altar to find him in her housekeeping."

The family fortunes suffered when antipapal forces swept into Rome in 1408 and again in 1410. On the first occasion, Lorenzo was stabbed but recovered, and on the second he was forced to flee. After the assault of 1410, Frances managed the family affairs and continued her good works from a corner of their ruined palace. When Lorenzo returned, a broken man, she nursed him until his death in 1436 and then joined a foundation of devout women she had earlier established. She served as their superior for the four remaining years of her life. Feast: March 9.

Francis de Sales, St.

(1567-1622. B. at Thorens, Savoy; d. at Lyons, France.) De Sales was so open-hearted, cheerful, and tuned to the will of God that he seemed a testimonial to his own advice: "Do not wish to be anything but what you are, and try to be that perfectly." He achieved near-perfection as a priest and the bishop of Geneva at a time of intense religious conflict following the Protestant Reformation.

In 1594, shortly after he was ordained, he went as a missionary to try to win the formerly Catholic, now Calvinist, population of the Chablis district back to the church. The effort seemed foredoomed—others had tried and failed. But through clear preaching, courage, tact, and genuine love of the people, he won over the majority. "Truth is always charitable," he said. "Bitter zeal does more harm than good." He also wrote pamphlets explaining Catholic teaching and distributed these to Calvinist homes.

On becoming bishop of Geneva in 1602, de Sales at once set out to reform his difficult diocese, which was struggling with the effects of the

Reformation. He preached at every opportunity and brought his clergy up to a very high standard. He taught catechism classes for children and offered spiritual direction to many. His advice—which could be firm, when necessary—was always sensitive to the human need for encouragement. "Be patient with everyone, but above all yourself," he counseled. "Whatever happens, never let go; hold steadfastly to God." He also championed the cause of the deaf and for this, is the patron saint of the deaf.

In 1604, he met St. Jane de Chantal and they began a devoted friendship ("With you I speak as I do with my own heart," he wrote to her). Together they founded the Order of the Visitation, a congregation for women.

Above all, de Sales was a pastor intent on helping not only religious but also laity to holiness. "It is an error or rather a heresy," he wrote, "to wish to banish the devout life from the regiment of soldiers, the mechanics shop ... or the home of married people." He wrote *Introduction to the Devout Life* for a married woman who wanted guidance for living as a Christian in the world. ("Marriage is a great sacrament. ... Its origin, its end, its uses, its form and its matter are holy," he wrote.) It was a best-seller and was followed by *The Treatise on the Love of God*. Both are still available and widely read.

De Sales suffered a stroke in 1622, and as he lay dying, a nun asked for some final words of advice. Taking a piece of paper, he wrote: "Humility, humility, humility." He is a Doctor of the Church and the patron saint of writers. Feast: January 24.

Francis of Assisi, St.

(1182-1226. B./d. at Assisi, Italy.) Francis' early life was one of wealth and comfort as the son of a well-to-do silk merchant. Francis learned the trade and became a "cautious businessman but a very showy spender," according to a contemporary. He fought as a soldier in a war with neighboring Perugia, was taken prisoner, and released after a year. He became seriously ill but recovered and returned to war, only to have a vision in which Christ invited him to "follow the master rather than the man."

After his conversion, Francis turned to a life of prayer. One day, in the church of San Damiano, he seemed to hear Christ say from the crucifix, "Francis, go and repair my church which as you can see is in ruins." Taking this literally, he sold some of his father's cloth to finance the work. His father, troubled by his son's turn toward religion, threatened to disinherit him and took him to court to recover his money. In a dramatic scene, Francis repaid his father, renounced his inheritance, then stripped off his clothes and returned them as well.

Francis was ordained a deacon but refused the priesthood out of humility. He attracted many followers to his simple life of poverty and preaching and in 1210 Pope Innocent III officially recognized them as a religious order, the Order of Friars Minor (Franciscans). Around 1212, together with St. Clare, Francis founded an order for women. In 1221, he started the Third Order for men and women who shared the Franciscan spirit but chose to remain in the world. Between 1210 and 1219, Francis made several missionary journeys and strengthened the organization of his order, particularly by fighting a movement from within to mitigate the poverty and simplicity of his rule.

Francis' warmth, intense love for the person of Christ, devotion to the Eucharist, poverty, emphasis on a more personal spirituality, and commitment to the church contributed to a much-needed renewal of thirteenth century religious life. Although today he is widely admired for his gentle spirit and love of nature, the driving force of Francis' life was his total surrender to God. "We should make a dwelling place within ourselves where he can stay," he wrote, "he who is the Lord God Almighty, Father, Son and Holy Spirit."

In 1224, while at prayer, Francis received the stigmata, the wounds of Christ's passion, on his hands, feet, and side. He tried to keep these hidden but they bled at times, were painful, and are well documented. Francis suffered from a variety of afflictions toward the end of his life and died after telling his assembled friars, "I have done my part; may Christ teach you to do yours." Feast: October 4.

Francis Xavier, St.

(1506-1552. B. near Pamplona, Spain; d. at Shangchwan, an island off the coast of China.) One of the first Jesuits and a close friend of St. Ignatius Loyola, Xavier is considered the greatest missionary since the apostles, even though his missionary activity lasted only ten years. His ministry, encompassing Japan and the East Indies, took him thousands of miles to the most remote areas under terrible conditions and frequent threat from "open enemies and not too trustworthy friends."

Francis was ordained with Ignatius in 1537 and was with him in Rome when the pope formally approved the Jesuit Society. In 1541, Ignatius sent him to Portuguese Goa, on the southwest coast of India. The principal obstacle to evangelization there was the greed, debauchery, and brutality of the colonists. Francis said that the treatment of the native people at the hands of one another and the Portuguese was "a permanent bruise on my soul."

He labored throughout the area for

the next eight years, traveling endlessly from Goa to Cape Comorin in the tip of India, Ceylon (Sri Lanka), the Malay peninsula, and the Molucca islands near New Guinea. He preached effectively against immorality, prayed with lepers, visited the sick and imprisoned, taught the faith, and baptized thousands. In 1549, he introduced Christianity to Japan, founding communities there that would later endure through terrible persecution. He returned to Goa in 1551, where he was appointed the first provincial of the Jesuits' newly formed province of India and the East.

In 1552, Xavier made arrangements to be smuggled into China, at that time closed to foreigners. He became ill and died off the coast of that country on the island of Shangchwan, attended only by a young Chinese Christian who had come with him from Goa.

Francis' life was one of unending hardship, travel (in spite of frequent sea-sickness), and loneliness, a constant theme in his many letters—he signed one, "The least and most lonely of your brothers." Still, he said that the dangers he experienced and the work he did for God brought him "spiritual joy." He met with unusual success due not only to his zeal but also to his compassion for and selfless identification with those he served. He is the patron saint of foreign missions. Feast: December 3.

Frassati, Bd. Pier Giorgio

(1901-1925. B./d. at Turin, Italy.) Frassati's father was a senator, an ambassador, and the founder of the liberal newspaper *La Stampa*. He was also an agnostic. Frassati's mother was a not-particularly-devout Catholic and a painter with a high-strung and critical personality. Frassati, nevertheless, turned out to be exceptionally pious and combined a deep spirituality with an outgoing, athletic nature and a love for art, theater, and music. He was a mountain climber and an avid skier who claimed, in the confines of town, to have "left my heart on the mountain peaks."

Frassati was a member of the St. Vincent de Paul Society and so generous to the poor that he helped support the children of a sick widow and often used his train fare for the needy. When his father offered him either money or a car on his graduation, he chose the money and gave it to the poor.

In 1918, he enrolled in the Royal Polytechnic of Turin to become a mining engineer in order "to serve Christ better among the miners." He was active in Catholic-oriented student and political organizations and was an outspoken opponent of fascism. He sometimes ended up in jail for his participation in religious processions that came under attack by political opponents. Once, he single-handedly beat off fascists who broke into his home to attack the family. "Cowards! Assassins!" he shouted as he chased them out the door.

In 1922, Pier joined the Dominican Third Order. In 1925, he contracted polio, apparently as a result of nursing a poor person who had the disease. He died five days later. Thousands attended his funeral, and shortly after, the poor of Turin petitioned the archbishop to begin the cause for his canonization. Feast: July 4.

G

Gabriel, St.

One of the seven archangels. In the Book of Daniel, Gabriel explains Daniel's visions to him (see Dn 8:15-27; 9:21-27). In the New Testament, he foretells the birth of John the Baptist to his father, Zechariah (see Lk 1:11-20). We know him best as the messenger who announces to Mary that she is to be the mother of the Savior (see Lk 1:26-38). Feast (with the Archangels Michael and Raphael): September 29.

Gapp, Bd. Jakob

(1897-1943. B. at Watten, Austria; d. at Berlin, Germany.) Gapp was a priest of the Marianist Order who ministered as a teacher, chaplain, and religious education director. He had a finely tuned social conscience born partially of his experience growing up in a working class family and partially from his familiarity with the church's social encyclicals. He sacrificed to help the poor, refusing to heat his room in the winter, for example, in order to give fuel to the needy.

During the rise of national socialism, Gapp studied Nazi documents to judge the validity of their philosophy. His research confirmed "the abhorrent nature of Nazism and its total irreconcilability with the Catholic faith," he

said. When the Germans took over Austria, Gapp refused to use the Nazi salute, to wear a swastika, or to promote Nazi ideas in the classroom. Consequently, he was not allowed to speak to students.

He moved back with his family, became a catechist, and again was silenced after telling his students, among other things, "God, not Adolf Hitler, is your God." Forbidden to teach, he eventually made his way to a Marianist school in Spain. There, in 1942, he applied for a visa to England. The Gestapo in Spain kept Jakob under surveillance and sent several agents to him posing as potential converts. He met with them for religious instruction and one day accepted their invitation to go on a picnic. The trip turned into an abduction as the agents spirited Gapp across the border into German-occupied France. There, the Nazis arrested him and sent him to Berlin. Charged with treason, he refused to compromise knowing, he said, that the Nazis intended to destroy the church. He was beheaded at Berlin-Plotzensee. Feast: August 13.

Garnier, St. Charles

(c. 1605-1649. B. at Paris, France; d. at St. Jean, Canada.) Garnier's Jesuit superior said of him that "his very laugh spoke of goodness." Garnier volunteered for the Jesuit mission in Canada after his ordination in 1635, but his father, reluctant to see him go, managed to delay his son's departure for a year. Upon his arrival in Quebec, he ministered to the Huron and Tobacco Indians for thirteen years. In December 1649 he was the only priest present at the village of St. Jean when the Iroquois, traditional enemies of the Hurons, attacked. Garnier assisted the dying, baptized catechumens, and was himself shot. Nevertheless, he made three attempts to crawl to a wounded man he wanted to help. Before he could reach him, Garnier was killed with a blow from a tomahawk. Feast (of the Martyrs of North America): October 19.

Giaccardo, Bd. Timothy

(1896-1948. B. near Narzole, Italy; d. at Rome.) Giaccardo was ordained as the first priest of the Society of St. Paul, a religious order established to promote the gospel through modern means of communication. In collaboration with the founder, Fr. James Alberione, Giaccardo guided the fledgling community, helping to establish its headquarters in Alba, opening the first house of the Society in Rome, and serving as vicar general of the congregation. He organized the society's publishing house, guided the young men who entered the order, visited the sick, and advised the many who sought his direction. A sensitive man, he concerned himself with the small needs of those in his care. When he discovered that a brother distributed religious booklets in front of church on bitterly cold winter mornings, he sent the man hot bricks on which to rest his feet and thermoses of warm milk.

He was "humble, simple, recollected, mortified, and very charitable," according to a contemporary. He had a "profound and continuous spirit of prayer ... and he united ... his evidently intense interior life with ... love and delicate religious courtesy." Giaccardo died of leukemia at the age of fifty-two. Feast: October 22.

Girolamo, St. Francis di

(1642-1716. B. at Grottaglie, Italy; d. at Naples.) Girolamo, "the apostle of Naples," was a Jesuit priest with a highly effective pastoral ministry. Acclaimed for his preaching—he was "a lamb when he talks but a lion when he preaches"—he brought many to conversion. He sought out the needy in prisons, hospitals, and ships' galleys and visited the roughest parts of the city, where he was sometimes assaulted. He once felt led to preach at night in a deserted part of town, and the next day a prostitute who had heard him through her window came to his confessional to repent. Perhaps his most remarkable penitent was Mary Alvira Cassier, a Frenchwoman who had murdered her father and then enlisted in the army, disguised as a man. Healings took place through his ministry, but he attributed all to the intercession of St. Cyrus, to whom he was devoted. Francis suffered physically toward the end of his life, and when he died, the poor turned out in great numbers for his funeral. Feast: May 11.

Giuliani, St. Veronica

(1660-1727. B. at Mercatello, Italy; d. at Citt' di Castello.) Giuliani's mystical experiences included the stigmata, ecstasies, and numerous visions, all well attested. These do not make her nearly as appealing as the common sense that guided her life and her balanced, practical holiness. She was a Capuchin nun, already noted for her spirituality when she entered the convent. ("She will one day be a saint," the bishop told her not-entirely-receptive fellow nuns.) Her superiors treated her harshly, and she was severely tempted to abandon ship but stayed and found herself increasingly drawn to the suffering Christ. After she received the stigmata in 1697, the bishop had her wounds bound and sealed, refused to allow her to receive communion, and put her under twenty-four-hour watch. When nothing he did

prevented the wounds from appearing, he allowed her to resume normal convent life.

She served as novice mistress for thirty-four years and forbade her novices to read any books of mysticism. Instead, she had them cultivate the essential virtues of humility, obedience, and charity. She was the abbess for the last eleven years of her life and in that position had water pipes laid to the convent and enlarged the buildings. She read voraciously and kept a journal at the order of her confessor. It ran to twenty-two thousand pages and is a rich source of material on the mystical life. She died of a stroke after fifty years as a religious. Feast: July 9.

Gonzaga, St. Aloysius

(1568-1591. B. in Lombardy; d. at Rome.) Aloysius' father, the marquis of Castiglione, was in the service of King Phillip II of Spain. He set his son apart for the military but by the age of seven, Aloysius' religious convictions led him elsewhere. A bout with kidney disease when he was eleven permanently undermined his health but gave him an excuse to limit his activities and devote himself to prayer and reading the lives of the saints.

Over the next few years his austerities became more rigorous—he fasted three times a week and rose at midnight to pray—and he decided to join the

Jesuits, a move his father vigorously opposed. In 1585, his father relented and Aloysius entered the Jesuit house in Rome, where he proved to be an ideal novice. During an epidemic in 1591, he nursed the sick with zeal and fell ill himself. Having earlier had a revelation that he hadn't long to live, he prepared himself for death and died at the age of twenty-three, after receiving the anointing of the sick from his confessor, St. Robert Bellarmine. He is a patron saint of Catholic youth. Feast: June 21.

Gonzales, St. Roque, and Companions

(1576-1628. B. at Asuncion, Paraguay; d. at Caaro, Brazil.) Roque was born to Spanish settlers of the nobility and became a priest when twenty-three. He immediately began to work among the Indians and after ten years entered the Jesuits in order to have greater missionary opportunity. He helped establish the famous Jesuit "reductions" in the area. These were settlements of Christian Indians protected by the missionaries from Spanish colonizers intent on selling the native people into slavery.

Roque worked patiently for two decades, establishing half a dozen reductions in spite of outright hostility from European settlers and the inherent dangers of the apostolate. A contemporary who knew both the priest and the terrain said that Roque endured danger, not only from hunger and extreme weather but from primitive travel that had him swimming across rivers and wading through bogs. Only a man as "holy as this priest was," the contemporary said, "could have born these trials with such fortitude."

In 1628, two young Jesuits joined him, and they founded a new reduction near the Ijuhi River. Fr. Juan de Castillo stayed there while Frs. Roque and Alphonsus Rodriguez went to Caaro in what is now southern Brazil to establish the All Saints reduction. There, a medicine man, jealous of the priests' influence, led an attack in which the priests were clubbed to death. Two days later, Juan de Castillo was stoned to death in a similar raid.

An Indian chief said of Roque that all the Christians among the Indians loved the priest, and mourned his death. "He was the father of us all." Feast (The Martyrs of Paraguay): November 17.

Goretti, St. Maria

(1890-1902. B. near Ancona, Italy; d. near Nettuno.) Goretti's father, a farmer, died when she was ten. Her mother struggled to maintain their farm while Maria, devout and good-natured, took care of the household chores. Alessandro Serenelli, the eighteen-year-old son of her father's partner, had harassed her on several occasions, and one day, while the rest of the family was in the fields, he attempted to rape her. She resisted and he stabbed her repeatedly. She died the next day. Maria endured her agonizing suffering heroically and when asked what had happened said simply, "He wanted to make me do wrong and I would not. May God forgive him," she said of her murderer, "because I already have forgiven him."

Alessandro was sentenced to thirty years in prison and spent the first eight unrepentant. He then had a dream in which he saw Maria in a field of flowers holding out white lilies to him. He repented, reformed his life, and asked forgiveness from Maria's mother. Pope Pius XII canonized Goretti as a martyr for Christian virtue. Feast: July 6.

Goupil, St. René

(1606-1642. B. at Anjou, France; d. at Osserneon, New York.) Goupil was a layman, served as an assistant to the Jesuit missionaries in Canada, and was the first to die of the group known as the North American Martyrs. He attempted to join the Jesuit order in his native France but failed due to poor health and instead became a surgeon. He went to Canada at his own expense and worked with St. Isaac Jogues. Mohawk Indians captured the two men while they were on a supply-gathering trip to Quebec, took them to their vil-

lage near present-day Albany in New York, and subjected them to severe torture. These included ripping out their hair and nails, beating them, and cutting off a thumb from each man. After two months, they killed Goupil with a tomahawk when he made the sign of the cross over some children. Within the year, Jogues escaped. He wrote of his companion, whose martyrdom he witnessed: "He was a man of unusual simplicity and innocence of life, of invincible patience and very conformable to the will of God." Feast (of the Martyrs of North America): October 19.

Grassi, Bd. Anthony

(1592-1671. B./d. in Fermo, Italy.) Grassi, a priest of the Oratorian order, was noted for his intellectual acumen and serenity of spirit. He spoke quietly and encouraged others to do the same, once saying to a fellow priest, "Please, Father, only a few inches of voice." In 1621, Grassi was struck by lightning while kneeling in prayer at church. The heat was overwhelming, he later said, and he thought it would destroy his heart. He couldn't move. Someone lifted him into a chair but he fainted. "...My head and arms and legs were dangling uselessly and my sight and speech had failed though my hearing was acute." The strike scorched his underclothes, healed him of chronic indigestion, and left him with a profound sense that his life belonged entirely to God.

Grassi was an extremely effective confessor and could often read the conscience of a penitent, naming the specifics of a situation without being told. He served as superior of the Fermo Oratory from 1635 until his death, elected repeatedly by his appreciative community. He discouraged rigorous bodily penances—"Humbling the mind and will is more effective than a hair-shirt"—but encouraged a very high level of holiness. He achieved this end primarily through personal example, encouragement, and gentle correction. Among his last acts were the reconciliation of two feuding brothers and the miraculous restoration of sight to a priest who was then able to celebrate Mass for the first time in nine years. Feast: December 13.

Gregory the Great, Pope St.

(c. 540-604. B./d. in Rome.) As Pope, Gregory chose to call himself the "Servant of the Servants of God," a title still used by the papacy fourteen centuries later. He was born to wealth and served as an administrator of Rome for two years, but upon the death of his father he turned over his estates to the church and founded seven monasteries. He himself joined the seventh, St. Andrew's, in 574. He was ordained in 578 and served as papal nuncio in Constantinople, where he continued to live an austere life. He returned to Rome in about 586, and in 590, to his great horror, he was unanimously elected pope, the first monk to hold that office. He appealed to the emperor to block his nomination, wanting only to pursue a simple monastic life. That failed and Gregory submitted to his consecration.

For the next fourteen years, he energetically and fearlessly reformed the church and restored Rome to a semblance of order in the absence of an effective civil government. He cared for victims of famine and plague, appointed governors, negotiated treaties, upheld the primacy of the Roman see in his dealings with the East, and disciplined the clergy. Gregory personally sent missionaries—headed by St. Augustine, prior of St. Andrew's—to England to refound the church there and guided them by letter in the enterprise. He contributed considerably to the development of the liturgy and is so closely associated with liturgical music that plainsong is known as Gregorian Chant.

Gregory was humble and practical, traits much in evidence in his many writings including 854 letters that survive. His *Dialogues*, an uncritical, credulous lives of the saints, served as a model for medieval hagiographers. His *Pastoral Care* offers advice to bishops in carrying out their duties. He is considered the father of the medieval papacy for his role in shaping that institution. He is a Doctor of the Church. Feast: September 3.

Guadalajara, Bd. Martyrs of

(D. 1936) In 1936, during the Spanish Civil War, Communist troops murdered three Carmelite nuns at Guadalajara, Spain. They were: Sr. Maria of the Angels of St. Joseph (born Marciana Valtierra Tordesillas), thirty-one years old; Sr. Maria Pilar of St. Francis Borgia (Jacoba Martinez Garcia), fifty-eight; Sr. Teresa of the Child Jesus (Eusebia Garcia y Garcia), twenty-seven.

On July 22, with soldiers roaming the city, the eighteen nuns of the Monastery of St. Joseph scattered through the streets disguised in secular clothes. Some found shelter with Catholic families, and Srs. Maria of the Angels, Maria Pilar, and Teresa, along with two other nuns, hid in the basement of the Hibernia Hotel. Two days later, the five left the hotel, two going to a nearby boarding house, the three martyrs making their way up a street. A soldier eating lunch in a parked jeep recognized them and shouted to her companions, "Shoot them! They are nuns!"

Sr. Maria of the Angels died instantly when a bullet struck her in the heart. Sr. Maria Pilar, also hit, cried out, "Viva Cristo Rey (Long live Christ the King)!" The soldiers, furious at the pious exclamation, shot her repeatedly and slashed her with a knife. She died, having lost most of her blood, saying, "My God, pardon them. They don't know what they're doing." Sr. Teresa was not harmed, and a soldier, pretending concern, gathered some of his companions and led Teresa to a nearby cemetery, apparently intending to rape her. As they went, she spoke out fearlessly against them, and they angrily insisted she praise communism. To each of their commands she cried, "Viva Cristo Rey!" Told to walk a few steps ahead, she spread her arms in the form of a cross and was shot in the back. Feast: July 24.

Guanella, Bd. Louis

(1842-1915. B. at Franciscio di Campodolcino, Italy; d. at Como.) As a young priest, Guanella's work with the poor earned him the enmity of anticlerical politicians. These feared the poor as potential revolutionaries and blacklisted Guanella, forcing him out of parish ministry. He went to Turin in 1875, and for several years assisted St. John Bosco, a man whose work for neglected boys made him, too, a target of Italy's rab-idly anti-Catholic factions. Recalled by his bishop, Guanella set up a school for poor children at Traona with the same results as before, but this time the authorities ordered him to a tiny parish in the Alps. Here he began his life's work of service to the sick poor, becoming involved in an orphanage and hospice in the area.

In 1886, he and his collaborators moved the work to Como and named it the Little House of Divine Providence in honor of the institute by the same name established by St. Joseph Cottolengo at Turin. Guanella was so completely devoted to the poor that once, when coworkers tried to restrict his generosity, he threw money out the window to a needy man below. On another occasion, he threw out a pair of shoes. "The heart of a Christian ... cannot pass by the hardships ... of the poor without helping them," he said. The work of the Little House flourished, and Guanella founded the orders of the Daughters of Divine Providence and the Servants of Charity to man the operation. In 1915, he received a gold medal from the government in Como for his work with the wounded during World War I. He died of a stroke the same year. Feast: October 24.

Guerin, Bd. Theodore Mother (Anne-Thérèse)

(1798-1856. B. at Etables, France; d. at St. Mary of the Woods, Indiana.) Guerin's journal describing her perilous trip to America for missionary work disappointed her religious superiors back in France. "We have read your little account of the voyage with interest but to be frank ... we would have preferred it if you had written in a style less romantic and more pious."

Fortunately, Guerin ignored this advice, and her subsequent journals and nearly five thousand letters give a lively account of life in mid-nineteenth century America. Her immensely attractive personality is evident everywhere, whether she's commenting on a whale sighting on the Atlantic ("...as big as a house") or describing a stage coach trip through a river: "The horses were swimming rather than walking.... The water poured in on us ... but the driver, without losing his American coolness ... set the carriage up again."

Guerin had been a member of the Sisters of Divine Providence of Ruille-sur-Loir for seventeen years when she led a group of five fellow sisters to Indiana. Their mission was to educate children of pioneer families and care for the sick poor. They arrived in 1840, and were immediately plunged into poverty. The sisters in France, with little money to spare, could offer scant assistance. Anti-Catholic settlers occasionally pelted them with rocks and eggs, spread malicious rumors, and now and then denied them credit at their stores. Two years after they arrived, their barns mysteriously caught fire and burned down ("This ... seems to be the result of a crime," Guerin wrote). Day in, day out, she responded with a quiet charity that impressed all. "Everybody wished to speak to her," one of the nuns said. "On the streets, they followed her for a word of advice."

The sisters persevered, opened schools, received novices, and slowly won the residents over. Meanwhile, Guerin did protracted battle with t he local bishop who, jealous of his authority, attempted to wrest control of the congregation from her. Although she never said an uncharitable word against him, she steadily resisted what she called "the caprices of a disordered imagination." The affair reached its nadir in 1847, when Guerin refused to accept his unreasonable demands and he locked her in a room while he went to dinner. Shortly after this incident, Rome relieved him of his duties, appointed a new bishop, and the order flourished.

The sisters established schools throughout the state and founded two orphanages and several pharmacies prior to Guerin's death from years of ill health. The order, now separate from the original congregation in France, is known as the Sisters of Providence of St. Mary-of-the-Woods. Its members minister in the United States, China, Taiwan, and other countries. Feast: October 3.

Guyart, Bd. Marie (Mary of the Incarnation)

(1599-1672. B. at Tours, France; d. at Quebec, Canada.) Guyart, in deference to her parent's wishes, married at the age of seventeen in spite of a preference for the religious life. She and her husband, Claude, had a son. When Claude died two years later, Marie made a private vow of chastity and worked to support her child. In 1632, leaving her twelve-year-old boy with her sister, she entered the Ursuline order and went as a missionary to Canada in 1639.

Guyart established a school for the Indians and opened the first Ursuline convent there in 1641. Her ministry was extraordinarily effective in spite of a fire that destroyed the convent in 1650, and danger during the Iroquois War from 1653-63. She wrote Algonquin and Iroquois dictionaries and carried on an extensive correspondence encouraging missionaries and helping them with problems. Her twelve thousand surviving letters provide much information about life in early Quebec. Guyart led an austere, penitential life, was a mystic, and experienced the presence of Jesus and Mary as well as revelations and consolations. Her son, Dom Claude Martin, became a Benedictine and wrote a biography of her. Feast: April 30.

Helen, St.

(c. 255-330. B. probably at Drepanum, Asia Minor; d. at Nicomedia.) Helen was the mother of the Emperor Constantine, the Roman emperor who first championed Christianity. A tradition making her a native of England probably confuses her with another Helen who was married to an emperor of Britain and had a son, also named Constantine.

Helen, of lowly birth, married the Emperor Constantius Chlorus, and their son was born in 274. Her husband abandoned her in 290 in favor of a political marriage to the stepdaughter of the Emperor Maximian. When Constantine became emperor in 306, he treated his mother with great honor. She enthusiastically promoted the Christian cause although it is not known when she became a Christian.

When she was about seventy, Helen went to the Holy Land, helped establish several churches there, and devoted her time to caring for the needy, redeeming prisoners, and setting up shrines. According to late tradition (c. 385-400), she shared in the discovery of the cross on which Christ was crucified. It came to light during excavations for a basilica Constantine ordered built on Mount Calvary. Feast: August 18.

Hilda of Whitby, St.

(614-680. B. at Northumbria, England; d. at Whitby.) After she became a nun at the age of thirty-three, Hilda ruled the double monastery of Whitby with great success for nearly twenty-five years. In such monasteries, which were common at the time, the monks and nuns gathered daily to sing the prayers of the church but otherwise they led entirely separate lives.

According to her biographer, St. Bede, Hilda—grandniece of the king of Northumbria—lived "most nobly in the secular state" before entering the religious life. As an abbess, first at the double monastery at Hartlepool and then at Whitby, she insisted on the importance of education. Her monks and nuns read Scripture, copied books by hand, illuminated manuscripts, studied literature, and worked at mathematical riddles. She encouraged the work of Caedmon, the first English religious poet, who was initially a herdsman and then a monk at Whitby. Hilda herself was renowned for her learning, charity, and diplomacy. "Not only ordinary people, but even kings and princes sometimes asked and accepted her advice," Bede said. Probably because of her reputation and also because of the location of the abbey, the famous synod of 663-664 met there to settle issues of church practice. "Her life was a bright example ... to all who desired to live well.... All who knew her called her Mother, such were her wonderful godliness and grace." Feast: November 17.

I

Ignatius of Antioch, St.

(c. 35-c. 107. D. at Rome.) According to tradition, Ignatius was a very early bishop of Antioch and may have been a disciple of the apostles. Condemned to death for his faith, he traveled under guard from Antioch to Rome to be thrown to the beasts at the games. On the course of his journey, he wrote letters to the churches at Ephesus, Magnesia, Tralles, Rome, Philadelpia, and Smyrna, and a short personal letter to Polycarp, bishop of Smyrna, who later was also a martyr.

The letters are invaluable for shedding light on theological development in the early church, particularly in the areas of clerical authority, heresy, and martyrdom. They also reveal the warm, gentle character of the bishop and his passionate devotion to Christ. In his letter to the Romans, he pleads with them not to seek a pardon for him. "Leave me to be a meal for the beasts.... I am his wheat, ground fine by the lions' teeth to be made purest bread for Christ.... He who died for us is all that I seek; he who rose again for us is my whole desire." It is probable but not certain that he died at the Coliseum. Feast: October 17.

Ignatius of Loyola, St.

(1491-1556. B. near Azpeitia, Spain; d. at Rome.) Ignatius was born into the Basque nobility, chose a career in the military, and was a typical young man of the times, with a lively interest in women, gambling, and sword play. In 1521 he was wounded in the battle of Pamplona when a cannon ball passed between his legs, tearing open the left leg and breaking the right. He was taken to the family castle at Loyola to recover, but the leg was badly set, causing the doctors to break and reset it, a painful procedure that Ignatius bore stoically. Unfortunately, a bone protruded from under his knee and, in another painful operation that Ignatius again bore heroically, the doctors sawed off the protrusion.

During his lengthy convalescence, Ignatius asked for romantic tales of chivalry to read but settled for a life of Christ and the lives of the saints, the only books available. Inspired by these, he decided to dedicate himself to God's service. In 1522, he went to the shrine of Our Lady at Monserrat, hung up his sword at the altar, and spent the next year in retreat at Manresa. This was a time of both spiritual desolation and consolation during which Ignatius began to write his famous *Spiritual*

Exercises. This practical guide, designed to help individuals overcome self-interest and give themselves to God, has had a profound impact on Christian spirituality and is still widely used.

After a trip to the Holy Land in 1523, Ignatius spent the next eleven years as a student, first in Spain and then at the University of Paris, graduating as master of arts. During these years, he evangelized and converted many and was even briefly imprisoned in Spain, where the authorities were suspicious of such ministry on the part of a layman.

In Paris, Ignatius laid the groundwork for the Society of Jesus (Jesuits) when he and six companions, including Bd. Peter Favre and St. Francis Xavier, took vows of poverty and chastity. They also vowed to preach in the Holy Land or, failing that, to submit themselves to the service of the pope. Most of the men were ordained in 1537. When the trip to the Holy Land proved impossible due to political instability, Ignatius went to Rome to place the group at the service of the pope. On the way there, he had a vision in which he saw Christ in a bright light, loaded with a heavy cross, and heard the words: "I will be favorable to you in Rome." Pope Paul III approved the society in 1540, and Ignatius became its first general superior.

Ignatius spent his remaining years in Rome guiding his company of men, which numbered one thousand at the time of his death. From the start, the Jesuits were active in the missions, played a key role in the Counter Reformation, and began the work of education for which they are so famous. Ignatius himself also directly served the poor, ministering to prostitutes, orphans, and the sick. He had a gift for friendship, a profound prayer life, and a deep humility. He died suddenly at Rome, but his influence in the church continues, most notably through his still-thriving Society. Feast: July 31.

Imbert, Bd. Laurence

(D. 1839. B. at Aix-en-Provence, France; d. near Seoul, Korea.) "I am overwhelmed with fatigue and in great danger," Imbert wrote from Korea, where he was a priest of the Paris Foreign Missionary Society. Previously assigned to China for twelve years—he had been a bishop there—he left for his new assignment in 1837. He entered Korea secretly, since the Korean government banned Christianity. For two years, he gave himself up to an apostolate that was so grueling he had little fear, he said, of the "sword-stroke" that might soon end it.

Imbert stayed undercover in Catholic homes, generally working from 2:30 A.M. through to 9 P.M. with only a brief rest at midday. He heard confessions, celebrated Mass, catechized, counseled, and administered other sacraments as necessary. The Korean Christians who had gathered secretly for his ministry then dispersed before daybreak. He repeated this pattern again and again, staying in the same place no more than two nights. He suffered a great deal from hunger. "I have always led a hard and very busy life but here I think I have reached the positive limit of work," he wrote. During the persecution of Christians that swept Korea in 1839, he and two other priests surrendered to authorities in an effort to avert a general massacre of the laity. The men were beaten and beheaded. Feast (with the Martyrs of Korea): September 20.

Irenaeus of Lyons, St.

(c. 130-200. B. at Smyrna; d. at Lyons.) Irenaeus tells us that as a child he had heard the great St. Polycarp and treasured his words "not on paper but in my heart (for the things we learn from our very childhood grow on with our soul and are a part of it)."

Irenaeus was a priest at Lyons in 177 when, on behalf of the clergy there, he carried to the pope a letter that requested leniency toward Montanist heretics of the area. While he was away, persecution of Christians broke out and many were martyred, including the bishop. Irenaeus was named bishop on his return. He is one of the great figures of the era, boldly opposing heresy and in the process writing down the first exposition of the fundamentals of Catholic doctrine. He combined an astute mind with deep faith, broad education, and an appreciation of tradition. His "name means 'peaceable' and ... by temperament [he] was a peacemaker," Eusebius wrote in his *History of the Church* (c. 323).

His main surviving work is *Adversus Haereses* (*Against the Heresies*) in which he described the errors of the Gnostics. ("It is by exposing their systems that we conquer them.") In opposition to those errors—and for the first time in the history of the young church—he clearly delineated Catholic belief. For this, he is sometimes called the Father of Catholic Theology. Irenaeus also insisted on the importance of tradition, stating that the true teaching of the church is that which has been passed down in an unbroken chain by the apostles. "...The oldest church ... founded and established at Rome ... can rightly lay claim to apostolicity." According to uncertain tradition, Irenaeus died a martyr at Lyons. Feast: June 28.

Ivo of Brittany, St.

(1235-1303. B. at Kermartin, France; d. at Lovannec.) A parish priest who was also a lawyer, Ivo distinguished himself in both fields. A verse from the time said of his work as an attorney that he "was not dishonest—astonishing in people's eyes" (lawyers, apparently, have long had to battle a negative press). Even as a student, he lived an ascetic life, fasting, wearing a hair shirt, and sleeping little. He served as judge in the church courts at Rennes and Treguier and won there the title "the poor man's advocate." He refused bribes, frequently represented the indigent in court, visited the imprisoned, and always attempted to reach settlement prior to trial, sparing his clients an expensive lawsuit.

In 1284, he was ordained a priest and shortly after left the practice of law to devote himself entirely to his parishioners. His preaching was simple and effective and much appreciated at a time when preaching was often neglected. He frequently arbitrated differences between people, and his advice was nearly always accepted. He built a hospital, cared for the sick, and personally brought food and money to the needy. Ivo was weak and ill when he said his last Mass and had to be held up by others. Nevertheless, he ministered one last time in the confessional and died shortly after. Feast: May 19.

J

Jacques of Jesus, Servant of God Père (Lucien-Louis Bunel)

(1900-1945. B. at Barentin, France; d. at Linz, Austria.) This member of the French Resistance was, before all else, a Carmelite priest. He died a victim of the Nazis for sheltering three Jewish students at his school, the Petit-College d'Avon near Paris.

Born to a devout working-class family during a time of labor strife, Jacques grew up with a strong commitment to social justice. "I come to you as a worker and the son of a worker to speak to you about Jesus, the worker," he once announced in a sermon at a prosperous parish in Le Havre. Ordained as a diocesan priest, he followed his inclination for the contemplative life by joining the Discalced Carmelites in 1931. Three years later, the Carmelites asked him to found and direct a boys' preparatory school. It was there, in 1943, that the Gestapo arrested him and the three students. The boys died not long after at Auschwitz.

Jacques himself ended up at Mauthausen concentration camp. His contemplative life flourished there, strengthening him for an active, clandestine apostolate. He shared his meager rations with the sick, heard confessions, provided spiritual direction, prayed with the dying, befriended communists and atheists, and helped lead an internal resistance network. A fellow prisoner said he was "proof of the living God." Worn out by his ministry and by ill-treatment, he developed tuberculosis and was seriously ill when the Americans liberated the camp in April 1945. Evacuated to Linz, Austria, he died on June 2. Pope John Paul II opened the cause for his canonization in 1990. Louis Malle's celebrated film, *Au Revoir, Les Enfants,* tells the story of the school and the arrest of Jacques and the boys.

James "the Great," St.

(first century. D. at Jerusalem.) James and his brother John were apostles and sons of Zebedee with whom they worked as fishermen. Jesus called the brothers "Boanerges," sons of thunder, probably to indicate ardent, fiery temperaments. They assured Jesus they could suffer with him and wanted to sit on either side of him in his kingdom, thereby stirring the indignation of the other apostles (see Mt 20:20-28). James was with Peter and John at the raising of Jairus' daughter from the dead, the Transfiguration, and the agony in the Garden. He was the first of the twelve to die as a martyr, beheaded at the order of Herod Agrippa I in the early forties (see Acts 12:2). A tradition dating to the seventh century says that he preached in Spain, a story that conflicts with early church tradition that places the apostles in Jerusalem until after the martyrdom of James. It is said that his relics are buried in Spain at the shrine of Santiago de Compostela, the most popular pilgrimage site in medieval Europe. Feast: July 25.

James "the Less," St.

(first century) James, the son of Alphaeus, was one of the twelve apostles and is sometimes designated "the Less" because he was supposedly younger than the other apostle James. He appears in the lists of apostles but nothing is known of him. He is sometimes identified as the James known as "the brother of the Lord" but most scholars agree that these are separate individuals. Feast: May 2.

Januszewski, Bd. Hilary

(1907-1945. B. at Krajenki, Poland; d. at Dachau concentration camp.) Januszewski was a Carmelite priest and professor of dogmatic theology and church history for the Polish Carmelite province at Cracow. He was appointed prior of that community in 1939, the year of the German invasion of Poland. Within a short time, the Nazis began arresting large numbers of priests and

monks including Januszewski, who, in 1940, offered himself in place of an older, sick friar. He did time in prison and several concentration camps before finally arriving at Dachau.

In 1945, on the eve of liberation, typhoid fever swept through the camp. The victims were left to die in Hut 25 in inhumane conditions. The authorities challenged the Polish priests to put their faith into practice and care for the sick, many of whom were Russians, traditional enemies of the Poles. Over thirty priests responded, including Januszewski, who told a friend as he left, "You know, I won't come out of there alive." He died of typhoid after twenty-one days. When the Americans liberated the camp a few weeks later, they found Hut 25 filled with hundreds of corpses.

On the occasion of Januszewski's beatification in 1999, the Carmelite Prior General wrote that had it not been for his heroic death, the quiet, prayerful prior would probably have been forgotten. However, in the face of a culture that valued only the usefulness of people he "opted radically for the dying, the useless ... [and] testified to the sacred value of human life, for itself and in itself." Feast: March 25.

Jaricot, Ven. Pauline

(1799-1862. B./d. in Lyons, France.) Jaricot was a wealthy teenager, secretly engaged to be married, when an accident—she fell from a stool while reaching for a box—disrupted her plans. She lingered near death for several months due less to her injuries than to mis-guided medical care. After her recovery, she dedicated her life to God when she heard a priest preach about the sin of vanity. She gathered a group of women around her—the Penitents, she called them—and together they served the poor. Pauline then founded the Propagation of the Faith to raise money for the missions, but her system of fund-raising was so ex-tremely effective that some clergy and missionary groups resented her success. (Pauline later recommended that the Propagation move to Rome to be administered under papal authority.)

She also started the Living Rosary, organizing people in groups of fifteen, each of whom said a decade of the rosary a day. Collectively, the group prayed all the decades of the rosary every day, a system still in use.

Pauline's concern for the working poor led her into a deal intended to finance a model factory town. Her business partners conned her, leaving her with a huge debt for the purchase of the factory property. She spent the rest of her life in extreme poverty, trying to repay her loans and suffering the hostility of many who regarded her as a naïve meddler. She was sustained in her trials by the friendship of St. John Vianney, the Curé of Ars, and her identification with the suffering Christ.

Javouhey, Bd. Anne

(1798-1851. B. at Jallanges, France; d. at Paris.) Javouhey was only ten years old when the French Revolution started, but over its course she secretly provided religious education for children and hid priests who risked their lives to minister to the people. She made a vow of celibacy in 1798 and decided to dedicate her life to the poor and the education of children. A vision she had of black children in need of help strongly influenced her later work. She began her ministry with several other young women, and in 1812 they were recognized as the Congregation of St. Joseph of Cluny.

Anne soon established houses not only in Europe but also in Africa, South America, India, and elsewhere. She worked extensively and successfully in French Guiana and in the 1830s drew up and imple-mented plans for the resettlement of five hundred newly freed slaves there. The project was a model of intelligent planning. Anne helped the former slaves turn the jungle into a prosperous town, much to the outrage of their former owners, who hoped eventually to gain their slaves back.

Throughout her life, Anne suffered opposition from certain misguided clerics, including one who denied her the sacraments for two years in Guiana. She showed heroic virtue in the face of these and other obstacles: "The cross of Christ is to be found wherever there are servants of God," she said, "and I rejoice to be reckoned among them." Feast: July 15.

Jerome, St.

(c. 345-420. B. at Strido, Dalmatia; d. at Bethlehem.) Jerome combined scholarship and piety with an unfortunate talent for invective, making him a most unusual saint. He was raised as a Christian, received an excellent education at Rome, and was baptized at eighteen, delayed baptisms being customary at the time. Several years later, he became a monk in Syria, remaining there about four years. In spite of his extreme asceticism, he experienced strong sexual temptation that he quelled by a singular method—he studied Hebrew, a language difficult enough to distract him. ("I could not conquer my burning passions.... As a last resource, I put myself under the tutelage of a certain monk, a Jew ... [and] began to learn the Hebrew alphabet.")

Jerome was ordained at Antioch but never exercised a priestly ministry. He studied Scripture briefly at Constantinople under the great St. Gregory Nazianzen and moved to Rome in 382, where he served as secretary to Pope St. Damasus I. At Damasus' direction, he began his translation of the Bible into Latin, a monumental achievement that eventually gave the church a uniform version of Scripture (the Vulgate) and ended the great disparities in biblical texts circulating at the time. He also wrote biblical commentaries and, at the same time, took on the spiritual direction of a group of pious Roman women, including the widow St. Paula. Jerome made enemies for himself in Rome—as he seemed to do everywhere—through his caustic pen and unsparing bluntness. He said of one man, for example, that "if he would conceal his nose and keep his mouth shut, he might be taken for both handsome and learned."

He left Rome for the Holy Land in 385, after the death of Damasus. Paula and other devout women soon followed Jerome there. In Bethlehem, they developed monastic communities of men and women and Jerome continued his work on Scripture. He devoted the remainder of his life to this work, to guiding his community, and to assisting the refugees who flooded the Holy Land during the barbarian invasions of Europe.

Jerome's irascibility led to broken friendships and disedifying controversy. On the other hand, he lived a life of extraordinary sacrifice and fruitfulness on behalf of the faith, putting his enormous erudition entirely at the service of the church. If he was at times intem perate in his observations, he most often employed his formidable intellect to advance orthodoxy in an age marked by heresy. He practiced great austerities, was compassionate to the needy, and enjoyed the devoted affection of his followers. He is a Doctor of the Church. Feast: September 30.

Joan of Arc, St.

(1412-1431. B. at Domremy, France; d. at Rouen.) Joan was born during the Hundred Years War when her native France was ruled for the most part by the English. The Dauphin (heir to the throne) was the indecisive Charles, as yet uncrowned, a dispirited ruler lead- ing a dispirited people. Joan was a devout thirteen-year-old peasant when she began to hear the voices of various saints urging her to save France from the enemy. For three years the voices persisted. Finally, convinced she should act, she obtained an audience with the Dauphin in 1429. She won his support and, two months later, rode out at the head of the French army and routed the English at Orleans. Her role was that of moral leader—she insisted the soldiers all go to confession and all prostitutes remain behind—and encour- ager. She provided the inspiration the French sorely needed and led the Dauphin to Rheims, where he was

crowned as Charles VII.

Shortly after, following several mili- tary defeats, Joan was captured by the Burgundians (allies of England) and sold to the English. A church court made up of politically motivated clergy tried her as a witch and heretic. Her condemnation was a foregone conclu- sion, but she defended herself with spirit and intelligence, a teenager before a panel of several hundred dignitaries. Charles VII made no attempt to help her. Under torture, she made a confes- sion that she promptly retracted upon recovery. She was burned at the stake at the age of nineteen, but twenty-five years later the pope reopened the case and condemned the verdict. She was canonized four hundred years later, not as a martyr but as a woman of virtue and a model of integrity and courage in responding to God's call. Feast: May 30.

Jogues, St. Isaac

(1607-1646. B. at Orleans, France; d. at Ossernenon, New York.) Jogues—a Jesuit priest—became a missionary, a captive of Indians, a victim of torture, an escapee, and finally, a martyr. He left his native France in 1636 to join his fel- low Jesuits in what is now Canada to minister at a variety of missionary posts. In 1642, a Mohawk war party ambushed Jogues, his coworker St. René Goupil, and several others, then tortured them savagely, killed Goupil, and held Jogues as a slave. His hair and nails were ripped out and his fingers crushed. Other wounds that covered his body became so infected "that worms dropped from them," he said.

He reported all this in a letter to his superior, adding that his left thumb had also been cut off. "I thank God that they left me the one on my right hand," he said, so that he could write to his confreres. While he was on a fishing expedition with his captors, the group passed through a Dutch village where the settlers helped Jogues hide on a boat and escape to France. There, a fellow Jesuit reported, "He is as cheerful as if he had suffered nothing and as zealous to return among the Hurons, amid all those dangers, as if perils were to him securities."

Jogues did return in 1644. While acting as an ambassador of peace to the Iroquois in New York, he and his companion St. Jean de la Lande were attacked, beaten, and killed with tomahawks. Feast (of the Martyrs of North America): October 19.

John, St.

(c. 6-c. 104. D. at Ephesus.) John and his brother James were among the first apostles called by Jesus. They were fishermen at work with their father, Zebedee, but on Jesus' invitation, "abandoned boat and father to follow him" (Mt 4:22). He named them "Sons of Thunder," no doubt because of their impetuous temperaments, and they were among his inner circle. With Peter, they were present at momentous events such as the transfiguration of Jesus. John is traditionally considered "the disciple whom Jesus loved" who "reclined close to him" at the Last Supper (Jn 13:23). From the cross, Jesus entrusted John with the care of his mother (see Jn 19:26-27). After Jesus' burial, when Mary Magdalen reported that his tomb was empty, Peter and John set out to check but John "outran Peter and reached the tomb first." He peered in and "saw and believed" (Jn 20:1-10).

John and Peter were imprisoned briefly by hostile authorities (see Acts 4:1-22) and then went to Samaria, where they prayed with people to receive the Holy Spirit (see Acts 8:14-19). Along with James, they were considered the pillars of the church in Jerusalem (see Gal 2:9).

John is traditionally identified as the author of the fourth Gospel, the Book of Revelation, and three biblical letters. Scholars debate the authorship of these works, suggesting, among other possibilities, that disciples of the apostle are respon-sible for some of this material. John is thought to have settled at Ephesus and died there well into his nineties. Feast: December 27.

John of God, St.

(1495-1550; B. in Portugal; d. at Granada, Spain.) John led a dissolute life as a soldier before experiencing a conversion around the age of forty and devoting himself to the care of the sick poor. His conversion began when he was accused of stealing some of the army's booty. Condemned to hang, he won a pardon and in gratitude spent two days in prayer before a wayside crucifix. Casting about for direction, he worked as a shepherd and peddled religious books from town to town. He went to Granada in 1536 after having a vision of Christ who offered him a pomegranate (the symbol of the city of Granada) surmounted by a cross and said: "John of God, Granada will be your cross."

Once there, he heard a sermon on repentance by Bd. John of Avila and was so overcome by remorse for his past that he gave away his possessions and ran through the streets tearing his hair as though insane. Confined to a mental hospital, he recovered instantly when John of Avila visited him and told him to do something useful with his life. He rented a house and turned it into a hospital that was clean, well-run, and a model of compassionate care. Critics accused him of harboring troublemakers when he opened a homeless shelter and a home for prostitutes, but he said that he knew of only one bad character

and that was himself. He died—overcome by fatigue and illness—after attempting unsuccessfully to rescue a drowning man. His followers formed the Brothers of St. John of God (Brothers Hospitallers) after his death. Feast: March 8.

John of the Cross, St.

(1542-1591. B. near Avila, Spain; d. at Ubeda.) St. Teresa of Avila recruited John—a Carmelite priest in his midtwenties—to assist her with the reform of the then-lax Carmelite Order. In 1577, Carmelites opposed to reform kidnapped John and locked him in a tiny, windowless cell in their monastery at Toledo. After nine months of brutal treatment, he escaped by tying strips of his blankets into a rope ladder, loosening the bolts in his door, and letting himself out through a window. He was then allowed to continue his work unmolested. John held various offices in the reformed order, until disagreement broke out among the monks of the reform. He sided with the moderates, was banished when the extremists took control, and died shortly after at a remote monastery.

John of the Cross was a poet, writer, and artist whose intense love of God found expression in writings today regarded as classics: *Dark Night of the Soul; Spiritual Canticle; Living Flame of Love;* and *Ascent of Mount Carmel.*

His life was one of extreme suffering, abandonment to God, and union with him, themes he explored in his writing. "I would not consider any spirituality worthwhile that wants to walk in sweetness and ease and run from the imitation of Christ," he wrote.

On the other hand, as a spiritual director, he worked to steer those in his care away from anxiety, toward a spirit of hope and of trust in God's mercy. He had great compassion for the sufferings of others and has been called "patron of the afflicted" for his readiness to help ease their burdens, both spiritually and materially. "At the evening of life," he said, "we shall be judged by love." He is a Doctor of the Church and cofounder (with St. Teresa of Avila) of the Discalced (barefoot) Carmelite Order. Feast: December 14.

John XXIII, Bd. Pope (Angelo Roncalli)

(1881-1963. B. at Sotto Il Monte, Italy; d. at Rome.) Roncalli was ordained in 1904 and began a career that seemed destined for diplomatic backwaters and obscurity. After nine years as secretary to the bishop of Bergamo, a social activist, he served as an army chaplain during World War I and as spiritual director of the seminary at Bergamo. In 1921, the pope chose him to reorganize the Congregation for the Propagation of the Faith and in 1925 made him a bishop and assigned him to Bulgaria as apostolic visitor. He spent the next twenty years in diplomatic outposts seemingly forgotten by the Vatican, apparently because he was suspected of unorthodox views. He fell under suspicion in part because, in his warm concern for people, he overlooked religious or political differences and, in one case, extended his friendship to an excommunicated priest. (Years later, when he was pope, a priest complained to him about the narrow thinking among some Vatican officials. Pope John responded with disarming simplicity: "...When you face Jesus Christ in eternity ... he is not going to ask you how well you got along with the Roman curia but how many souls you saved.")

In Bulgaria and later as apostolic delegate to Turkey and Greece, Roncalli distinguished himself as a pastor, ecumenist, and statesman. When earthquakes devastated Bulgaria, he slept in tents among the refugees, readily available to those in need. He worked steadily to diminish the hostility between Orthodox and Catholics, visiting Orthodox clergy and praying at their altars: "Whenever I see a wall between Christians," he once said, "I try to pull out a brick." During World War II, Roncalli saved thousands of Jews, intervening on their behalf with authorities and issuing false baptismal certificates.

His unaffected goodness and diplomatic skills won him the position of nuncio to Paris in 1945. In 1953, he became a cardinal and patriarch of Venice and in 1958, at the age of seventy-eight, was elected pope. He immediately put his own stamp on the papacy, lamenting at first that "the gifts of the Holy Spirit do not include the gift of papal style." He refused to wear the velvet slippers traditionally worn by the pope—they didn't suit his active lifestyle—and made frequent unscheduled visits to prisons, hospitals, seminaries, parishes, and shrines. "I have pressed my heart against yours," he told the cheering prisoners at one jail.

Three months after his election, he announced plans for an ecumenical council, to the dismay of some prelates who hoped that, given his age, his papacy would be uneventful. The intent was to foster unity among Christian denominations, he said, and to renew the church, "helping it to look to the present, to new conditions ... which have opened avenues to Catholic apostolate." He convened the first session of the council in October 1962 but died of cancer eight months later. The council continued under Pope Paul VI and closed in 1965, its groundbreaking effects still felt in the church today. Pope John's writings include the encyclicals *Mater et Magistra* (on the church's concern for the poor) and *Pacem in Terris* as well as his diary, *Journal of a Soul,* which he kept from the age of fourteen until shortly before his death. Feast: June 3.

Joseph, St.

(first century) "No one will ever be able to worthily praise Joseph," St. Ephraim said in the sixth century. St. Joseph's role as the husband of Mary and foster father of Jesus played out quietly in Scripture—little is recorded there of his life—but he is one of the most revered of saints. We can surmise from biblical evidence that he was a thoughtful, courageous, just, compassionate man, finely attuned to the will of God.

Joseph was of the house of David, a carpenter by trade, when he became betrothed to Mary. Distressed to discover she was pregnant and knowing that he was not the father, he decided to divorce her quietly. His compassionate response would shield her from death by stoning, the penalty for infidelity in such cases. An angel appeared to him in a dream and told him not to be afraid to take Mary into his home. She was pregnant by the power of the Holy Spirit and "will bear a son and you are to name him Jesus, because he will save his people from their sins" (Mt 1:18-25).

Joseph obeyed and was with Mary in Bethlehem for the birth of Jesus and visit of the Magi (see Lk 2:1-20). At the

instruction of an angel, he took his little
family to Egypt to escape the deadly
intentions of Herod (see Mt 2:13-15)
and returned with them to Israel after
another angelic visitation. They settled
at Nazareth in Galilee, Joseph having
been warned in a dream to avoid Judea,
where Herod's son now ruled (see
Mt 2:22-23). Joseph and Mary
presented Jesus at the temple, according
to the Law, and were amazed at the
prophetic words of Simeon ("My eyes
have seen your salvation," Lk 2:30).
Joseph appears for the last time in
Scripture when he and Mary search for
Jesus after the Passover in Jerusalem and
then take him home to Nazareth, where
he "was obedient to them" (see Lk
2:41-52).

Joseph almost certainly died before
the crucifixion of Jesus—there is no
mention of him in the accounts of those
final days—but there is no record of the
event. It is assumed that he died with
Jesus and Mary at his side, and for this,
is the patron of a happy death. For his
privileged and obviously successful role
in the Holy Family, he is the patron of
fathers. He is also patron of workers
(feast: May 1) in tribute to his career as
a carpenter ("Good St. Joseph," St.
Thérèse of Lisieux wrote, "… How
many times did [others] refuse to pay
him for his work!"). Joseph was named
patron of the universal church in 1870,
and in 1962, Pope John XXIII added

his name to the canon of the Mass.
Feast: March 19.

Joseph of Cupertino, St.

(1603-1663. B. at Cupertino, Italy;
d. at Osimo.) Joseph was born in such
dire poverty that his mother gave birth
to him in a shed. His father was, at the
time, selling the family's home to pay
off debts. Joseph was not bright and his
family considered him a burden. He
used to wander the village with his
mouth open and for this, was nicknamed "the gaper."

When he turned seventeen he tried
twice—unsuccessfully—to enter religious orders. In despair, his mother
arranged for the Franciscans to take him
on as a servant. He flourished among
them, and his superiors, impressed with
his holiness and humility, decided to
prepare him for the priesthood.
Understandably, his studies did not go
well. But he was unusually fortunate at
test time. On one occasion, the bishop
was so impressed after examining several candidates for the priesthood that he
passed the rest of the group, including
Joseph, without further questioning.

Joseph was ordained in 1628. From
that point until his death thirty-five
years later, his life was a remarkable
series of ecstasies, miracles, and supernatural events that took place on a large
scale and are well documented by trustworthy eyewitnesses. He frequently

levitated, particularly during Mass. The distraction caused his superiors to forbid him to say Mass in public, to eat with his fellow monks, or to attend public functions. He was also said to have command of animals as St. Francis did, and was often lost in contemplation, insensible to his surroundings.

For the last decade of his life, the Franciscans kept him strictly enclosed and moved him from friary to friary, one step ahead of the pilgrims who flocked to him as soon as they learned he was nearby. The supernatural manifestations continued on a daily basis until he died after a brief illness at the age of sixty. Feast: September 18.

Jude, St.

(first century) Jude appears as an apostle in Luke 6:16 and Acts 1:13. He is thought to be the same person as the apostle named Thaddeus in the lists in Matthew 10:3 and Mark 3:18. We know nothing further of him. For various reasons, scholars generally agree that he was not the author of the Epistle of St. Jude. An apocryphal story links Jude and Simon as missionaries to Persia, where they were beaten to death. Jude has become popular as the patron of impossible causes, although the origin of this patronage is unclear. Feast: October 28.

Julius the Veteran, St.

(D. c. 304, at Silistria, Bulgaria.) As a soldier, Julius served in seven campaigns over twenty-seven years and held an unblemished military record. He refused to sacrifice to the gods, however, and for that he had to appear before the prefect Maximus. At his interrogation, he said that throughout his career he had always worshiped in reverence the God who made heaven and earth and that he served him right up to that moment. Maximus offered him a bonus if he would sacrifice and give the impression of acting voluntarily. Julius refused and said that Christ "died for our sins to give us eternal life. This same man, Christ, is God and abides forever and ever."

When Maximus pressed him again, saying that to sacrifice would save his life, Julius replied: "To live with you would be death for me.... I have chosen death that I may live with the saints forever." Before he was beheaded, he prayed: "Lord Jesus Christ, I suffer this for your name. I beg you to receive my spirit together with your holy martyrs." Feast: May 27.

K

Kafka, Bd. Maria Restituta

(1894-1943. B. at Brno, Czech Republic; d. at Vienna, Austria.) Restituta grew up in Vienna and entered a nursing order, the Hartmann Sisters (Sisters of Christian Charity) in 1915. She developed a reputation as an excellent operating room nurse and anesthetist with a good sense of humor and a love for the poor. After the German occupation of Austria in 1938, she firmly rejected Nazism and defied the ban on religious activities in hospitals, praying with the dying and placing crucifixes in the rooms of a new ward. She called Hitler "a madman" and made copies of an anti-Nazi poem. "A Viennese cannot keep her mouth shut," she said of herself.

The Gestapo arrested her in 1942, and a year later sentenced her to death by beheading. Martin Borman, Hitler's secretary, refused to commute the sentence, saying the execution of the death penalty was "necessary for effective intimidation." Feast: March 30.

Kalinowski, St. Raphael

(1835-1907. B. at Vilnius, Lithuania [formerly Russian Poland]; d. at Wadowice, Poland.) Kalinowski took the unusual path to the priesthood of first serving in the military and then enduring ten years of exile in Siberia for subversive activities. Although he was of Polish heritage, at the time of his birth. Russia had occupied and dominated Poland for forty years. He studied military engineering in Russia (because the occupying power had closed all universities in Poland) and abandoned religious practices. However, he "did not find interior peace this way," he said, and gradually returned to his faith.

During his service in the Russian military, he experienced a growing awareness of how unjust the occupation was. It was enough to make him resign his commission and join an insurrection against the Russians. He was captured and sentenced to the salt mines at Usole, Siberia. By this time an ardent Catholic, he took with him into exile *The Imitation of Christ,* the Gospels, and his crucifix. Besides his daily share of hard physical labor, for the next ten years he cared for orphans, taught the poor, consoled fellow exiles who were often near despair, helped the sick and needy, and reached his decision to become a priest.

When the Russians freed him, Kalinowski entered the Discalced Carmelites. At the age of forty-seven, he was ordained at Czerna in the only Polish Discalced Carmelite monastery remaining after the suppression of the order during the occupation. For the next twenty-five years he worked to restore the Carmel in Poland, held positions of increasing responsibility, and was known for his devotion to Mary and skill in the confessional. A penitent said that Kalinowski was "extraordinary. At every hour of the day and at every call, he was ready to go down to his confessional. All this was founded on a deep love of God.... He saw the image of God in every human being." He died at Wadowice thirteen years before the birth there of Karol Wojtyla, Pope John Paul II, who would later canonize him. Feast: November 15.

Kim Hyo-im, St. Columba
(1814-1839);
Kim Hyo-ju, St. Agnes
(1816-1839) (B. in Hanyang, Korea; d. in Yongmuri.) The founding of the Catholic Church in Korea was entirely a lay undertaking, begun when Korean diplomats in China brought Catholic books back to their country in the eighteenth century. Shortly after, a scholar and layman, Yi Sung-hun, went to Beijing in 1784, was baptized a Catholic, and returned to Korea, where he catechized and baptized many. A Chinese priest finally entered the closed kingdom in 1794, and discovered four thousand Catholics awaiting his arrival. Catholicism was illegal, as were all for-

eign influences, and over the next one hundred years, thousands of Catholics were martyred, the majority of them laymen, women, and children.

Columba and Agnes, sisters, died in the persecution of 1839. Betrayed by a fellow villager, they were repeatedly tortured, remaining silent as soldiers beat them with spiked clubs and twice burned incantations into their backs. In an effort to destroy their virginity, guards stripped them and threw them into a cell with male criminals, who refused to harm them. Columba complained to a judge about the stripping and imprisonment, saying that not only were they against the law but "the chastity of a woman has the right to be respected." He agreed, and as a result future female prisoners were spared similar treatment. Agnes was beheaded on September 3, and Columba on September 26. They are representative of the 103 Korean martyrs whose feast day is September 20.

Kim Tae-gon, St. Andrew
(1821-1846. B. in Solmoi, Korea; d. in Saenamt'o.) Kim Tae-gon came from a family of martyrs and was the first native-born Korean priest in the then sixty-year history of the Korean Catholic Church (see Kim Hyo-im, Columba, above, for founding of Korean church). In 1837, at the age of sixteen, he left for Macao to study for

the priesthood. His superiors found him "very promising ... eloquent ... obedient but daring," with a strong will and good judgment.

While still a seminarian, he slipped back into Korea twice to arrange a way to smuggle priests into the country, including the newly appointed bishop, Joseph Ferreol. In February 1845, after a harrowing boat trip plagued by storms and pirates, he arrived in Shanghai to meet the new bishop. Ferreol ordained him there on August 17, 1845, and they left shortly after for Korea, where Kim Tae-gon began his priestly ministry. He was making arrangements to smuggle more missionaries into the country when he was arrested in June 1846. He wrote a letter to his people from prison, encouraging them "to be patient, seek always eternal glory and be very, very cautious." He was beheaded by twelve half-drunk executioners who took turns slashing at him. "Losing him," wrote Bishop Ferreol, "is a great calamity and an irreparable loss for the Korean church." Feast (with the Martyrs of Korea): September 20.

Kitbamrung, Bd. Bunkerd Nicholas

(1895-1944. B. at Nakhon Pathom Province, Thailand.; d. at Bang Kwhan Central Prison.) Kitbamrung grew up as a Catholic in predominately Buddhist Thailand and was ordained a diocesan priest in 1926. He was noted for his generosity, helping Salesian missionaries adjust to the culture, for example, and teaching them the Thai language. He worked in a number of parishes and had a special concern for fallen-away Christians and for religious education, refusing to baptize those who were not yet firm in their faith.

The rise of Thai nationalism in 1940 contributed to persecution of the Catholic Church, considered too closely identified with the French colonizers: "Those who worship that religion are also the enemy of the [Thai] nation." On January 11, 1941, Fr. Nicholas traveled to St. Joseph's Church in Ban Han, where he led the parishioners in night prayer and invited them to Mass the next day. He rang the church bells at 8:30 in the morning to summon them despite a government ban on ringing church bells. He was arrested, falsely accused of being an agent of the French government, and sentenced to fifteen years in prison. To the anger of the authorities, he continued his priestly ministry in jail, catechizing the prisoners and baptizing sixty-eight. He was denied his prayer book but often prayed the rosary. His health undermined by ill-treatment, he developed tuberculosis and died three years after his arrest. Feast: January 12.

Kolbe, St. Maximilian

(1894-1941. B. at Zdunska-Wola, near Lodz, Poland; d. at Auschwitz concentration camp.) Kolbe was thirteen when he had a vision in which Mary offered him two crowns, a white one representing purity and a red one representing martyrdom. When she asked which he wanted, he chose both. Shortly after, he entered the seminary, studied in Rome, and was ordained a priest of the Franciscan order in 1918. His interest in the role of Mary in salvation led him to found the Knights of Mary Immaculate to promote devotion to her.

Kolbe earned doctorates in both theology and philosophy and taught at a seminary in Poland before launching a monthly magazine in 1922, the *Knight of the Immaculate*. Overcoming tremendous financial odds and serious ill health due to tuberculosis, Kolbe eventually established what amounted to a small publishing house. It was headquartered at Niepokalanow—City of the Immaculate—a Franciscan community founded by Kolbe that ultimately numbered nearly eight hundred Franciscans. Always interested in technology, he also started a radio station there. In 1930, he established another City of the Immaculate in Nagasaki, Japan. (Sheltered by a hillside, it survived the atomic bombing of the city.) In 1936, Kolbe returned to Poland

and was superior at Niepokalanow when the Germans invaded the country in 1939. Openly critical of Nazism, he was arrested in 1941 and sent to Auschwitz concentration camp. He carried on his priestly ministry secretly, hearing confessions and exhorting the prisoners to forgiveness, saying "hatred is not creative." He distinguished himself for his compassionate aid to his fellow prisoners. One later commented: "He was a priest every inch of his burned-out body."

In July 1941, a prisoner escaped. In retribution, the men from Kolbe's barracks were lined up and ten chosen at random to die in a basement starvation cell. When one of the men cried out in despair for his family, Kolbe offered to take his place. In the bunker, he led the men in prayer and hymns, calming, comforting, and encouraging them. Two weeks later, still fully conscious, he was killed with an injection of carbolic acid. Francis Gajowniczek, the man whose place he took, was present at his canonization in 1982. Feast: August 14.

Kowalska, St. Faustina

(1905-1938. B. at Glogowiec, Poland; d. at Lagiewniki.) Faustina worked as a maid when her parents refused to allow her to become a nun. Discouraged by their resistance, she briefly abandoned the spiritual life, but in 1924, while attending a dance, she had a vision of the suffering Jesus who said: "…How long will you keep putting me off?" Faustina left the dance hall, went to a nearby church, prostrated herself before the tabernacle, and prayed. She heard an interior voice say: "Go at once to Warsaw; you will enter a convent there." She joined the Sisters of Mercy in Warsaw shortly after.

Faustina experienced frequent visions of Christ that increasingly focused on the mercy of God. In response, she offered herself and her sufferings for "the conversion of sinners, especially those souls who have lost hope in God's mercy." As instructed in her visions, she promoted the Feast of Divine Mercy, now celebrated on the first Sunday after Easter, to be preceded by the Novena of Divine Mercy.

She understood her vocation as reaffirming for an unbelieving age God's compassion for sinners and the need to trust in him. She died of tuberculosis on the eve of World War II, having prophesied that great suffering would come to Poland. At her beatification, Pope John Paul II said: "Her mission … is yielding astonishing fruit…. Where, if not in the Divine Mercy, can the world find refuge and the light of hope?" Feast: April 30.

Kowalski, Bd. Joseph

(1911-1941. D. at Auschwitz concentration camp.) Kowalski, a Salesian priest, served as secretary to the Salesian provincial at Cracow. After the Nazi invasion of Poland, he was arrested and sent to Auschwitz where, at great personal risk, he ministered to fellow prisoners. "I met Fr. Joseph Kowalski in … Auschwitz in 1941, in a place where [prisoners] were praying," one witness later said. "At half past four in the morning, about eight people would meet for prayer in the darkness at some hidden place. The group increased despite the risk and Fr. Joseph was the soul of it." He also secretly celebrated Mass, heard confessions, and preached. The Nazis drowned Kowalski in a cesspool on July 3, 1941.

Kozal, Bd. Michael

(1893-1943. B. at Ligota, Poland; d. at Dachau concentration camp.) Kozal was a parish priest and a high school teacher with a strong commitment to young people. For twelve years he served as rector of the seminary at Gniezno and in 1939, on the outbreak of World War II, became bishop of Wloclawek. In their drive to destroy the church in Poland, the Nazis arrested Kozal on November 7, 1939, a few days after he celebrated his only solemn Mass as bishop. He was confined and brutally treated at Wloclawek, Lad, Szczeglin, and Berlin before finally arriving at Dachau on April 25, 1941.

Kozal was calm and brave, refusing

any preferential treatment from fellow inmates: "I'm only a number here, too, and I'm determined to carry my cross along with the rest of you." He was a steady inspiration and guide to other prisoners, especially priests. When he could, he celebrated Mass in secret, telling his battered congregation: "I give you the greatest gift, Jesus in the Eucharist. God is with us. God will never abandon us." In prayer, he offered his life as a sacrifice for the church in Poland. The Nazis murdered him by lethal injection. Feast: January 26.

L

Labouré, St. Catherine

(1806-1876. B. at Côte d'Or, France; d. at Paris.) Labouré received visions of Mary as a young nun but lived an otherwise completely unremarkable life. Even her identity as a visionary was hidden from virtually everyone. In 1830 she joined the Sisters of Charity, who sent her to their convent at the rue du Bac in Paris. Almost immediately she experienced a series of visions in which Mary asked her to promote what was to become known as the miraculous medal.

On November 27, 1830, Mary appeared to Catherine standing on a globe with shafts of light coming from her hands. Surrounding her were the words: "O Mary conceived without sin, pray for us who have recourse to thee." On the reverse side of the vision appeared a capital M with a cross above it and two hearts below, one crowned with thorns, the other pierced by a sword. Catherine understood that Mary wanted her to have this image struck on the medal, offering blessing to those who wore it in a spirit of devotion. With some difficulty, working through her confessor, Catherine did as Mary asked, and in 1836, after canonical investigation, the visions were approved as authentic.

Catherine spent the remaining forty-five years of her life in complete obscurity, caring for elderly men at a hospice and serving there in various menial positions. She told no one but her confessor of the visions and refused to allow him to reveal her identity in spite of the enormous and instant popularity of the medal. Catherine, described by others as quiet, "unexcitable," and "rather insignificant," told her superior about her extraordinary experiences only shortly before her death. Feast: November 28.

Labre, St. Benedict Joseph

(1748-1783. B. at Amettes, France; d. at Rome.) Benedict is the patron saint of homeless people and tramps, whose lifestyle he adopted as his own for his last dozen or so years. The oldest of fifteen children, Benedict was born to good parents who maintained a comfortable living as shopkeepers. He attempted to join the Trappists, Carthusians, and Cistercians with no success and began to live as a wandering holy man. For several years he stayed on the road, making pilgrimages on foot to shrines in France, Spain, Italy, Germany, and Switzerland. In 1774, he settled in Rome, sleeping in the ruins of the Coliseum at night and praying in various churches during the day. He was particularly attracted to the Forty Hours devotion.

His confessor described his first encounter with Benedict, which took place after Mass. "I noticed a man close beside me whose appearance ... was decidedly unpleasant and forbidding.... His clothes were tied round his waist with an old cord. His hair was uncombed, he was ill-clad ... he seemed to be the most miserable beggar I had ever seen." However, he soon became aware of Benedict's intense holiness, knew him for the last year of the saint's life, and wrote a biography about him.

Benedict collapsed while leaving the Madonna dei Monti church and died in the nearby home of a butcher. The people of the city immediately hailed him as a saint. Feast: April 16.

Lalande, St. Jean de

(D. 1646. B. at Dieppe, France; d. at Ossernenon, New York.) We know all too little of Lalande beyond the circumstances of his death. He was a layman who served as an assistant to the Jesuit missionaries in Canada. He was on a trip to visit the Iroquois with St. Isaac Jogues when Mohawk Indians ambushed the men and took them captive. Other Indians tried to protect them, but their captors tomahawked them, Jogues on October 18, Lalande the following day. Feast (with the Martyrs of North America): October 19.

Lalemant, St. Gabriel

(1610-1649. B. at Paris, France; d. at St. Ignace, Ontario, Canada.) As a young Jesuit priest, Lalemant made a vow to offer his life in the missions, but his poor health initially stood in the way. In 1646—sixteen years later—his superiors allowed him to leave for Canada. Even then his fellow missionary, St. Jean de Brébeuf, said of him: "He was almost without strength other than what his zeal and fervor supplied him." Lalemant ministered side by side with the more experienced Brébeuf, and they enjoyed considerable success among the Huron Indians.

Their ministry played out against a background of warfare. The Iroquois, enemies of the Hurons, decimated Huron settlements and on March 16, 1649, raided the village of St. Louis. Lalemant and Brébeuf helped women and children escape into the forest and stayed behind to take care of the men who remained to fight. The missionaries plunged into the mayhem, baptizing catechumens, caring for the wounded, and giving absolution. The Iroquois destroyed the village, captured Brébeuf and Lalemant, took them to St. Igance, and subjected them to a particularly savage martyrdom. They beat and burned them, "baptized" them with boiling water, cut off the martyrs' flesh, and ate it before their eyes. The frail Lalemant called on God for strength and died after seventeen hours when hit in the head with a hatchet. Feast (with the Martyrs of North America): October 19.

Lawrence, St.

(D. 258 at Rome.) All we know for certain of Lawrence is that he was one of the seven deacons of Rome, was closely associated with Pope St. Sixtus, and was martyred four days after the pope himself was beheaded. Both men, as well as many others, were executed under the anti-Christian persecution initiated by Emperor Valerian in 257.

As a deacon, Lawrence helped in the distribution of alms. According to tradition, the authorities asked Lawrence to turn over to them the treasures of the church. He gathered the poor, homeless, orphans, lepers, and other needy and presented them to the prefect, saying: "These are the treasures of the church." It is said that for his punishment he was slowly roasted to death on a gridiron, cheerfully telling the executioner to turn him when he was done on one side. In fact, he was probably beheaded. He is buried in the Cyriaca cemetery on the Via Tiburtina, site of the present basilica of St. Lawrence-outside-the-Walls. His cult is ancient, and it is said that his death led to the end of paganism in Rome. Feast: August 10.

Laziosi, St. Peregrine

(1260-1345. B./d. at Forli, Italy.) Laziosi was ill-disposed toward the church and a supporter of the antipapal Ghibelline party during the conflict between the Guelfs and Ghibellines. The pope asked St. Philip Benizi, superior of the Servite order, to act as mediator between the two groups. He did so, but at a meeting tempers flared and the Ghibelline leaders assaulted him. Laziosi punched him in the face, but when Benizi literally turned the other cheek, he repented and reformed his life. He spent hours each day in prayer at a chapel of Our Lady and had a vision in which she told him to go to Siena to join the Servites.

Laziosi was ordained a Servite priest and was known for the zeal with which he pursued his priestly ministry, particularly his work of preaching and sacramental reconciliation. Later in life, he developed such severe varicose veins in one foot that the doctors decided to amputate. Laziosi spent the night in prayer, slept lightly, and woke to find his foot completely healed. Already revered as a holy man, the healing, attested to by his doctors, enhanced his reputation. Upon his death, miracles were reported through his intercession. Feast: May 1.

Leisner, Bd. Karl

(1915-1945. B. at Rees, Germany; d. near Munich.) An early opponent of the Nazis, Leisner was a seminarian who ministered to young people. When the Nazis took control of all youth work, he circumvented their restrictions by taking the teenagers camping in Belgium and the Netherlands where they could freely discuss Catholicism. Denounced for criticizing Hitler, Leisner was sent to several concentration camps, arriving at Dachau, his final destination, in 1941. There, fellow inmate French Bishop Gabriel Piquet secretly ordained him on December 17, 1944. Other prisoners conspired in the effort, managing to provide everything from vestments to a paten as well as a ring and pectoral cross for the bishop. Leisner was so sick at the time that it was a week before he could celebrate his first Mass. He was suffering from tuberculosis when the camp was liberated in 1945, and died four months later on August 12 at a sanitarium near Munich.

Lestonnac, St. Joan de

(1556-1640) Joan, a niece of the writer Montaigne, was born in Bordeaux, France. Although her father was a staunch Catholic, her mother embraced Calvinism and urged Joan to as well. She refused, married Gaston de Montferrant, a Catholic, and they had four children. After twenty-four happy years, the marriage ended with Gaston's death in 1597. In 1603, at the age of forty-seven, she entered a Cistercian convent in Toulouse, but the austere life undermined her health and she left, apparently intending to found a religious congregation.

Several years later, she cared heroically for plague victims in Bordeaux, assisted by a band of like-minded young women. Advised by two Jesuits, in 1608 she founded the Sisters of Notre Dame of Bordeaux, devoted to teaching girls. Education, she felt, would help to counter the spread of Calvinism. The order flourished but Blanche Herve, one of the nuns, spread false stories about Joan and she was removed as superior by the archbishop. Blanche was appointed in her place and for three years treated Joan with complete contempt, even physical violence. Perhaps moved by Joan's patient endurance, Blanche finally repented and the women were reconciled. Joan spent several years visiting the twenty-six houses of her order and then lived in retirement until her death. Feast: February 2.

Leszczewicz, Bd. Anthony (1890-1943); Kaszyra, Bd. George (1904-1943) (D. at Rosica, Belarus.) By the mid-1930s, the communist government of the Soviet Union had either

killed or expelled all priests in Belarus (formerly part of Poland, occupied successively by Russia and Germany). The Germans gained control of the area during World War II, and religious returned to reopen churches and catechize the neglected population. Priests of the Marians of the Immaculate Conception established a mission at Rosica, but within a year, the Nazis threatened to suppress the work, claiming that Soviet supporters were operating in the region.

At the end of 1942, the authorities warned the priests to leave but they refused to abandon their people. On February 15 they repeated the warning but the priests again chose to stay. The Nazis immediately began to burn buildings in surrounding areas, shot those trying to escape, and detained the rest in the church at Rosica. They shipped the stronger prisoners to work camps and kept the others at the church. The priests moved among the people, hearing confessions, praying, celebrating Mass, baptizing converts, and preparing all for death. On the afternoon of February 17, Fr. Leszczewicz and some others were locked in nearby buildings that the Germans doused with gasoline and set on fire. The next morning, Fr. Kaszyra distributed communion to the remaining people, and then he and about thirty detainees were driven to a wooden house. The Nazis locked them inside, tossed in grenades, opened fire on the building, and then set it ablaze. Feast: June 12.

Lewoniuk, Bds. Wincenty, and Companions

(D. 1874 at Pratulin, Poland.) These thirteen martyrs died in an area of eastern Poland that at the time was dominated by Russia. As Byzantine-rite Catholics in communion with Rome, they were the target of Russian attempts to incorporate Eastern Rite Catholics into the Orthodox Church. The Byzantine bishop and priests had been deported to Siberia, and on January 24, 1874, soldiers poured into the village of Pratulin to transfer the parish to the Orthodox Church. The laity gathered around the church in protest, rejecting threats of punishment as well as offers of favors from the czar for converting. The officer in charge ordered his troops to prepare their weapons, the people knelt down, praying and singing hymns, and the soldiers opened fire. The thirteen laymen who died ranged in age from nineteen to fifty. Most were married and had children. We know little about them beyond the fact that they were ordinary people of very strong faith.

Libermann, Ven. Francis

(1802-1852. B. in Saverne, France; d. in Paris.) Libermann was a Jew rigorously trained by his father, the chief rabbi of Saverne, for the rabbinate. Instead, Francis converted to Catholicism ("...The Lord's wrath be upon you," his father wrote). He entered the seminary but fell victim there to blinding headaches and frequent seizures, tempting him to contemplate suicide. Through it all, a friend said, he remained calm and gave himself "entirely to God." The seminary reluctantly dismissed him due to his health, and soon after Libermann began to plan a new missionary order, the Congregation of the Holy Heart of Mary. Free from seizures and his health much improved, he was ordained in 1841, and the pope approved the order. The society was ahead of its time—it aimed to develop an indigenous clergy in missionary territories and to serve native people not, primarily, colonists— and was so successful that it aroused the opposition of jealous clergy.

In particular, the then languishing Congregation of the Holy Ghost declared open war upon Francis. In spite of this hostility, Libermann recognized the potential of this rival missionary group and in 1848 orchestrated a merger of his congregation with theirs, insisting, with his customary diplomacy, that the new order be known as the Congregation of the Holy Ghost under the protection of Mary. He is considered the second founder of the Holy Ghost Fathers.

Libermann met the challenges of his life, including the humiliation of his poor health, with unfailing sweetness of temperament. "His judgement was excellent," a contemporary said, "and he was vividly, keenly, delicately sensitive. When he had to act, he mentally exchanged places with the people concerned and tried to imagine how he would feel if someone treated him as he intended to deal with them." Libermann's health collapsed completely in 1851, and he suffered greatly before dying on February 2, 1852.

Lichtenberg, Bd. Bernard

(1875-1943. B. at Ohlau, Silesia [now in Poland]; d. at Hof, Bavaria.) At great personal risk, before and during World War II, Lichtenburg—a parish priest in Berlin—condemned Nazi treatment of the Jews. In 1933, he tried without success to get the head of the German bishops' conference to oppose the Nazi boycott of Jewish merchants. Two years later, he personally appealed to Hermann Goering on behalf of the Jews in concentration camps but was dismissed as naïve and finally arrested. Released from custody, Lichtenberg secretly distributed Pope Pius XI's banned encyclical, *Mit brennender Sorge* (With Burning Anxiety), a bitter denunciation of Nazi policy. After witnessing Kristallnacht (November 9, 1938), the destruction of Jewish stores and synagogues, he denounced Nazi treatment of Jews from his pulpit at St. Hedwig's Cathedral. "Outside, a temple is burning," he told the congregation, "and it, too, is a house of God."

For three years, Lichtenberg continued his campaign and dedicated regular evening prayer at St. Hedwig to Jewish as well as Christian victims of the Nazis. The Germans arrested him in 1941, imprisoned him for two years in appalling conditions, and released him to the Gestapo for "re-education." He died en route to Dachau at a hospital in Bavaria, his health undermined by ill-treatment. Four thousand people followed his funeral procession in Berlin despite Nazi disapproval and threats from air raids. Feast: November 5.

Liguda, Bd. Aloysius

(1898-1942. B. near Opole, Poland; d. at Dachau concentration camp.) Liguda entered the Society of the Divine Word (SVD), was ordained in 1927, and received a master's degree in philology from the University of Poznan. He was rector of the Society's community in Gorna Grupa when the Nazis invaded Poland in 1939. The Germans took over the SVD house and imprisoned priests and seminarians there.

Early in 1940, the Nazis sent the prisoners, including Liguda, to Dachau, where he was singled out for mistreatment because of his friendly attitude to all, including the German guards. Nevertheless, he wrote: "People may treat me as base but cannot make me base. Dachau can rob me of all my rights and titles [but] the privilege of being a son of God no one can take from me." In December 1942, the Nazis drowned Liguda, who had grown somewhat weak in the barbarous conditions, at the camp reservoir. When they came to get him, he told observers: "If I lose my life, you will know full well that they have murdered a healthy man."

Liguori, St. Alphonsus

(1696-1787. B. at Marianella, Italy; d. at Nocera.) Liguori was a lawyer whose brilliant career began at nineteen and ended in disaster eight years later. He had argued a client's case to great effect, but the opposing counsel pointed out that he misunderstood a key piece of evidence. Stunned, he acknowledged his mistake, conceded the case, and never practiced law again. A devout, charitable man, he was visiting hospital patients shortly after when he heard an interior voice say, "Leave the world and give yourself to me."

He became a priest and worked as a missionary in the Naples area. In 1732, he began an order of priests, the Congregation of the Most Holy Redeemer (Redemptorists), to preach in rural areas (he also helped found the Redemptoristines, an order of nuns).

Almost immediately, he had to deal with internal dissension and the interference of civil authorities, who for years attempted to suppress the order. Through it all, the congregation grew and Liguori himself conducted extremely effective missions. He published prolifically on moral, theological, and devotional topics including, notably, his *Moral Theology* and *Glories of Mary*.

At the age of sixty-six, he was appointed bishop of a languishing diocese served by numerous clergy living indifferent and in some cases evil lives. He reformed the seminary, corrected and suspended priests, and organized successful missions to the laity. Struck down by rheumatic fever, he nearly died but recovered, partially paralyzed and with a permanently deformed back that pushed his chin toward his chest.

To his physical sufferings were added, during the last twenty years of his life, ongoing battles with civil authorities and betrayal from within his own congregation. In 1780, in an attempt to gain royal approval of his rule and settle his troubles with the government, he signed a rule that, unbeknownst to him and with the connivance of his own vicar general, completely altered the original. At the time, he was eighty-five and nearly blind, and the altered rule was written in tiny handwriting. He read only the opening lines. Accused of destroying his order, he accepted the blame saying, "It was my duty to read it myself, but ... I find it difficult to read even a few lines."

The order was divided, the pope recognizing only those in the papal states, the king of Naples only those in his region. Liguori himself was essentially excluded from his own congregation. For a year and a half he experienced deep spiritual depression and temptations to despair but emerged into a period of peace marked by ecstasies, visions, and prophecies. He died two months short of his ninety-first birthday, his order still in disarray. It was reunited after his death and flourishes today. Feast: August 1.

Line, St. Anne

(1565-1601. B. at Dunmow, England; d. at London.) Anne was born to an English Protestant family during a period of anti-Catholic persecution. Her parents disinherited her when she became Catholic. She married a fellow convert who was also not only disinherited but then imprisoned for his faith and forced into exile in Belgium. His death there in 1594 left her "without friends in this world," but she was "full of kindness and very discreet," according to a contemporary, and thus the ideal candidate to run a large house of refuge for priests in London. It was an extremely dangerous assignment since both priests and those who aided them faced the death penalty. Despite the risk, Anne managed the finances, cared for guests, and dealt with inquisitive strangers, even though in chronic ill health herself.

When the house came under suspicion, she moved, continued her ministry, and was present during a raid as a priest prepared to say Mass. He escaped but Anne was taken prisoner. At her trial, when asked if she harbored priests, she simply said: "… Nothing grieves me more but that I could not receive a thousand more." Although the case against her was insufficient and she was so sick that she had to be carried into court, Anne was sentenced to death. At her execution she knelt, kissed the gallows, and prayed "until the hangman had done his work." Feast: February 27 and also, as one of the Forty Martyrs of England and Wales, October 25.

Lioba, St.

(c. 700-780. B. at Wessex, England; d. near Mainz, Germany.) At a time when travel was extremely dangerous and time-consuming, Lioba was sent from her convent in England to work as a missionary in Germany.

She had been educated at the monastery at Wimborne in Dorcetshire and chose to stay on and become a nun when she grew up. Her cousin St. Boniface left to evangelize Germany in 722, and sometime afterward Lioba struck up a correspondence with him ("I would ask you … to send me a few kind words which I eagerly look forward to as a token of your good will"). Their correspondence continued until, in 748, he asked the abbess to send Lioba and others to help in the mission field. She led a group of thirty nuns to Germany, where Boniface settled them at Mainz. Under Lioba's leadership, the group grew rapidly and soon opened other houses in the area.

A monk of Fulda named Rudolph wrote the story of Lioba's life sixty years after her death, based on the testimonies of four of her nuns. She was said to have been warm, pleasant, and smiling, patient, intelligent, and kind. A sensible woman, she refused to allow her nuns to practice severe austerities such as depriving themselves of sleep. Church and state leaders relied on her for advice, as did ordinary people of the neighborhood. Boniface, before he left for his final mission and martyrdom, asked that she be buried near him on her death so that they could await the resurrection together. She died after serving as abbess for twenty-eight years. Feast: September 28.

Louis IX of France, King St.

(1214-1270. B. at Poissy, France; d. at Tunis.) At times, Louis seems more monk than king. He wore a hair shirt, scourged himself, and personally washed the sores of lepers and served meals to the poor. "He ransomed friendless prisoners, buried the dead and assisted all, both virtuously and abundantly," his confessor wrote. His friend and biographer, John de Joinville, recalled that Louis once asked him if he would rather be a leper or commit a mortal sin. De Joinville, who said he couldn't tell a lie, answered that he would rather commit thirty mortal sins than suffer leprosy. The king, raised to prefer death to sin, chided him for this response.

Louis became king at the age of twelve, on the death of his father, Louis VIII. His mother, the astute and devout Blanche of Castile, ruled ably in his stead until he turned twenty-one. By that time, Louis had already led troops in battle—three times, at the age of fifteen—and was married. He and his wife, Margaret Berenger, had eleven children and a happy marriage though Louis was, inevitably, a man of his times. He once berated his wife for attempting to organize a pilgrimage on her own, even though he constantly urged his family to pursue piety. On the other hand, he told the men of his court to "dress well, so that your wives will find you all the more attractive."

As king, Louis was famous for his even-handed justice and his often successful efforts to end the private wars of feudal lords. He forbade the practice of usury, made serious efforts to free serfs, and supported trade guilds for the protection of workers. He frequently arbitrated the legal cases of ordinary people so that they might bypass a lengthy court procedure. Unfortunately, Louis was not free from the prejudices of his age as, for example, in his negative attitude toward Muslims and Jews. During his reign, the Talmud was twice burned publicly in France and Jews were required to wear red badges.

Louis was involved in two crusades, both disastrous. He was captured during the first but ransomed himself and his men. He died of dysentery during the second. His reign was notable not only for his personal integrity but also for a general flowering of culture. He built the St. Chappelle to house the supposed crown of thorns, supported the founding of the Sorbonne University, built the first French navy, and befriended theologians such as St. Thomas Aquinas. Feast: August 25.

Luke, St.

(first century) Luke, the author of the third Gospel and the Acts of the Apostles, was Paul's "dear physician" (Col 4:14) and companion on some of his journeys. Little is known for certain of Luke's life although Eusebius, in his *History of the Church* (c. 323), says that he was born at Antioch. He was a gentile, and according to very early tradition, he wrote his Gospel in Greece and died there, unmarried, at the age of eighty-four. Luke is the patron saint of doctors and painters, the latter because he was said to have painted a picture of the Blessed Virgin that actually dates to a later age. Feast: October 18.

M

MacKillop, St. Mary

(Mary of the Cross) (1842-1909. B. at Melbourne, Australia; d. at Sydney.) MacKillop is Australia's first native-born saint. She worked as a governess, helping to support her family, but felt called to the religious life, particularly to the service of the poor. In 1866, together with Fr. Julian Woods, Mary founded the Sisters of St. Joseph of the Sacred Heart, dedicated to education, to the care of orphans, and to other charitable works. The order grew rapidly, but Mary suffered tremendously from others who meddled in its affairs, most notably a bishop who excommunicated her after relying on some bad advice. The following year he apologized and removed the excommunication. In the face of this and other injustices, Mary never judged, criticized, or blamed her persecutors, excusing them and praising their good qualities instead.

Mary's order offered numerous social services that at the time were not provided by the government. The sisters, who lived in extreme poverty, were well-loved by Catholics and Protestants alike. Mary was something of a pioneer in her work, was concerned for the welfare of the aboriginal people, and fostered conservation. She suffered from ill health in her final years but indefatiga-bly served the order, which at the time of her death, had spread beyond Australia to New Zealand and Peru. Feast: May 25.

Macrina the Elder, St.

(B. at Capadocia; d. c. 340.) St. Basil the Great attributed his sound faith and unshakable orthodoxy to the instruction of his grandmother, Macrina the Elder, who raised him. Macrina and her husband fled their home during the persecutions of Galerius and Maximinus and hid in the hills for seven years. According to St. Gregory Nazianzen, their grandson's good friend, they were frequently hungry and ate wild animals that miraculously allowed themselves to be caught. During another persecution, the state confiscated the couple's goods. Macrina survived her husband but the exact date of her death is uncertain. Feast: January 14.

Makhlouf, St. Charbel

(1828-1898. B. at Beka-Kafra, Lebanon; d. at Annaya.) On the day the monk Charbel was buried, his superior made an unusual entry in the monastic records. "Because of that which [Fr. Charbel] will do after his death, I need not give any details of his life. Faithful to his vows and of exemplary obedience, his conduct was more angelic than human."

Charbel was a member of the Maronite Baladite Order (the Maronite Church is one of the Eastern churches in communion with Rome). He was ordained a priest in 1858 and spent sixteen years as a monk before withdrawing to a hermitage attached to his monastery. He ate little, prayed constantly, refused to touch money, and lived in obedience to the men who occupied the other three cells in the hermitage. He remained there for twenty-three years, sought out by many for prayer and counseling. At the age of seventy, he suffered a stroke while celebrating Mass and died eight days later, on Christmas Eve.

For forty-five days after his burial, a mysterious bright light shone around his grave. His body was exhumed on several occasions over the next sixty years and found to be incorrupt, flexible, and lifelike. It exuded a bloody sweat. After his beatification in 1965, the body decomposed. Many miracles have been—and still are—claimed through his intercession.
Feast: December 24.

Malla, Bd. Ceferino Jimenez

(1861-1936. B. at Fraga, Spain; d. at Barbastro.) Malla is the first Gypsy beatified by the church. He was married, worked as a horse dealer and, though he was illiterate, Gypsies and others frequently sought his advice. He was known for his charity to the poor and his honesty. Once, he was unjustly accused of theft and imprisoned but finally declared innocent. His lawyer said that he was no thief but "San Ceferino, the patron of Gypsies." Malla was arrested for his religious activities during the Spanish Civil War when the church was heavily persecuted. He continued to openly practice his faith in prison and refused to stop praying the rosary, even when offered his freedom in return. He was executed by firing squad, dying with his rosary in his hands. Feast: August 2.

Mandic, St. Leopold

(1866-1942. B. at Herceg Novi, Bosnia-Herzogovina; d. at Padua, Italy.) Leopold was very small (4'6"), spoke with a stutter, and suffered from poor eyesight, stomach problems, and crippling arthritis. In spite of these difficulties, he entered the austere Capuchin Franciscan order in Italy. After his ordination in 1890, he requested assignment to eastern Europe as a missionary (he was particularly interested in church unity). Instead, he was assigned the task of spiritual direction. For nearly forty years, he fulfilled this ministry primarily through sacramental reconciliation: "God's mercy is beyond all expectation," he said of the work. When fellow monks reproached him for his lack of severity with penitents, he said: "If the Lord wants to accuse me of being too lenient toward sinners, I'll tell him that it was he who gave me this example...."

Leopold had a special concern for children and expectant mothers and was devoted to Mary, calling her "Parona benedeta" ("my holy boss"). He remained active until his death from cancer of the esophagus in 1942. During World War II, Leopold's church and monastery were bombed but his confessional was untouched, as he had predicted: "Here God has exercised so much mercy for people, it must remain as a monument to God's goodness." Feast: May 14.

Marcella, St.

(325-410. B./d. at Rome, Italy.) St. Jerome's wide circle of friends included the incomparable Marcella. "Whenever I picture to myself her ardor for study, her vivacity of mind, and her application, I blame my idleness. I who ... am unable to accomplish what a noble woman accomplishes in the hour she snatches from the cares of a large circle and the government of her household."

Marcella was widowed after seven months of marriage and refused to remarry. She turned her mansion in Rome into a center for women who, like herself, chose an austere life of prayer, learning, and works of mercy.

She studied Greek and Hebrew in order to better understand Scripture and questioned Jerome closely on religious matters both when he was living in Rome and, after he left, by mail. Sixteen of his letters to her survive and are our main source of information about her. She was not intimidated by the sometimes difficult saint, challenging his arguments and chastising him for his hot temper.

Marcella was captured by the Goths during the invasion of Rome and tortured to force disclosure of the location of her fortune. This she had long since distributed to the poor. She died shortly after of the effects of the abuse. Feast: January 31.

Margaret of Cortona, St.

(1247-1297. B. at Laviano, Italy; d. at Cortona.) Margaret suffered ill-treatment from her stepmother and ran away to become the mistress of a nobleman. She remained with him for nine years and they had a son. Her lover was murdered while on a business trip, prompting Margaret to repent of her life and return to her father who, at the urging of his wife, refused to accept her. Margaret found help through the Franciscans and soon began to practice severe penance, joined the Third Order of St. Francis, and eventually sent her son away to school (he later joined the Franciscans). She spent the early years of her conversion wrestling with temptation and told a priest who urged her to mitigate her penance: "Between me and my body there must needs be a struggle till death."

Margaret founded a hospital and organized some women of the Third Order into a community, the Poverelle, to help the sick poor. She endured fierce gossip that cast aspersions on her relationship with the Franciscan friars, but the accusations proved false. Toward the end of her life, she had great success leading sinners to repentance, healing feuds, and attacking vice. Her reputation for sanctity spread as far as France and Spain, many came to consult her, and healings were reported through her intercession. Feast: February 22.

Margaret of Metola, Bd.

(c. 1286-1320. B. at Metola, Italy; d. at Citta-di-Castello.) Margaret was born blind and abandoned by her parents when a hoped-for healing at a shrine failed to occur. A group of women cared for her until a couple adopted her. She then joined a local convent, where her piety and austerities so annoyed the lax community that they treated her badly and in the end threw her out.

She went back to her adoptive family and, on becoming a Third Order Dominican, taught the local children,

visited the sick and imprisoned, and continued her intense prayer life and severe penances. Miracles were attributed to her both before and after her death at the age of thirty-three. She is also known as Margaret of Citta-di-Castello, the town near Metola where she settled. Feast: April 13.

Margaret of Scotland, St.

(c. 1045-1093. D. at Edinburgh, Scotland.) Margaret was the granddaughter of Edmund Ironside, the English king, and was probably born in Hungary where her family was in exile. They returned to England in 1057 but fled to Scotland after the Norman conquest.

In spite of leanings toward the religious life, Margaret married Malcolm III, king of Scotland, in 1070. The marriage proved exceptional, both in the mutual devotion of Malcolm and Margaret and in the positive influence she exerted over Scottish affairs, including the reform of the church. Her effect on Malcolm, who was rough and illiterate, was considerable. She helped soften his temper, led him to a concern for the needy, and generally helped him and his court achieve a higher standard of civilization. Her biographer wrote that Malcolm "could not but perceive that Christ dwelt within her.... He readily obeyed her wishes in all things; whatever pleased her he also loved for the love of her."

Margaret personally tended the sick and gave alms, fasted regularly, slept little, prayed frequently, and was particularly noted for her love for the poor. She arranged for church synods that regulated marriage laws, restored order to practices such as the Lenten fast and Easter communion, and ended simony. Worn out by her austerities, she died at the age of forty-seven, shortly after receiving word that Malcolm and their son, Edward, had been killed in battle. Feast: November 16.

Marillac, St. Louise de

(1590-1660. B. at Auvergne, France; d. at Paris.) Louise was born to an aristocratic French family although her birth seems to have been out-of-wedlock, between her widowed father's first and second marriages. Her father claimed her as his daughter, but she appears never to have been fully accepted by his family. She married Anthony Le Gras in 1613 in spite of an inclination to the religious life. The couple had one child and their marriage was happy although troubled by job loss and financial constraints. Louise endured a time of temptation, depression, and loss of faith when Anthony became ill and died in 1625. Shortly after, she came under the influence of St. Vincent de Paul, who became her spiritual director and with whom she worked the rest of her life.

She oversaw the work of his Ladies of Charity—well-to-do women who cared for the poor and needy—and helped transform them into a more effective organization. In 1633, she took four young women into her own home in Paris and trained them for direct service to the poor. This was the beginning of the Sisters of Charity, officially approved as a religious order in 1646. St. Vincent described them as "a community with no other monastery than the houses of the sick, with no cells but ... the poorest room ... with no cloister other than the streets...." Guided by Vincent and with the energetic, devout, and intelligent Louise as superior, the order expanded rapidly. The sisters were enormously effective in ministering to orphans, the mentally ill, wounded soldiers, condemned criminals, the hungry, the abandoned, and all in need. Louise died in 1660 after telling her sisters to serve the poor and "to honor them like Christ himself." Feast: March 15.

Mark, St.

(first century) Mark is traditionally identified as the author of the second Gospel and the John Mark who was the son of a Christian at Jerusalem named Mary (see Acts 12:12). He was a cousin of St. Barnabas and accompanied Barnabas and St. Paul on their first missionary journey. Mark left them at

Perga, however, and returned to Jerusalem, evidently having offended Paul in some way. He then went with Barnabas to evangelize Cyprus (see Acts 15:36-39) and later, back in Paul's good favor, was with Paul in Rome during his first imprisonment (see Col 4:10). It is thought that he wrote his Gospel at Rome, where he was also a disciple of St. Peter (see 1 Pt 5:13). According to Papias (c. 135), he was the interpreter or secretary to Peter. This association helped shape his Gospel which, scholars believe, was used as a source by both Matthew and Luke.

Various traditions that claim Mark went to Alexandria, was its first bishop, and was a martyr are unsubstantiated. He is the patron saint of Venice, his relics supposedly brought there in the ninth century. Feast: April 25.

Martin of Tours, St.

(c. 315-397. B. at Sabara, Pannonia [now Hungary]; d. at Tours, France.) Martin became a catechumen at the age of twelve against the wishes of his pagan parents. His father, a soldier, was stationed with the family in Italy, and Martin, when fifteen, was conscripted against his will. One winter, when billeted in Amiens, he came upon a half-naked beggar, trembling in the cold. Martin cut his cloak in two, gave half to the beggar, and that night, had a dream in which Jesus appeared, clad in half of Martin's cloak. "Martin, while still a catechumen, gave me this to cover me," Jesus said. Martin responded by immediately seeking baptism and shortly after, left the army: "I am a soldier of Christ," he said, "and I am forbidden to fight."

He joined Bishop St. Hilary of Poitiers, was ordained, visited his parents where he brought about the conversion of his mother but not his father, and rejoined Hilary in 360. He lived as a monk for ten years, pioneering the monastic life in Gaul, until, at the demand of the people but against his will, he was made the bishop of Tours. He continued to live as a monk, visited the most remote parts of his diocese on foot, donkey, and by boat, and was a zealous missionary. He was involved in doctrinal disputes, particularly with a sect known as the Priscillianists, and actively opposed the emperor's interference in that matter as well as his threat to put members of the sect to death. Sulpicius Severus, his friend, wrote Martin's biography, which was widely read and helped to make him one of the most popular saints in the Middle Ages. Feast: November 11.

Marto, Bd. Jacinta (1910-1920. B. at Aljustrel, Portugal; d. at Lisbon.) **and Bd. Francisco** (1908-1919. B./d.at Aljustrel.) The Blessed Virgin appeared at Fatima to Jacinta and Francisco, sister and brother, as well as to a third child, Lucia Santos (as of the year 2000, Lucia was still alive and a Carmelite nun). The six apparitions began on May 13, 1917, ended on October 13, and took place at the Cova da Iria where the three pastured sheep. Mary told the children to urge people to do penance for sin and pray the rosary because otherwise great suffering would come to the world. Jacinta, age six, and Francisco, eight, would soon die, she said, but Lucia would live to promote devotion to the Immaculate Heart of Mary.

Jacinta was sensitive and outgoing and for the rest of her short life offered her prayer and sacrifice for sinners, to preserve them from hell. She also developed a special concern for the pope, praying for him daily. Francisco was quiet, submissive, and friendly. He was a compassionate boy and offered much of his prayer and suffering to Mary and Jesus to console them over humanity's sinfulness. Both children became ill during the worldwide flu epidemic, and Francisco died on April 4, 1919. Jacinta developed complications, was in and out of hospitals, and died after great suffering on February 20, 1920. Her last words were: "Pray for the priests."

Mary Magdalen, St.

(first century) Mary was from Magdala, a village on the west coast of the Sea of Galilee. She was among the women who ministered to Jesus. He drove seven demons from her (see Mk 16:9; Lk 8:2); she was present for his crucifixion and burial (see Mt 27:56, 61; Mk 15:40, 47; Jn 19:25); and she was one of the women who discovered the empty tomb (see Mt 28:1-10; Mk 16:1; Lk 24:10). In John's account, Mary went to the burial site alone after the Crucifixion, saw that the stone had been moved away, and ran to tell Peter and the "disciple Jesus loved." They went to the tomb, verified Mary's story, and returned home. Mary, who remained behind weeping, turned and saw Jesus standing beside her. She mistook him for the gardener until he said, "Mary!" "Rabboni" (teacher), she responded. He told her not to cling to him but to go announce his resurrection to the disciples (see Jn 20:1-18).

In the past, Mary Magdalen has been identified as the same woman as Mary of Bethany (sister of Martha and Lazarus) and the unnamed penitent who anointed Jesus' feet (see Lk 7:36-48). Current biblical scholarship has led the church to recognize the three as separate individuals. Biblical research also rejects the traditional identification of Mary as a reformed prostitute. Scripture merely states that she was freed from seven demons and makes no reference to sexual sin.

Mary is rightly seen as a woman who received and responded to God's mercy. In this and in her privileged encounter with the risen Christ, she is a sign of hope and a witness to the triumph of life over death. Feast: July 22.

Mary of the Cross, Bd. (Jeanne Jugan)

(1792-1879. B. at Cancales, Frances; d. at Saint-Perm.) Jugan's life was unusual in that she discovered her vocation quite late, practiced it actively for only twelve years, and then lived in seclusion for twenty-seven. Born to poverty, she supported herself as a maid and hospital worker and devoted herself as well to the poor, possibly as a member of the Third Order of the Heart of the Admirable Mother. She was forty-seven when she took in an elderly, destitute, blind widow and began what proved to be her life's work. Assisted by two helpers, she soon expanded the ministry and founded the Little Sisters of the Poor, devoted especially to the elderly and sick. In 1845 the prestigious French Academy honored her for her widely acclaimed work.

Shortly after she established her community, the spiritual director, Fr. Le Pailleur, deposed Jugan as superior. In 1852, he banished her to the motherhouse, where she lived in obscurity until her death twenty-seven years later. He took control of the order and rewrote its history, naming himself as founder, a deception not corrected until after Jugan's death. He did this so skillfully that the fraud was detected by few other than Jugan.

She, for her part, never complained, choosing, she said, to be "grafted onto the cross." Her exile was spent among the young women entering the order, and she passed on her vision and spirit to them, creating an exceptionally firm foundation for the community. "She lived in the presence of God," one of them recalled. "She would be on fire when talking to us about [him]." After Jugan's death, Le Pailleur grew increasingly dictatorial and Rome, becoming aware of the situation, investigated. Authorities removed the priest from office eleven years after Jugan died. Feast: August 29.

Mary of the Incarnation, St. (Barbe Acarie)

(1566-1618. B. at Paris; d. at Amiens.) The devout and charming Barbe married Peter Acarie, an aristocrat and treasury official, when she was seventeen. She and her husband, a charitable, pious man, had six children, including three daughters who entered the Carmelite order and one son who became a priest.

Peter plunged the family into heavy debt by his support of the Catholic League against the Protestant Henry IV (who later converted to Catholicism). When the still-Protestant Henry became king, Peter's property was seized, he was banished, and his family fell into complete poverty. Barbe went to court on her husband's behalf, conducted his defense herself, proved that he was innocent of conspiracy, and was able to restore some of their fortune.

Barbe's charities were far-flung and her wisdom and piety so widely admired that others entrusted her with alms for distribution at her discretion. She is said to have had two visions of St. Teresa of Avila, reformer of the Carmelite order, which inspired her to introduce the Discalced Carmelites into France. Though married, she helped train women for that life and received spiritual advice at this time from St. Frances de Sales and Pierre Berulle, founder of the French Oratorians. On the death of her husband in 1613, she entered the Carmelites as a lay sister and died four years later. Feast: April 18.

Mary of Jesus Crucified, Bd. (Mary Baouatdy)

(1846-1878. B. at Abellin, near Galilee; d. at Nazareth.) Mary was a Christian Arab and member of the Greek Melkite rite, an Eastern rite church in union with Rome. She is honored as a model of humility—"When you want to be big, make yourself little," she said.

Mary was orphaned and raised by an uncle who arranged a marriage for her when she was twelve. She refused the match and asked a servant to contact her brother in Nazareth on her behalf. Instead, the servant attempted to convert her to Islam. When she declared her faith in the Catholic Church, he sliced her neck with a scimitar and dumped her in an alley. She was rescued and healed, she said, by a woman dressed in blue and was convinced that this was Mary, the mother of Jesus.

Mary left her adoptive family, became a servant, and took a vow of chastity. Eventually, she moved with her employer to France. She entered the Carmelite Order at Pau where, true to her desire to remain unnoticed, she did menial chores but also experienced mystical graces, including the stigmata. She was sent to help found the first Carmel in India and in 1872 felt inspired to open a Carmel in Bethlehem. She started another Carmel at Nazareth, but before it was finished, she fell, broke her arm, and died when the wound became infected with gangrene. The last years of her life were marked by ill health and mystical prayer followed by a period of spiritual desolation. Throughout, she remained a "little sister to everyone," always ready to serve in spite of her own fatigue. She had a special devotion to the Holy Spirit, praying that the Spirit would "let me understand Jesus."

Feast: August 26.

Mary, the Mother of Jesus

Mary has been honored in the church from ancient times, preeminent among the saints as the Mother of God. Her titles include Blessed Virgin Mary, Blessed Mother, and Queen of Heaven. It is primarily as mother, model, and intercessor that Catholics revere her. "It's good to speak of her privileges," St. Thérèse of Lisieux wrote, "but it's necessary above all that we can imitate her."

Mary was a young Jewish woman when the angel Gabriel appeared to her and announced that through the power of the Holy Spirit, she would become the mother of Jesus. Trusting in God, without demanding details, she consented: "Let it be done to me as you say." In so doing, she modeled perfect abandonment to God's will. She visited her cousin Elizabeth, who greeted her as the mother of the Lord, prompting Mary to respond with praise of God's mercy: "My being proclaims the great-ness of the Lord."

She married Joseph and gave birth to her son in Bethlehem, where the couple had gone to take part in a census. Shortly after, the family fled to Egypt to avoid the murderous anger of King Herod, who feared the child as a rival to the throne. When the danger passed, they settled at Nazareth. Nothing is recorded of Mary's life there except for the presentation of Jesus at the temple and his brief disappearance while on a trip to Jerusalem (see Lk 1–3; Mt. 1–2).

The strength of Mary's relationship with her Son is later evident at the wedding at Cana. Prompted by her intervention, he performed his first miracle by changing water into wine (see Jn 2:11). She was present at Jesus' crucifixion, where he entrusted her into the care of the disciple John—"Behold thy mother" (Jn 19:25-27)—and was with the disciples in Jerusalem at Pentecost (see Acts 1–2). This is the last mention of her in Scripture.

According to tradition, Mary died either at Ephesus or Jerusalem. In 1950, the church declared the doctrine of Mary's Assumption, stating that following her natural death, she was taken body and soul into heaven (feast: August 15). This is a very early Christian belief, widely observed as a feast by the sixth century. The doctrine of the Immaculate Conception, promulgated in 1854, declares that Mary was free from original sin from the moment of her conception. Under the title of the Immaculate Conception, Mary is patron of the United States (feast: December 8). The Catholic Church also honors Mary for her perpetual virginity.

The church has approved only a small number of the reported appearances of Mary. Some of these are the appearances at Lourdes (see Bernadette Soubirous), Fatima (Marto, Francisco and Jacinta), Paris (Alacoque, Margaret Mary), and Mexico (Diego, Juan). The approved Marian appearances are not considered articles of faith.

The Catholic Church stresses Mary's role as intercessor, an ancient tradition witnessed to by a prayer dating to the late third to early fourth century. The importance of this role has been consistently reinforced. "The Church ... sees Mary maternally present and sharing in the many complicated problems which today beset the lives of individuals, families, and nations and sees her helping the Christian people in the constant struggle between good and evil" (*Redemptoris Mater*, Pope John Paul II).

Mary of Providence, Bd. (Eugenie Smet)

(1825-1871. B. at Lille, France; d. at Paris.) From an early age, Eugenie had a strong concern for the suffering souls in purgatory. She decided that the church needed a religious order committed to those souls and felt called to start one. Eugenie had enormous confidence in God, received encouragement from St. John Vianney, and in 1856, after several false starts, founded the Helpers of the Holy Souls. She took the name Mary of Providence, reflecting her trust in God's bounty. The order's aim, she said, was "through constant prayer and the practice of the works of mercy, to relieve and deliver the souls who are completing their expiation [in purgatory] before being admitted to the bliss of heaven."

The sisters began the practical side of their ministry by chance, when someone asked them to take care of a poor woman in the neighborhood. Soon they were caring for the sick and suffering poor, and in 1867 the rapidly expanding order sent six sisters to China. Sister Mary died of cancer in Paris during the Franco-Prussian War, her trust in God as strong as ever even though she was in terrible pain and the convent was short of food and fuel. Today, her sisters serve in twenty-five countries. Feast: February 7.

Mas y de Vedruna, St. Joachima de

(1783-1854. B./d. at Barcelona, Spain.) Several days after their wedding, Joachima told her husband Teodore that she was depressed because she had always wanted to be a nun but, in deference to her parents' wishes, had married. She now worried that she had failed God. Teodore said that he, too, had intended to enter the religious life but felt obliged to fulfill his duty as eldest son by marrying. They agreed that when they had raised a family they could enter religious orders and then went on to have eight children and a happy life.

During the Napoleonic wars, the family evacuated to Vich and Teodore enlisted in the army. In 1813, they all returned to Barcelona, but Teodore died suddenly three years later, his health undermined by his military tour of duty. Joachima continued to raise their children but also volunteered at the local hospital and cultivated a life of prayer and penance.

In 1826, she founded the Carmelites of Charity, a religious order devoted to teaching the young and visiting the sick. Within a few months, the sisters opened a hospital. The order spread throughout the area in spite of wars and persecution and, briefly, the arrest and imprisonment of Joachima by antireligious soldiers. In 1849, Joachima suffered the first of several strokes and died after five years of complete paralysis. During the Spanish Civil War of 1936-39, twenty-five of her order were martyred. Feast: August 28.

Matthew, St.

(first century) Matthew was a tax collector at the time Jesus called him to be an apostle. Scholars generally agree that he is the same individual named as Levi in Matthew 9:9; Mark 2:14; Luke 5:27-32. Luke says of him that at his call he stood up, left everything behind, and became Jesus' follower. He then held a large reception for Jesus attended by tax collectors and "those known as sinners" (Mt 9:10). He is traditionally regarded as the author of the Gospel of Matthew. Nothing is known with certainty of his later life, but Eusebius in his *History of the Church* (c. 323) claims he preached to the Jews. *The Roman Martyrology* says he was martyred in Ethiopia, but other accounts place his martyrdom in Persia or Pontus. Feast: September 21.

Matulaitis-Matulewicz, Bd. George

(1871-1927. B. at Luigine, Lithuania; d. at Kaunas.) Orphaned at age eleven, George developed tuberculosis of the bone when he was fifteen—a painful, lifelong condition. Ordained a priest in 1898, he was assigned to Warsaw and immediately turned his attention to issues of social justice, helping the poor, opening an orphanage, and assisting workers. His health deteriorated, and in 1905 he ended up in the paupers' ward of a hospital, close to death. He made a remarkable, unexpected recovery and, in gratitude, vowed to find a way to honor the Blessed Virgin.

George had been a student of the Marian Fathers of the Immaculate Conception as a teenager and in 1907 discovered that, due to persecution by the Lithuanian government, they had been reduced to one priest at one house in Mariampole. He decided to revive the order as a tribute to Mary, received permission from the pope, and in 1909 joined the sole survivor, Fr. Senkus, and professed vows as a Marian.

Because of government persecution, they had to operate in secret, but after moving to Fribourg, Switzerland, the order began to grow. By George's death in 1927, there were 250 members. Houses were opened around the world including Brazil, Rwanda, and Australia, and in 1913, George himself opened a house in Chicago. He also founded two communities for women, the Sisters of the Immaculate Conception and the Servants of Jesus in the Eucharist.

George served as bishop of Vilnius from 1918 to 1925, a position that caused him great suffering due to conflicting ethnic and religious differences among the people. On his deathbed he told his Marians: "Fall in line and sacrifice yourselves." Two Marian priests who did that and died at the hands of the Nazis were beatified by Pope John Paul II in 1999 (see Leszczewicz and Kaszyra). George died following surgery for his tuberculosis. Feast: January 27.

Maximilian, St.

(D. 295. at Theveste, Numidia [now Tebessia, Algeria].) Maximilian, a soldier's son, refused to serve in the Roman army as required by law for all sons of veterans. His father, Victor, appeared with him at court when he explained that he could not be a soldier of this world because he was already a soldier of Christ. Victor refused to interfere with his son's decision even when the proconsul ordered him to do so: "He knows what he believes and can take his own counsel on what is best for him."

Maximilian asserted that he was following his own conscience and the inspiration of Christ in the matter. Even when threatened with death, he didn't waver: "I shall not die. If I go from this earth my soul will live with Christ my Lord."

The court condemned the twenty-one-year-old, and he was beheaded almost immediately. His father "went home joyfully, thanking God for having allowed him to send such a gift to heaven."

The account of the trial and execution of this early conscientious objector is authentic, ancient, and free from embroidery. Feast: March 12.

Mayer, Bd. Rupert

(1876-1945. B. at Stuttgart, Germany; d. at Munich.) Mayer had a particularly happy childhood—"a wonderful youth such as is rarely experienced," he said. His parents were very committed Christians who encouraged their six children to develop spiritually, intellectually, and socially. Mayer was a gifted student and athlete (his favorite sport was horseback riding), played the violin, and felt inclined toward the priesthood. He was ordained, entered the Jesuits, and in 1912 was assigned to Munich, the primary site of his ministry for the rest of his life.

During World War I, he was a chaplain at the front for the German army and received the Iron Cross, Germany's highest military honor. He had "a spirit of unbelievable sacrifice," a general said. "When the fighting was fiercest he was always ... at the front line. During the most severe bombardments he went from one man to another, crawling along the ground," consoling the men or, when necessary, preparing them for death. He was wounded by a grenade in 1916, forcing the amputation of his left leg and military retirement.

He returned to Munich, where he cared for workers and the poor—he led Caritas, the charitable organization— and ministered to university students through the Sodality of Our Lady. The

organization grew from three thousand to seven thousand members under his guidance. It was a powerful influence in parish life. In the volatile postwar climate, he spoke out against communism while also closely following the development of the National Socialist (Nazi) Party. He followed the meetings Hitler held every two weeks, spoke out at them, and once, after Hitler gave a speech, said of him that he was a great speaker and very popular but "stirs up the people by distorting the truth." As early as 1923 he stated at a debate that "no German Catholic can ever be a National Socialist."

When the Nazis finally came to power, they found the priest a thorn in the side but had to tread lightly in view of his enormous popularity. Nevertheless, in 1937 they banned him from speaking and when he preached anyway, arrested him. Released with a suspended sentence and advised by his superiors to remain silent, he received their permission to speak out when the Nazis publicly slandered him. ("Priests are all the same.... Rattle the keys of the concentration camp [and] they subside ... and shut up.")

He was rearrested, sent to Sachsenhausen concentration camp but, when his health collapsed in 1940, was reassigned to house arrest at Ettal monastery in Bavaria. The Nazis, fearing martyrdom would make him a hero, kept him alive but totally isolated for the remainder of the war. He found this exile extremely hard to endure, "much worse than actual death for which I had prepared myself so many times."

Mayer was liberated by American troops on May 6, 1945, and returned to Munich but died of a stroke on November 1, while preaching at Mass. His last words were: "The Lord ... the Lord ... the Lord...." Feast: November 1.

Mazzarello, St. Mary

(1837-1881. B. at Mornese, Italy; d. at Nizza Monferrato.) Mary was born into a peasant family and spent the first part of her life working in the fields beside her brothers and sisters. She was attractive, funny, intelligent—though uneducated—and a member of the Daughters of Mary Immaculate, a sodality in her parish. In 1860, the sodalists nursed the victims of a typhoid epidemic and Mary caught the disease, almost dying. Her health was permanently undermined, but she turned to dressmaking, starting a business that employed local girls.

Meanwhile her contemporary, St. John Bosco, was aware of the need for an order of women to provide the same sort of educational and work opportunities for girls that he provided for boys. He met Mary and they collaborated on founding the

Daughters of Mary Help of Christians (the Salesian sisters), formally instituted in 1872. Mary was appointed superior. She had a gift for governing and the same encouraging, gentle approach to others that was characteristic of Bosco and his Salesian priests. Her order expanded rapidly, but in 1881, after a trip to Marseilles to oversee the departure of some of her sisters to South America, she became seriously ill. She died not long after being anointed, saying to the priest: "Now that you have given me my passport, I suppose I may leave at any time at all?" Feast: May 14.

Menni, St. Benedict

(1841-1914. B. at Milan, Italy; d. at Dinan, France.) As a teenager, Benedict volunteered to be a stretcher-bearer carrying soldiers wounded in a local battle to the hospital of the Hospitaller Brothers of St. John of God. Impressed by their devoted care, he joined the order and was ordained (each community of brothers had a priest acting as chaplain). In the 1830s the order had been suppressed in Spain due to anti-clerical legislation, but in 1866 Benedict was chosen to reestablish the brothers there. Although political instability led to threats on his life and, briefly, expulsion from the country, Benedict and the brothers opened hospitals for sick and abandoned children as well as numerous psychiatric hospitals. He was superior of the order in Spain and provincial of a newly established Spanish-American province.

Benedict's motto was "Pray, work, suffer, forbear, love, silence," and much of his suffering came at the hands of members of his own congregation. He had founded an order of women, the Hospitaller Sisters of the Sacred Heart, and some brothers resented them, seeing the sisters as competition. Others resented his insistence on conformity to church doctrine and his removal from office of those he felt fell short of that goal. The brothers ousted him from the order's headquarters in Rome in 1912 and forbade him to seek shelter even with the sisters. He died of a stroke in 1914. His life was completely devoted to the sick, especially the mentally ill, and he felt that by serving them he directly served Christ. Feast: April 24.

Merlo, Ven. Thecla

(1894-1964. B. at Castagnito d'Alba, Piedmont, Italy; d. at Albano.) At a time when women were not prominent in the field of communications, Merlo helped to found the Daughters of St. Paul, a religious order devoted to spreading the gospel through publishing, radio, television, film, and other means of communication. "Life passes quickly," she said to her sisters, "let's be smart"—and they began their work by reviving a diocesan newspaper, learning

along the way the technical aspects of typesetting, printing, and distributing their product.

Merlo worked closely with Fr. James Alberione, founder of the Society of St. Paul and cofounder of the Daughters. He initially invited her to direct a workshop sewing clothes for soldiers during World War I. Under Fr. Alberione's guidance, Merlo and several women of the workshop took preliminary vows in 1918 and revived the diocesan newspaper at his invitation. With Merlo as their superior, the ministry quickly spread worldwide. The sisters manned printing presses, wrote books, opened bookstores and worked in them, drove cars, rode bicycles—revolutionary behavior for sisters at the time. In 1953, the Vatican formally recognized them as a religious congregation. Merlo died of a stroke on February 5, 1964, with Fr. Alberione and some of her sisters at her side.

Michael, St.

Michael, an archangel, appears four times in Scripture. In the Book of Daniel, he is mentioned twice, once as "one of the chief princes" (10:13) and once as "the great prince," guardian of God's people (12:1). In the Book of Revelation, he waged war against Satan and his angels, overpowering them and hurling them down to earth (12:7-9). The obscure reference to Michael in the

Epistle of Jude is based on a story from the apocryphal Assumption of Moses. Michael disputes with the devil over the body of Moses but "did not venture to charge him with blasphemy" (9), leaving the judgment of the devil to God.

Michael was held in great esteem by the Jewish people and from the beginning of Christian history. He is regarded as the protector of believers against the devil, especially at the hour of death, and as the helper of Christian armies. Feast (with the Archangels Gabriel and Raphael): September 29.

Miki, St. Paul, and Companions

(1564-1597. Japan) Paul was of the Samurai warrior caste, the son of a prosperous military chief. He lived near Kyoto, Japan, and studied with the Jesuits who, under the leadership of Francis Xavier, had begun to evangelize Japan in 1549. In 1587, the authorities ordered all missionaries out of Japan, fearful that they were precursors of foreign conquest. Most went underground and the church continued to flourish.

In 1596 the first of a series of intense persecutions began, and Miki, who had a reputation as a powerful preacher, was arrested. He was three months short of his ordination as a Jesuit priest. A few weeks later, he was executed along with twenty-six others—three Jesuits, six Franciscans, and seventeen laity. Among the latter were catechists, interpreters, a soldier, a doctor, and three boys who were altar servers. Most of the martyrs had part of their left ear cut off and, with blood smearing their faces, were taken through towns to intimidate Christians and potential converts. They were crucified near Nagasaki by being bound to crosses and then speared in the side almost at the same instant, each by his own executioner. Feast (as the Martyrs of Japan): February 6.

Milleret, Bd. Marie-Eugenie

(1817-1898. B. at Metz, France; d. at Paris.) Milleret was baptized into a nonpracticing Catholic family, and her parents, whose marriage was unhappy, separated when she was a teenager. Her mother, with whom she lived in Paris, died shortly after in a cholera epidemic. Placed with a socially prominent family, the fifteen-year-old found the fashionable life tedious and felt drawn to religious faith. She received the inspiration she needed in a series of sermons preached by the famous Dominican Lacordaire, who struck a nerve when he said: "It is prayer that re-establishes our relationship with God."

As a result of this personal revival of faith, Milleret decided to consecrate herself to God. A priest asked her to help start a religious order for women that would be contemplative in character but dedicated to the education of women. In 1839, they began the

Congregation of the Religious of the Assumption. She guided her congregation firmly in spite of the meddling of others, some of whom disapproved of her interest in social issues or simply wanted to control her. The interference drove her to exclaim: "The further I go, the less sympathy I have for priests or pious lay people.... Their hearts do not beat for anything broad-minded. Do I have to modify our style so as to take out of it everything that shocks narrow minds?"

By 1844, the first members were professed, and in 1850, the order began to expand abroad. Rome formally approved the congregation in 1866 following one last attempt by a cleric to discredit it and expel the sisters from Paris. Milleret, who was completely committed to the church and convinced of the importance of education in cultivating faith, said: "It is fire, passion, and ardent love for the Church and this society, so far away from God, which has given birth to this work. The irreligiousness of three-quarters of the people necessitates a work of education. Serious studies will put us in a position to make Jesus Christ known." Feast: March 10.

Molla, Bd. Gianna Beretta

(1922-1962. B./d. at Milan, Italy.) Gianna was a medical doctor who specialized in pediatrics. She was devout, active in Catholic Action, and a daily communicant. Thinking she might have a vocation to the religious life, Gianna made a pilgrimage to Lourdes seeking discernment and, upon her return, met and fell in love with Pietro Molla. She took this as an answer to her prayers and married Pietro in 1955. Soon they had three children, Gianna successfully blending her career and family life.

She was diagnosed with a uterine growth shortly after becoming pregnant again in 1961. At that time, treatment was limited, but Gianna refused to have a hysterectomy or any other procedure that would interfere with the life of the baby. "I have entrusted myself to the Lord in faith and hope," she said. The doctors successfully removed the growth, but the pregnancy continued to be high-risk. Before the birth, Gianna told her husband: "If they should ask you which of the two lives they should save, do not hesitate.... First, the life of the child." She had a successful cesarean delivery but died of peritonitis a week later.

Gianna was beatified not simply for her willingness to sacrifice her life for her unborn baby but also, as the beatification announcement notes, because she was "a woman of exceptional love, an outstanding wife and mother, a witness to the power for good of the gospel in everyday life." Feast: April 28.

Monica, St.

(c. 331-387. B. at Tagaste; d. at Ostia.)
Monica was the mother of St.
Augustine, who wrote extensively about
her. His frank assessment reveals a
woman whose intense Christian piety
together with her extreme affection for
her wayward son created a mother
determined to win him for Christ.

Monica's married life was difficult.
Her husband, Patricius, had a temper,
was unfaithful, and was not a Christian
although he became one shortly before
his death in 371. Her mother-in-law
lived with them as well, and she, too,
became a Christian under Monica's
influence. The couple had three children whom Monica tried to raise in the
faith. We know little of the others, but
Augustine went to study at Carthage
when he was sixteen and began to live a
profligate life. Eventually he joined the
Manichaean sect and settled down with
a mistress with whom he had a son.

Although Augustine tried to elude
her, Monica followed him to Rome in
383 and then to Milan. She prayed
intently for his conversion and asked
others to do the same, prompting one
exasperated bishop to tell her: "It is not
possible that the son of so many tears
should be lost." Monica persuaded
Augustine to send his mistress away and
arranged a suitable marriage for him.
Before anything could come of that,
Augustine embraced Christianity and

Monica "rejoiced triumphantly," her
son wrote, because God had "granted
her much more than she had asked
for in her tears, prayers, plaints and
lamenting."

Monica died shortly after as she,
Augustine, and their friends were on their
way back to Africa. Feast: August 27.

More, St. Thomas

(1478-1535. B./d. at London, England.)
More was a married man, father, writer,
lawyer, Lord Chancellor of England,
and martyr. He was known for his
intellectual brilliance, wit, and integrity
undergirded by a deep personal piety.
More was "born and made for friendship" according to his contemporary,
Erasmus—his character was like his
face, Erasmus said, cheerful and ready
to smile.

More was from London, England,
the son of a lawyer. He studied at
Oxford, prepared for the law at
Lincoln's Inn, and was admitted to
the bar in 1501. He lectured in law
and, in 1504, entered Parliament.
Drawn to the monastic life, he lived
near the Carthusians, participated in
their spiritual exercises, wore a hair shirt
(a lifelong practice), and followed an
ascetic, penitential life.

Ultimately, he decided to pursue a
secular career, and in 1505, he and Jane
Colt married and had three daughters
and a son. Their home became a center

of culture, attracting the leading intellectual figures of the day. When Henry VIII took the throne in 1509, he launched More on a brilliant career of public service beginning with an appointment as undersheriff of London.

At almost the same time, More's wife died, and within the month he married Alice Middleton, a widow seven years his senior and a good pragmatic choice as a stepmother to his young children. His family was of great concern to More, and he not only formed his children in the faith but also provided each of his daughters with an excellent education, an uncommon practice at the time. His home life was lively and cultured, and when More traveled he regretted his time away from his children, writing to them nearly every day.

More finished his famous book, *Utopia*, in 1516, went on several diplomatic missions for the king, was knighted in 1521, and filled a series of high offices until, in 1529, Henry appointed him Lord Chancellor. At the time, King Henry was agitating to have his marriage to Catherine of Aragon declared invalid, which would free him to marry Ann Boleyn. More defended the validity of the first marriage, to the great anger of the king, and in 1532 resigned as Chancellor, thereby losing his income and plunging his family into poverty.

He refused to attend the coronation of Anne Boleyn and lived quietly for a year and a half until summoned to swear to the Act of Succession, which involved, in part, the repudiation of papal religious authority. He refused, was accused of treason, and was imprisoned in the Tower of London for fifteen months. He spent the time in prayer and penance, wrote devotional books, and resisted the entreaties of his family (led by his beloved daughter, Margaret) to conform. He was beheaded on July 6, 1535, declaring to the crowd: "I die the king's good servant, but God's first." Feast: June 22.

Morosini, Bd. Pierina

(1931-1957. B./d. near Albino, Italy.) A devout young factory worker, Morosini helped support her family when her father became ill. She was active in Catholic Action, devoted to the Sacred Heart, joined the Third Order of St. Francis, taught catechism, and visited the sick. Each workday, she rose at four to attend Mass before arriving at the factory at six. In 1947 she attended the beatification in Rome of St. Maria Goretti, who had died while repelling a rapist. She was attracted by Goretti's purity and wanted to be "a little apostle of all those girls who are led astray by the world."

Morosini was walking home through the forest on the afternoon of April 4,

1957, when she was assaulted by a twenty-year-old man. She resisted the attack but the assailant, who had been harassing her for a year, beat her, raped her, and left her in a coma. Her brother found her but she died two days later at the hospital without regaining consciousness. The doctor who cared for her said, "Now we have a new Maria Goretti."
Feast: April 6.

Moscati, St. Joseph

(1880-1927. B. at Benevito, Italy; d. at Naples.) The example of his parents—they attended daily Mass with their nine children and frequently, on family walks, dropped in at church for brief visits—stuck with Moscati throughout his life. He studied medicine at the University of Naples, graduated with top honors, became a doctor, and approached his career as a vocation through which he could minister to the whole person, body and spirit. He worked at the United Hospital and distinguished himself by his concern for his patients. When Mt. Vesuvius erupted in 1906, he raced to the branch hospital near there and began to evacuate it himself, many of the staff having already left. Shortly after he and some remaining staff members removed the last patient, the roof collapsed under the weight of volcanic ash.

Alongside his hospital work, Moscati became a university professor, served as chair of the clinical chemistry department at the Institute of Physiological Chemistry, wrote numerous articles for medical journals, avidly pursued research, and held prestigious posts in the medical community. He considered joining the Jesuits but chose instead to dedicate himself to his profession, remaining single as well. He treated the poor for free and kept a basket in his waiting room with a note attached: "If you can, put in whatever you wish; if you cannot and are in need, take whatever is necessary."

Moscati was forty-seven years old when, telling others he felt slightly ill, he sat down in his favorite wingback chair, folded his arms, and quietly died. A huge crowd attended his funeral. An admirer said: "We mourn him because the world has lost a saint, Naples has lost an example of every virtue and the sick poor have lost everything." Feast: April 12.

Mzyk, Bd. Louis

(1905-1940. B. at Chorzaw, Poland; d. in Poznan.) Mzyk was a priest of the Society of the Divine Word (SVD) and director of novices at Chludowo when the Nazis invaded Poland. He made plans to move the novices out of Poland to safety and discussed his efforts, unwittingly, with an undercover agent planted by the Gestapo. They arrested him and imprisoned him in a twenty-five-foot-square room with eight other priests. The guards mocked and tortured Mzyk, but he responded with courage. The camp director shot him, along with two other priests, at point- blank range, and tossed the bodies into the snow.

Namuncura, Ven. Zepherín

(1886-1905. B. in Argentina; d. at Rome.) The Araucano Indians lived on the pampas of Argentina, and Namuncura was the son of the chief, destined himself to be chief. Shortly before his birth, European colonists defeated the Indians in war. A Salesian priest the tribe trusted negotiated the peace treaty, and when Namuncura was two years old, his father asked this priest to raise his son as a Christian. The boy ended up at the Salesian mission school in Buenos Aires, where his outgoing nature, kindness, and love of sports made him a favorite. Occasionally, however, he experienced unintended prejudice, such as the time a student asked him what human flesh tasted like. Namuncura, although hurt, ignored the question.

He decided to become a priest in order to bring the Christian faith to his people. Popular at the seminary as well as devout, he frequently prayed before the Blessed Sacrament or said the rosary for his tribe. In 1903, he developed tuberculosis, and in 1904, hoping that the change of climate would help, the bishop asked him to accompany him on a trip to Rome and remain there to continue his studies. But his illness progressed and, although he bore his suf-fering heroically and continued to pray constantly for his people, he died on May 11, 1905, at the age of eighteen. His body is buried in Argentina at the Salesian school of Fortin Mercedes.

Nengapeta, Bd. María Clementine Anuarite

(1939-1964. B. at Wamba, Zaire; d. at Isiro.) Anuarite was born to a pagan family but baptized because her father found Christianity impressive. She was devout but not academically inclined. She entered the Congregation of the Holy Family and finished college in 1962. She then taught in the sisters' school.

During civil war in 1964, rebel soldiers abducted Anuarite and other sisters, claiming they were protecting the women from American troops. A Colonel Ngala made sexual advances to Anuarite, who pleaded for her virginity and asked the sisters to pray for her, saying she would rather die than break her vow. After several days of uneasy standoff, a drunken soldier ordered her and another nun into a car. The sisters managed to elude him momentarily, but he beat them with the butt of his gun and then shot and killed Anuarite. The others were rescued shortly after. Anuarite's body had been tossed in a common grave, but the sisters knew her, despite her battered face, by a small statue of Mary she had slipped into her pocket when initially taken hostage. She is recognized as a martyr for purity. Feast: December 1.

Neri, St. Philip

(1515-1595. B. at Florence, Italy; d. at Rome.) From the start, Philip seems to have had the appealing, cheerful personality that made him so popular throughout his life. When he was eighteen, he joined his uncle's business firm but decided the life was not for him. Already devout, he apparently experienced an even deeper conversion at this time and set out penniless for Rome. There he lived almost as a hermit for several years, supporting himself as a tutor, studying theology, and spending his nights in prayer.

Eventually, he emerged from solitude and began an informal apostolate in the streets, leading many to reform their lives. His ever-increasing circle of friends went with him to visit the sick and to pray in the churches of Rome. In 1544, while praying alone in the catacomb of San Sebastian, Philip was overcome by God's love and saw a globe of fire enter his mouth and expand his heart. A permanent swelling the size of a fist remained there, and an autopsy later revealed that two ribs had fused in an arch to accommodate his unusually large heart. Afterward from time to time, he experienced interior heat and violent trembling of his heart, particularly when moved by the love of God.

Philip was ordained a priest in 1551 and had a powerful ministry through the confessional, bringing many to conversion. Eventually, he formed a religious order, the Oratorians, so named because initially his followers met in Philip's room or oratory for prayer, discussion, and music. By 1575, when the new society was formally approved, Philip was the most well-loved person in the city, "the apostle of Rome." He was known for miracles, visions, and ecstasies as well as common sense, good humor, and a penchant for practical jokes. He died at eighty after a normal day of hearing confessions and receiving visitors. Feast: May 26.

Neumann, St. John Nepomucene

(1811-1860. B. at Prachatitz, Bohemia [now in Czechoslovakia]; d. at Philadelphia, Pennsylvania.) Neumann studied for the priesthood intending to serve as a missionary to America's German immigrants. His bishop's illness caused postponement of his ordination, but Neumann left for America anyway, where the bishop of New York ordained him in 1836. He spent the next four years ministering upstate in the towns and wilderness around

Buffalo. He covered the vast territory on foot and horseback in snow, rain, and heat with little rest, gradually undermining his health. Once, he collapsed on the forest floor and Indians discovered him and carried him home.

In need of spiritual and fraternal support, John joined the Redemptorist order of priests in 1840. He continued his missionary work, now along the East Coast, became a pastor in Baltimore, Maryland, and was appointed superior of the American Redemptorists in 1847. Against his wishes, he was named bishop of Philadelphia in 1852. A zealous leader, he regularly visited all the parishes in his huge diocese. During his eight years as bishop, Neumann promoted the establishment of parochial schools (there were two when he became bishop, nearly one hundred when he died), increased the number of clergy by fifty, and dealt effectively with anti-Catholic groups in the area. Over seventy new churches or chapels were built during his tenure.

Through it all, he remained a pastor at heart: "My only consolation is the piety of the faithful of the diocese. Everything else is fear, hardship and work." He died at the age of forty-eight, shortly after suffering a stroke while crossing a street in Philadelphia. Feast: January 5.

Neururer, Bd. Otto

(1882-1940. B. at Piller, Austria; d. at Buchenwald concentration camp.) Neururer was ordained in 1907, served in various parishes, and in 1932 was appointed pastor in Gotzens. He fulfilled his priestly ministry with courage even after the German invasion of Austria in 1938 and the subsequent restrictions placed on the church.

A member of Neururer's parish, Elisabeth Eigentler, planned to marry George Weirather, divorced and a member of the notorious SA, a Nazi paramilitary organization. Otto recommended against the marriage and helped her compose a letter to that effect. Weirather reported Neururer—already under suspicion for his religious activities—to the Gestapo. They arrested him and sent him to Buchenwald, where he endured severe torture but nevertheless gave comfort and support to fellow prisoners.

Along with another priest, he talked with an inmate who was interested in converting to Catholicism. For this, the priests were sent to the camp torture center, and hung by their feet until dead. At the beatification ceremony, Pope John Paul II praised Neururer for defending the sanctity of Christian marriage and for "his sense of priestly duty that spurred him to give lessons in the faith, despite the severe prohibitions of the camp authorities." Feast: August 13.

Nicholas, St.

(fourth century; Asia Minor) Nothing is known of this popular saint other than that he was a bishop of Myra in Lycia in the fourth century. The earliest story of his life appeared in the ninth century. It is to this that we owe the legend of his saving three girls from prostitution by providing three bags of gold for their marriage dowries (the pawn-broker's sign of three gold balls appears to be based on this incident). He is also said to have raised three boys from the dead after they had been murdered by a butcher and pickled in brine.

Because of these stories, he is best known as a patron of children, so that the custom arose, especially in Germany, Switzerland, and the Netherlands, of giving children gifts in his name on his feast day. Dutch settlers introduced the custom to America (Saint Nicholas, in Dutch dialect, became Sinte Klaas). The character of Santa Claus was also influenced by details from such Nordic gods as Thor, who rode a chariot pulled by goats. Feast: December 6.

Nicholas of Flue, St.

(1417-1487. B./d. near Saschseln, Switzerland.) Nicholas had an early reputation for piety—a childhood friend said he often found him as a boy "on his knees in some solitary place, pray-ing." He grew into an affable, cheerful man who worked his family's farm and served as a soldier in two wars. In one conflict, he saved a convent from destruction and later reflected on the responsibilities of the military: "The honor of a soldier demands courage and gallantry in the struggle but after victory, mercy, kindness and disinterest-edness. Do not take advantage of the vanquished but act as Christians.... When necessary, defend your country and its liberty."

He married and he and his wife, Dorothy, had ten children. Nicholas continued his ascetic habits, and his son later testified that though his father went to bed when everybody else did, "every night I saw him get up again and heard him ... praying until morn-ing."

Nicholas continued to farm and also served as a local magistrate but quit when his fellow judges rendered an unjust judgment against a poor man in favor of a rich one. In 1467, after twenty years of marriage and with his wife's permission, he retired to a nearby her-mitage where he lived until his death.

People flocked to "Brother Klaus," as he was known, for guidance. In 1481, his reputation for sanctity well established, the authorities sought his advice in an effort to avoid an impending civil war. Both sides accepted his counsel, and the resulting compromise ensured Swiss unity. He has since been regarded as a national hero and is the patron saint of Switzerland.

Feast: March 21.

Odilo, St.

(962-1049. D. at Souvigny, France.)
Odilo ruled the monastery of Cluny
for fifty-four years. He led his monks
by combining firmness—he demanded
strict observance of the rule—and
gentleness—he said he would rather be
damned for being too merciful than
too severe. During the famine of
1006, he melted down the church ves-
sels and sold the crown King St.
Henry II had given the monastery in
order to buy food for the poor.

Under Odilo's leadership, a growing number of monasteries adopted
the Cluniac monastic reform and
joined in a centralized government
dependent on Cluny. They played a
decisive role in the leadership of the
medieval church. In an age of endless
petty warfare, Odilo helped establish
the "peace of God"—seasons and days
of the year (Friday through Sunday)
when fighting was forbidden. He was
also responsible for establishing the
feast now known as All Souls Day
(November 2)—initially a day set
aside to pray for deceased monks.
Odilo suffered from a variety of painful
diseases during the last five years of his
life. After receiving the Anointing of
the Sick, he died while lying on the
floor of the church, as he requested,
on a sackcloth sprinkled with ashes.
Feast: January 1.

Odo of Cluny, St.

(c. 880-942. B. at Tours, France;
d. at Tours.) Odo was the second in a
line of saintly abbots of the reforming
monastery of Cluny in France. Abbot
St. Berno received him as a monk at
the Baume-les-Messieurs monastery
and named him head of the monastery
school. In 909, Berno himself went on
to found a new monastery on a piece
of land given him by William of
Aquitaine at Cluny in Burgundy.
What Berno began as an unassuming
house following strict observance of
the Rule of St. Benedict developed
into a powerful movement of monastic
reform centered at Cluny. It exercised a
decisive influence on the spirituality of
the medieval church. At Berno's death
in 927, Odo became abbot of Cluny.
It was during his tenure that the abbey
began its astonishing growth as other
monasteries, attracted by its spirit and
simplicity, placed themselves under
Cluniac rule.

At the pope's request, Odo served
as a mediator in various papal affairs
and took advantage of the travel
involved to encourage reform at
monasteries along the way. Those he

encouraged did not always appreciate his efforts. On at least one occasion, resentful monks threatened him with death. Besides his reforming work, Odo also found time to write hymns, antiphons, and books, including moral essays and an epic poem on the redemption. Feast: November 18.

Olympias, St.

(c. 366-c. 408. D. at Nicomedia.) Olympias counted numerous saints among her friends, among them Gregory of Nyssa, Gregory Nazianzen, and John Chrysostom, who was bishop of Constantinople. She was a widow by the age of twenty—"the glory of the widows in the eastern church," Gregory Nazianzen said—and determined not to remarry.

Because of her enormous wealth and social standing (not to mention her great personal charm), that decision brought her into conflict with the Emperor Theodosius. When she refused to marry his cousin, Theodosius put her fortune under guardianship until she was thirty. She wrote him a somewhat pointed but gracious letter of thanks for relieving her of the burden of overseeing her money. She suggested he finish the job by dividing the funds between the poor and the church. Impressed, he restored her fortune to her in 391.

Olympias was consecrated a deaconess and lived an austere life at Constantinople with other devout women. She gave her money to the needy and with John Chrysostom opened an orphanage and hospital. When he was unjustly sent into exile, she was one of the last to say farewell and had to be taken from his presence by force. She was persecuted and exiled for her support of Chrysostom. She corresponded with him—seventeen of his letters to her from exile survive— and carried out various commissions for him. "I cannot cease to call you blessed," he wrote, praising her patience, dignity, prudence, wisdom, and charity. She suffered very bad health and died at about the age of forty-two. Feast: December 17.

Oriol, St. Joseph

(1650-1702. B./d. at Barcelona, Spain.) A loving stepfather and a woman who had nursed him in infancy prevented Oriol's early life from sinking into tragedy. His father died when Oriol was six months old, but his devoted stepfather carefully provided for his education and loved him as his own. He died when Oriol was about thirteen, but Oriol's nurse took the boy in to help ease the financial burden on his indigent mother.

A devout, sensitive man, Oriol was ordained a priest in 1676 and took a position as tutor in a wealthy family in order to support his mother. One day, while helping himself to some of the abundant food there, he felt an invisible force holding back his hand. He took this as a sign that he should live a simple life and severely restricted his diet. When his mother died in 1686, he became a parish priest and from then until his death exercised a remarkable ministry caring for everyone from soldiers and prisoners to businessmen, the poor, children, and the learned.

He was gentle, quiet, cheerful, and so loving that people instinctively trusted him. Joseph spent as much time as possible in the confessional, where he often knew people's sins before they revealed them. He led an extremely austere, penitential life, slept little (he didn't even own a bed), and gave all his money to the poor. Many healings were attributed to him. Joseph's compassionate, effective ministry as a parish priest anticipated the later, similar ministry of John Vianney. Feast: March 23.

Orione, Bd. Louis (Aloysius)

(1872-1940. B. at Pontecurone, Italy; d. at Tortona.) The short-tempered, impatient Orione—he fought these deficiencies all his life—was also kind, devout, and completely devoted to the abandoned and outcast. He was a student of St. John Bosco at Turin, and that relationship had a profound effect on Orione. He joined the diocesan seminary at Tortona and soon began to do works similar to Bosco's work among underprivileged boys. In 1891, four years before he was ordained, Orione established a school for 150 poor boys in San Bernardino and also ministered to the sick and suffering. When he was denied permission to visit prisoners, he stood outside the jail and played the mandolin for their entertainment.

Within a few years of becoming a priest, Orione's bishop approved his plan for a religious order, the Little Work of Divine Providence (papal approval came later). Since its aim was to serve the unfortunate, "it should flourish among them," he wrote. "This work should center its activities in working-class areas, preferably in the most run-down quarters of the great industrial cities." The congregation served needy children, the abandoned, the poor, the elderly, the sick, and also, troubled priests. Orione, who had a fiery personality, resisted any offers of aid from Italy's fascist government. "Our spirit and theirs have nothing in common," he said.

In 1915, he founded an order of nuns to assist in the work, the Little Missionaries of Charity, and later, the Sacramentine Sisters, a contemplative order of nuns, all blind. Orione, a diabetic and in poor health, suffered a series of strokes and died, repeating the name of Jesus. His communities continue to serve worldwide. Feast: March 12.

Owen, St. Nicholas

(c. 1550-1606. B. at Oxford, England; d. at London.) Trained as a carpenter, Owen entered the Jesuits as a lay brother in 1580. This was a time of intense anti-Catholic persecution in England, and Owen was the man for the hour. For twenty-six years, he put his skills to work constructing hiding places in houses for priests who, due to the political climate, ministered secretly, under threat of death.

His brilliantly designed closets, tucked behind walls in the houses of the laity, led a contemporary to say that it was difficult to find any priest who did not often owe his life to Owen's hiding places. "When he was about to design a hiding place," a friend said, "he began by receiving the Eucharist, sought to aid his work by continual prayer, and offered the completion of it to God alone."

Owen was arrested three times and is said to have been responsible for planning and executing the daring escape of Fr. John Gerard from the Tower of London. On the occasion of his final arrest, Owen was trapped in a raid with two priests and voluntarily gave himself up to divert attention from them. Tortured mercilessly on the rack, he refused to divulge any information. He died in agony on March 2. He was canonized in 1970 as one of the Forty Martyrs of England and Wales whose feast is observed on October 25. He also has a separate feast on March 22.

Ozanam, Bd. Frederick

(1813-1853. B. at Lyons, France; d. at Marseilles.) A happily married layman and primary founder of the St. Vincent de Paul Society, Ozanam combined a warm, sensitive nature with great intellectual gifts. He studied law at the Sorbonne in Paris, threw himself into the defense of Catholicism, which was then under attack, and helped revive a Catholic discussion club. He and fellow members of the club began to care for the poor as a way of putting their faith into action. This ministry eventually became known as the St. Vincent de Paul Society, named for that French apostle of charity.

Frederick received his doctorate in law, taught at the University of Lyons, and returned to the Sorbonne for his doctorate in literature. He then joined the Sorbonne faculty and became a popular professor of literature there. At the same time, he continued to guide his growing society and to defend Catholicism. He married Amelie Soulacroix on June 23, 1841, and throughout their married life the devoted Frederick presented her with a bouquet of flowers on the twenty-third of each month. They had a daughter, Marie, in 1845.

Worn out by his teaching, writing, and work for the poor, Frederick fell ill and nearly died. On a tour of Italy to recover his health, he encouraged the start of the St. Vincent de Paul Society there. He returned to his work and cared for the poor during a period of revolution and epidemic, but his health broke again and he died in 1853. "Social welfare is not to be learned in books," he wrote, "but in climbing the stairs to the poor man's garret ... [and] sharing the secrets of his lonely heart." Feast: September 8.

P

Pachomius, St.

(c. 290-346. B. near Esneh, Egypt; d. at Tabennisi.) Conscripted into the army when he was twenty, Pachomius sailed down the Nile under wretched conditions with other recruits. Christians from a nearby town treated the men with such compassion that Pachomius, as soon as the army disbanded in 316, returned home, enrolled as a catechumen, and was baptized. He immediately took to the desert and became a disciple of Palamon, a hermit, until 323. He then moved to an uninhabited area along the Nile called Tabbennisi, where he was joined by disciples.

Pachomius, a gifted administrator, soon had the men organized into a communal life centered around prayer and work, such as weaving and making pottery. He wrote a rule—the first monastic rule—but he regarded it as a minimum, encouraging his monks to go beyond it in the pursuit of holiness. He led by example, limiting his sleep, fasting rigorously, memorizing and constantly repeating passages from Scripture (his rule contains twenty-five hundred biblical quotes). He founded nine monasteries for men and two convents for women (his sister entered one), and at the time of his death, his followers numbered three thousand. He is considered the founder of communal monasticism.

St. Jerome translated Pachomius' rule into Latin in 404; this translation influenced St. Benedict and through him, the whole course of Christian monasticism. Pachomius died during an epidemic, which also carried off many of his disciples. Feast: May 9.

Pallotti, St. Vincent

(1795-1850. B./d. at Rome, Italy.) Pallotti was ordained a priest in 1818 after a devout childhood that moved unerringly into an even more devout adulthood. Before his ordination, he summed up his spiritual "method" in his diary: "Not the intellect, but God. Not the will, but God. Not the soul, but God. Not hearing, but God…. Not breath, but God…. Not the body, but God. Not air, but God…. Not riches, but God. Not honors, but God…. Not advancement, but God. God always and in everything."

He taught theology at Rome for ten years but left the academic world to do pastoral work, moved by compassion for the needs of ordinary people. "I think about and hear and see so many afflicted persons," he wrote. "…Worn out, burdened and occupied by their labor ... carpenters, bricklayers ... women afflicted with domestic cares ... fatherless children and unprotected widows ... the sufferings of the poor ... of slaves and those in prison...." He was regarded as the "apostle of Rome," similar in spirit to St. Philip Neri, and he counseled those who sought his advice, helped to found schools, revived guilds, befriended soldiers and prisoners, and provided direct help to the poor (he even gave away his own clothes, again and again).

In 1835, he founded the Society of the Catholic Apostolate, bringing together clergy and laity interested in spiritual growth and social justice. His emphasis on the role and importance of lay people in apostolic work was far ahead of its time, and deeply resented by some clergy. These harassed Pallotti—once a fellow priest even struck him—but he responded charitably (later, at the beatification process, one of these clerical opponents spoke on Pallotti's behalf).

He founded the Congregation of the Catholic Apostolate (Pallotine Fathers), an order of priests devoted solely to the work. Among other projects, priests and lay people provided for homeless children, visited the sick, assisted the missions, and helped prisoners. The Sisters of the Catholic Apostolate, now the Pallotine Missionary Sisters, evolved from the ministry of women to those affected by the cholera epidemic of 1837.

Pallotti was recognized as a saint in his own lifetime, known particularly for his ministry in the confessional and for bringing many back to the faith. He died of pleurisy at the age of fifty-five. Feast: January 22.

Pampuri, St. Richard

(1897-1930. B. at Trivolzio, Italy; d. at Milan.) Service in the medical corps during World War I interrupted Pampuri's studies to be a doctor. He was decorated for bravery and, after the war, completed his studies at Pavia, graduating in 1921. When he established a practice as doctor and surgeon, he wrote to his sister, a nun: "Pray that neither selfish indulgence nor pride nor any other evil passion prevent me from seeing in my patients Jesus who suffers, and from healing and comforting him."

Pampuri entered the Hospitaller Order of St. John of God at Brescia in 1927 (the Jesuits and Franciscans turned him down due to his poor health). He was in charge of the order's free dental clinic for the poor and sensitively provided for their needs. Once, after treating a malnourished boy, Pampuri asked for payment. When the boy said he had no money, Pampuri quickly handed him some saying, "Don't worry, if you can't pay me, I'll pay you." After a year, Pampuri became ill, was diagnosed with pneumonia, and died at the order's hospital in Milan. Healings took place at his tomb, and his cause for canonization proceeded quickly. Pope John Paul II said of him: "He was an extraordinary figure, close to our own times but even closer to our problems and sensibilities." Feast: May 1.

Patrick, St.

(c. 385-c. 461. B. in Roman Britain; d. in Ireland.) Patrick's family was Christian—his father was a deacon—but they were not particularly religious. They lived near the town of Carlisle in northwest Britain, where Patrick's father was a councilman. When Patrick was sixteen, Irish warriors raided the area, captured him, and took him to northwest Ireland, where he was enslaved for six years. He considered this turn of events punishment for his earlier disregard for the faith and turned to a life of prayer: "…Tending flocks was my daily occupation and constantly I used to pray…. Love of God and the fear of him increased more and more and faith grew and the spirit was moved…."

Patrick escaped to Britain when he was about twenty-two after receiving assurance in a dream that he would return to his own country. He studied for the priesthood, possibly in Gaul, and in response to another vision in which he heard the voices of the Irish pleading, "Come, and from now on walk with us," he returned to Ireland as a missionary bishop in about 432.

Patrick was not the first to bring the faith there, but believers were few and disorganized. He evangelized, baptized, established churches, developed a native clergy, and expressed humble amazement at his success. "I, Patrick, a sinner, am the most ignorant and of least account among the faithful…. I owe it to God's grace that so many people should through me be born again to him." His ministry was rife with danger, and he was at one point imprisoned and condemned to death. Worse, in his eyes, was the betrayal of a close friend, an event that shook his faith and almost caused him to despair.

All that we know with any certainty of Patrick we find in his moving autobiography, the *Confession*, and his letter to the soldiers of Coroticus protesting their raid on and enslavement of members of one of Patrick's churches. Many of the stories about him, such as his driving the snakes from Ireland, are from a much later period, no earlier than the late seventh century, and are of uncertain value. Feast: March 17.

Paul, St.

(first century) Paul was a Jew from Tarsus, a cosmopolitan, Greco-Roman city in present-day Turkey. He was intelligent, a passionate defender of Judaism and a man of action—bold, courageous, and visionary. He opposed Christianity and was on his way to ferret out and arrest Christians in Damascus when he had a dramatic encounter with the risen Christ (see Acts 9:1-19). The event transformed him from a "zealot for my ancestral traditions" into the "apostle to the Gentiles" (Gal 1:13-15), a role for which he was well suited, given his broad background.

Much of his story is told in the Acts of the Apostles, from his approval of the killing of Stephen, the first Christian martyr (Acts 7:58-8:1), through his conversion and most of his missionary career. His letters, which make up a good part of the New Testament, also provide biographical information about him and give insight into his personality (when Peter refused to eat with non-Jewish Christians, Paul "opposed him to his face" [Gal 2:11]).

Paul's three missionary journeys spanned the years 45-58 and were carried out in the face of extreme difficulty. He was whipped five times ("forty lashes minus one"), beaten with rods three times, stoned once, and shipwrecked three times. "In dangers from rivers, dangers from robbers, dangers from my own race, dangers from Gentiles, dangers in the city, dangers in the wilderness, dangers at sea, dangers among false brothers ... through many sleepless nights ... hunger and thirst ... frequent fastings ... cold and exposure" (2 Cor 11:24-27).

Paul was arrested in Jerusalem when his presence caused a riot among the Jews. He spent two years in jail until he invoked his Roman citizenship and appealed for a trial at Rome. On the way there, Paul was shipwrecked at Malta but after several months on that island, proceeded under custody to Rome (see Acts 27:1-18). He was under house arrest at Rome for two years and either was tried and executed at this time or was acquitted only to be rearrested some time later. His movements are uncertain, and Acts ends without resolving the question.

There is a strong possibility that Paul went to Spain and revisited Ephesus about this time. According to tradition, he was beheaded at Rome in A.D. 67 during the reign of Nero. He is buried at the site of the basilica of St. Paul Outside the Walls.

Paul's influence on the church was definitive. His thinking has shaped all subsequent Christian theology. His life was completely dominated by his devotion to Christ and his single-minded efforts to win others for him: "I have been crucified with Christ; yet I live, no longer I, but Christ lives in me" (Gal 2:20).

The New Testament letters traditionally attributed to Paul are Romans;

1 and 2 Corinthians; Galatians; Colossians; Philemon; Ephesians; Phillipians; 1 and 2 Thessalonians; 1 and 2 Timothy; and Titus. Feast: June 29.

Paula, St.

(347-404. B. at Rome; d. at Bethlehem.) Paula is best known as the friend and confidante of St. Jerome. When she died, he said that he was "completely prostrated.... At one blow I lost all comfort." And when he tried to write something in her honor, "the stylus fell from my fingers."

Paula, a Roman of noble birth, was happily married to the senator Toxotius, with whom she had five children. She was thirty-three when her husband died, and "she mourned him so much that she almost died of grief," Jerome wrote. Under the influence of St. Marcella, a Roman widow who lived a semi-monastic life, and the spiritual direction of Jerome, she devoted herself to penance, prayer, and works of charity. In 385, she and her daughter, Eustochium, and a band of devout women accompanied Jerome to the Holy Land (shortly before, Paula had endured the death of her daughter, Blesilla). They settled in Bethlehem, where Paula founded a monastery and convent, built a hospice and several churches, and helped the poor.

Paula was an invaluable aid to Jerome in his work of biblical scholarship and learned Hebrew "so well," said Jerome "that she spoke the language without any Latin peculiarities." She died at the age of fifty-six, "noble by birth but far more noble by her sanctity." Feast: January 26.

Pelletier, St. Euphrasia

(1796-1868. B. at Noirmoutier, France; d. at Angers.) Pelletier's work with ex-prostitutes and abused, homeless, and delinquent girls was nothing if not clear-sighted. "Do not imagine that letting them suffer is going to convert them," she warned the nuns of her order.

Pelletier joined the Institute of Our Lady of Charity founded by St. John Eudes in 1814. The houses in that order were under the direction of local bishops, however, and Pelletier saw the need for centralized government. In spite of controversy and accusations of ambition, she left and founded the Institute of Our Lady of Charity of the Good Shepherd—the Good Shepherd Sisters. The congregation received papal approval in 1835.

The order grew rapidly, both clients and sisters responding to Pelletier's practical compassion. "I have no great talents, nor have I done anything great," she said. "I only loved, but I loved with all the strength of my soul." She urged her sisters not to preach at the women in their care but to appreciate the pain they endured in trying to turn from their former way of life. The nuns prepared their clients for productive work and provided religious and moral guidance.

In the long run, Pelletier told them, "What cannot be healed by work needs to be healed by prayer." By the time of Pelletier's death from cancer, there were almost three thousand Good Shepherd Sisters serving throughout the world. Today they work in sixty-seven countries helping girls and women who are homeless, abused, chemically dependent, leaving prostitution, or in jail. Feast: April 24.

Perboyre, St. John Gabriel

(1802-1840. B. near Montgesty, France; d. in Wuchangfu, China.) Perboyre was ordained as a priest of the Congregation of the Mission (Vincentians) in 1826. His superiors, recognizing his intellectual gifts, assigned him to teach at the seminary at St. Flour, postponing his boyhood dream of serving in the missions. After two years, he took charge of the minor seminary and in 1832 was named assistant novice master of the order's seminary in Paris. "In order to heal more effectively, he knew how to bide his time ... go easy when dealing with spiritual ills," one of his students said. "...His zeal was unhurried...."

In 1835, Perboyre finally left for China where, he said in a letter, he was "a very curious sight: my head shaved, a long pigtail, stammering my new languages, eating with chopsticks." He taught, gave a series of missions, and joined in the Vincentian work of rescuing abandoned children. He was arrested during an outbreak of persecution in 1839, betrayed by a catechumen. Over the year of his imprisonment he was tortured so relentlessly that "his flesh hung off him in strips," according to a priest who visited him disguised as a merchant. He was charged with entering China illegally to preach Christianity and was strangled to death.

Perboyre's life was one of single-minded identification with Christ: "After our death, we will not be asked if we were scholars, if we held prominent positions, if we have had people speak favorably of us," he wrote. "... We will be asked if we busied ourselves with the study and imitation of Jesus Christ." Feast: September 11.

Perpetua and Felicity and Companions, Sts.

(D. 203 at Carthage.) Perpetua and Felicity, two young mothers, were martyred along with three other catechumens, Revocatus, Secundulus, and Saturninus, and their teacher, Saturus. They were among the many victims of anti-Christian persecution during the days of the Roman Empire. The vivid, remarkable account of their sufferings has come down to us largely in their own words, much of it written by Perpetua. She was twenty-two years old, married, and the favorite of her pagan father. She resisted his repeated entreaties to renounce the faith, but his grief so troubled her that, once in prison, she wrote: "I thanked God for the relief of being, for a few days, parted from my father." Nevertheless, she admitted to being "tormented with anxiety" for her six-month-old infant until he was allowed to stay with her in jail.

Felicity, eight months pregnant, worried that she might not die with her companions since Roman law forbade the execution of pregnant women. Three days before the scheduled execution, after the prisoners prayed for the birth of the child, Felicity went into labor and delivered a girl who was adopted by another Christian.

The martyrs were condemned to the wild beasts at the games. They entered the amphitheater "cheerful and bright of countenance," according to the unknown author who completed the account. "You judge us: God will judge you!" they declared to the presiding official. Perpetua, her "piercing gaze abashing" the crowd, refused to wear a dress dedicated to the gods. All were attacked by the beasts and then, accord-ing to custom, had their throats cut. The novice swordsman missed the mark with Perpetua. She shrieked in pain and guided his hand to her throat. "Perhaps so great a woman," the author concluded, "could not have been slain unless she so willed it." Feast: March 7.

Peter, St.

(D. c. 64) The apostle Peter was a fisherman from Bethsaida, married, and the brother of Andrew, also an apostle. He was originally named Simon but Jesus called him "rock," *petros* (Peter) in Greek, *kepha* (Cephas) in Aramaic. The name indicated his role: "You are Rock and on this rock I will build my church, and the jaws of death shall not prevail against it" (Mt 16:18). Peter was the leader of the apostles, asked questions on their behalf, and answered, on their behalf, the question posed by Jesus: "Who do you say that I am?" "You are the Messiah," Peter said, "the Son of the living God" (Mt 16:15-16). At the Last Supper, Jesus told Peter to strengthen the others (see Lk 22:32).

Peter was impulsive, occasionally suffering the consequences of his impetuosity. When Jesus spoke of the coming suffering of the Son of Man, Peter remonstrated with him and earned a solid rebuke: "Get out of my sight, you Satan!" (Mk 8:33). He tried to walk on the water, became frightened, and started to sink (see Mt 14:28-31). At the Transfiguration, with Jesus in conversation with Moses and Elijah, he boldly proposed building booths on the site to accommodate them (see Mk 9:5). Peter claimed that even if everyone else were shaken in faith, he would stand by Jesus to the death (see Mk 14:29). When he ultimately did deny him, as Jesus had foretold, Peter "broke down and began to cry" (Mk 14:72).

After the Resurrection, Peter was the first to enter the empty tomb and the first apostle to whom the risen Christ appeared (see Jn 20:6; 1 Cor 15:5). Jesus told him three times that he should feed—be the shepherd of—his sheep (see Jn 21:15-17). Peter is the first to address the crowd after the events of Pentecost and took the lead in all the important decisions of the early church. He directed the election of a successor to Judas (see Acts 1:15-26); healed the lame man (see 3:1-10); passed sentence on Ananias and Sapphira (see 5:1-11); received the astonishing revelation that opened the church up to the gentiles (see 10:9-16); defended his policy toward the gentiles at the Council of Jerusalem (see 15:7-12); and was imprisoned by Herod Agrippa but miraculously released (see 12:1-19). Paul went to Jerusalem after his conversion to "get to know Cephas," indicating Peter's stature in the church (Gal 1:18).

Peter traveled as a missionary but Scripture is silent about his activities following his attendance at the Council of Jerusalem around the year 50 and visit to Antioch shortly before or after (Gal 2:11-14). Ancient tradition associates Peter with Rome, and scholars find no good reason to doubt it. Church fathers as early as Clement of Rome (c. 95) attest to the tradition, and Eusebius' *History of the Church* (c. 323) recorded that Peter was crucified upside down there during the persecution of Nero in 64. Excavations under St. Peter's Basilica on Vatican Hill in the mid-twentieth century have exposed an ancient cemetery, long thought to be the final resting place of the apostle. Scholars speculate that Constantine chose this site for the original basilica precisely because, according to earliest tradition, it held the body of Peter. Feast: June 29.

Philip, St.

(first century) Philip is listed as an apostle in the synoptic Gospels and in the Acts of the Apostles. In John he appears in several incidents and is identified as from Bethsaida, the same town as Andrew and Peter (see Jn 1:44). After Jesus called him, Philip persuaded Nathanael (see St. Bartholomew) to meet Jesus (see Jn 1:43-50); Greeks in Jerusalem who wanted to visit Jesus put their request to Philip (Jn 12:20-22);

and at the Last Supper, Philip said to Jesus: "Show us the Father and that will be enough for us" (Jn 14:8-9).

Philip the apostle has often been confused with Philip the deacon and evangelist (Acts 21:8). Only vague traditions surround the later life of Philip the apostle, including one that says he preached the gospel in Asia Minor. Feast: May 3.

Pietrantoni, St. Agostina

(1864-1894. B. at Pozzaglia Sabina, Italy; d. at Rome.) Pietrantoni entered the Sisters of Charity in 1886 and worked as a nurse at Rome's Santo Spiritu Hospital. She said she was "ready to do anything" for God, and when she contracted and then recovered from tuberculosis, she asked to be assigned to the tuberculosis ward to protect the other sisters from contact with the disease. The patients in this ward were notorious for their violent behavior, and Pietrantoni was sometimes spat upon, verbally abused, and once, badly beaten. She remained patient and cheerful, and prayed constantly for her charges. She had a particular devotion to Our Lady.

Giuseppe Romanelli, a patient with a criminal record who was evicted from the ward, blamed Pietrantoni and wrote her threatening notes. He slipped back into the hospital, confronted her in a hallway, stabbed her repeatedly, and

fled. She said, "Blessed Mother, help me," nodded when asked if she forgave her murderer, and died within minutes. Romanelli was arrested a few days later after a knife fight with police. Sentenced to life in prison, he died within a year, reconciled to the church. Pietrantoni was canonized for her Christian virtue, not as a martyr. Feast: November 13.

Pius of Pietrelcina, Bd. (Padre Pio)

(1887-1968; B. at Pietrelcina, Italy; d. at San Giovanni Rotondo.) Devout from childhood, Pio entered the Capuchin Franciscan order and was ordained a priest in 1910. In 1918, the stigmata—the wounds of Christ— appeared on his hands, feet, and side, and he suffered their persistent bleeding for fifty years. Other supernatural phenomena attributed to him include bilocation, prophecy, visions, cures, and the ability to read the thoughts of others, particularly in the confessional. He devoted his life to intense prayer, celebration of the Mass, counseling, spiritual direction, and hearing confessions for up to twelve hours a day. Pilgrims came by the thousands to his remote mountain monastery, including politicians, church and state dignitaries, and soldiers during World War II.

Padre Pio endured hostility from many, including some clergy, who accused him of everything from improper relations with women to fraud. Told that some believed his stigmata were psychologically induced, Pio replied: "Go out to the fields and look very closely at a bull. Concentrate on him with all your might. Do this and see if horns grow on your head." Opposition continued throughout his life but he met it with heroic virtue and humor. Pio regarded his own life as united with Christ in suffering for the salvation of humanity: "I am devoured by the love of God and the love of my neighbor." Feast: September 23.

Plunkett, St. Oliver

(1629-1681. B. at Loughcrew, Ireland; d. at London, England.) Plunkett was born to the nobility and ordained a priest at Rome in 1654. He was a distinguished professor there, took degrees in canon and civil law, and acted as representative of the Irish bishops at Rome. In 1669 he was named archbishop of Armagh and primate of all Ireland. When he returned to Ireland he was one of only two bishops residing there—the other one in hiding. Severe persecution had reduced the church to a state of disorder and sent clergy into exile. Plunkett confirmed ten thousand people in his first year there and set about restoring the church.

In 1673, renewed persecution forced the bishop to minister under conditions of great hardship, in abject poverty,

sometimes disguised as a country squire, British officer, or cattle merchant. He was arrested in 1679 on fabricated charges and transferred in chains to Newgate prison in London. His trial was a travesty, the judge finally admitting that he was on trial because of his Catholic faith. He was hung, and drawn and quartered at Tyburn, a particularly barbarous death which, he wrote from prison, "I ... joyfully embrace. Compared to the death of the cross ... [it] is but a flea biting." Feast: July 1.

Pole, Bd. Margaret

(1473-1541. B. near Bath, England; d. at London.) Nearly seventy years old when beheaded for her faith, Margaret, Countess of Salisbury, had served for many years in the household of King Henry VIII. Widowed in 1505, Margaret raised her five children and served as governess to Princess Mary. The king declared Margaret the holiest woman in all England, but she incurred his anger when she disapproved of his divorce and subsequent marriage to Anne Boleyn. He removed her from her post but she returned to court after Anne's death.

Her son Reginald, who would later become a cardinal, unwittingly compromised her safety when his treatise, *Pro Ecclesiasticae Unitatis Defensione,* denounced Henry's claim to be head of the church. Henry vowed to destroy the family and in 1539 executed two of Margaret's sons on grounds of treason. Margaret was arrested soon after but her interrogators, who admired her intelligence and dignity, failed to make a case against her. She was held in the Tower of London for two years and eventually condemned although never brought to trial. She walked calmly to the block but the executioner, who was a novice, botched the job, adding to her suffering. Feast: May 28.

Polycarp, St.

(c. 69-155. D. at Smyrna.) The bishop of Smyrna for nearly fifty years, Polycarp was a leading figure in the Asian church and an invaluable link between the age of the apostles and the theologians of the late second century. According to St. Irenaeus, who knew him, Polycarp was taught by apostles and was acquainted with many who knew Christ. St. Ignatius of Antioch wrote him a letter, which survives, as Ignatius made his way to Rome for his martyrdom. Polycarp's letter to the Phillipians also survives and is valuable in particular for its quotations from the New Testament, offering insight into the developing canon of Scripture. He was a fierce opponent of heresy. On one occasion, he came face-to-face with the heretic Marcion, who asked, "Don't you recognize me?" "I do indeed," Polycarp replied, "I recognize the first-born of Satan!"

Polycarp was martyred during an outbreak of persecution in Smyrna. He was arrested late at night at a house in the country, betrayed by a servant under torture. Calm and hospitable, he offered refreshments to his captors and spent some time in prayer, at which point many of the officials "began to regret this expedition against a man so old and saintly." During a lengthy interrogation, Polycarp refused to repudiate Christ: "For eighty-six years I have been his servant and he has done me no wrong. How then can I blaspheme my king and my Savior?" Regretful or not, his captors burned the venerable Polycarp at the stake, an end he had foreseen in a vision.

After the fact, an eyewitness wrote an account of his arrest and suffering at the request of a neighboring Christian community. It is a vivid document with a strong narrative drive, the earliest authentic story of a Christian martyrdom apart from the biblical account of the death of St. Stephen. Feast: February 23.

Porres, St. Martin de

(1579-1639. B./d. at Lima, Peru.) Martin was born of an interracial relationship between a Spanish knight and a freed Panamanian. His dark skin distressed his father, who acknowledged him and his sister as his children but eventually abandoned the family. Martin apprenticed to a barber when he was twelve, became a lay member of the Dominican order when he was fifteen, and so impressed his superiors that they invited him to become a friar when he was twenty-four.

Martin served his fellow Dominicans as infirmarian, barber, tailor, wardrobe keeper, and distributor of alms. He was devoted to the poor and sick, helped establish an orphanage and foundling hospital in Lima, and cared for the African slaves of the city. Animals, too, enjoyed his solicitude. He kept a dog and cat refuge at his sister's house, and it was said that many animals— including mice and rats—obeyed him. His holiness was evident to all, many miracles were attributed to his intercession, and on his death both the rich and the poor attended his funeral. Feast: November 3.

Possenti, St. Gabriel

(1838-1862. B. at Assisi, Italy; d. at Isola di Gran Sasso.) Possenti attended the Jesuit college at Spoleto and was a bright student, something of a ladies' man, and a good dancer. He was also a hunter, an expert marksman, outgoing, exceptionally cheerful, and had a large circle of friends. He became seriously ill, vowed to enter the religious life if he recovered, but failed to keep the vow. In 1855, during a procession in honor of Our Lady, he heard a voice within ask: "Why do you remain in the world? It is not for you. Follow your vocation."

In spite of his father's opposition, Gabriel entered the Passionist order in 1856 and was an ideal novice, his piety and attention to duty balanced by his cheerfulness and humility. His skill with a gun came in handy, too, during a period of political turmoil. When a band of men raided the nearby town, looting and burning, Gabriel confronted them, proved his expertise by shooting a lizard that had darted onto the road, and disarmed the band. He then ran them out of town.

Gabriel contracted tuberculosis after only four years as a religious. He remained good-natured and peaceful to the end, dying quietly at the age of twenty-three. Feast: February 27.

Potamon, St.

(c. 340) Potamon, bishop of Heraclea in Egypt, is distinguished for suffering twice for the faith, once at the hands of pagans and once—fatally—at the hands of the heretical Arians. In 305, during the persecution of Christians under Maximinus Daia, he was tortured, lost an eye, and was permanently crippled. He attended the Council of Nicaea in 325, where he shared stories of the persecution, and in 335 he accompanied Bishop St. Athanasius, under attack by Arian Christians, to the Council of

Tyre. Potamon defended the courageous, orthodox Athanasius, who was nevertheless deposed. For his loyalty, Potamon himself became a target of the Arians, who beat him to death during an outbreak of hostilities several years later. He is one of the many nearly forgotten heroes of the early church who fought for orthodoxy in the face of heretical movements that threatened to derail the faith. Feast: May 18.

Prat y Prat, Bd. Mercedes María

(1880-1936. B./d. at Barcelona, Spain.) As a teenager, Maria Mercedes served as a catechist and taught reading and writing to children of the poor. She entered the Company of St. Theresa and Jesus in 1905 and was known for her deep spirit of prayer. She made her profession in 1907, taught in Barcelona, and was provincial counsellor for her order.

During the intense anti-Catholic persecution of the Spanish Civil War, nuns were forced to leave their convents and seek shelter in private homes. Maria Mercedes did so but on July 23, 1936, she was arrested while going to another house. That night, along with other religious, she was taken into the street and shot. She survived, lying on the street in extreme pain, praying aloud. Her cries attracted the attention of passing militia who shot her again. She bled to death at about four in the morning.

A religious who was wounded but survived the massacre later testified on Maria Mercedes' behalf when the process for her canonization got underway in 1969. Feast (with the Martyrs of the Spanish Civil War): July 22.

Pro, Bd. Miguel

(1891-1927. B. at Guadalupe, Mexico; d. at Mexico City.) Pro's family lived in the silver mining region of central Mexico, where his father was a mining engineer. His parents, devout and charitable, provided a warm family life for their seven children. Pro himself was fun-loving with a flair for the guitar, acting, and comedy. As a teenager working in his father's office, he sometimes put on an impromptu show for the miners when they emerged from their shift.

Pro entered the Jesuit order in 1911, not long after the start of a revolution in Mexico. By 1914 the fighting and anti-Catholic persecution forced the community to escape to Spain. Pro was ordained in 1925 in Belgium, where he had gone to complete his studies. He was assigned to Mexico City in 1926, just as Catholicism was outlawed there.

Fr. Pro pursued his ministry by using a series of disguises, preaching a retreat to taxi drivers, for example, dressed as a mechanic. He had many narrow escapes. Once, while fleeing from the police, he saw a young woman he knew, took her arm, and successfully eluded his pursuers who, unsuspecting, passed by the couple. Pro ministered secretly to thousands of Catholics and also helped the poor.

When his superiors expressed concern for his safety, he said that followers of St. Ignatius—Jesuits—don't "run after the first shot is fired." He welcomed the prospect of martyrdom and in 1927, he was arrested and falsely charged with an attempt on the life of the president. Taken before the firing squad, he refused a blindfold. Pro forgave his enemies, stretched out his arms in the form of a cross, and cried out, "Viva Cristo Rey!" (Long live Christ the King). Feast: November 18.

Pucci, St. Anthony Mary

(1819-1892. B. in Poggiole, Italy; d. in Viareggio.) An outstanding parish priest and member of the Servite order, Pucci spent his entire forty-nine years of ministry at St. Andrew's parish in Viareggio. He was small—the parishioners called him "Il curatino" (the little parish priest)—extremely shy, ill-at-ease with the well-to-do, lacked conversational skills and oratorical gifts (he memorized his sermons), and had an unattractive voice.

For all that, he was an extraordinarily successful pastor due in large measure to his total, sacrificial commitment to his priestly duty. He visited his parishioners regularly, first praying before the Blessed Sacrament for a blessing on those he would see. He was known to levitate while at prayer and was always so absorbed at Mass that he once failed to notice an earthquake that shook the building. He spent more than half his day in the confessional to accommodate the throngs who besieged him.

During two cholera epidemics, he slept by his front door so as to be immediately available when summoned to the dying. In the anticlerical atmosphere of the times, there was some opposition to his ministry, and on at least one occasion he was lured to a false sick call only to be beaten and badly wounded. He refused to reveal the name of the assailant. He was provincial for the Servites' Tuscan province for seven years while working as a pastor and died at the age of seventy-three, active to the end. Feast: January 12.

Radbert, St. Paschasius

(c. 790-865. D. at Corbie, near Amiens, France.) Radbert was abandoned as an infant, left on the doorsteps of the nuns of Notre Dame at Soissons. The nuns adopted him and sent him to the monastery of St. Peter for his education. He later spent some time in the world before entering the monastery at Corbie, famous for its library, where he devoted himself to theological studies. He helped found a monastery at Corvey, served as novice master at Corbie, and was elected abbot in 843, a position that did not suit his studious nature. He gladly resigned in 849, and spent the rest of his life writing.

Radbert is particularly famous for his work *De Corpore et Sanguine Domini*, the first doctrinal treatise on the Eucharist. He affirmed the real presence of Christ in the Eucharist, specifying that this was the flesh born of Mary, crucified, risen, and multiplied through God's power at each consecration. He stated that this presence was spiritual but didn't elaborate on how this might be. His understanding, however, seems close to the later doctrine of transubstantiation. He also said that in receiving the Eucharist, people are incorporated into the mystical body of Christ, the church.

Radbert also wrote a life of the abbot Adelard, commentaries on Lamentations and the Gospel of Matthew, as well as the letter *Cogitis Me*. The latter is important in the history of the development of the doctrine of the Assumption. Feast: April 26.

Radegund, St.

(518-87. B. at Erfurt, Germany; d. at Poitiers, France.) Radegund's status as a Thuringian princess didn't shield her from the violence of her bleak era. Her father, a king, was assassinated by his brother, and shortly after, King Clothaire of the Franks kidnapped Radegund, then about twelve, and her brother.

Radegund became a Christian but at eighteen was compelled to marry Clothaire, a womanizer and murderer. He ignored her piety and good works and complained that he had married a nun, not a queen. The uneasy alliance weathered six years until Clothaire, for unknown reasons, murdered Radegund's brother. She left him and petitioned the bishop to let her enter a convent. She showed up to speak to the bishop already dressed as a nun, to stiffen his resolve should he feel intimidated by Clothaire's murderous reputation.

In 561, Radegund established the Monastery of Holy Cross near Poitiers. Here, for the next thirty years, she developed an oasis of culture, piety, scholarship, and works of mercy. She bathed the poor, fed the sick with a spoon, and even cleaned the latrines. She required her nuns to study for two hours every day and she herself read prodigiously. Her friendship with Venantius Fortunatus, priest and poet, yielded poems in her honor that survive and reveal her as a woman of humor, intelligence, and holiness. Her life was well documented by her contemporaries, including Fortunatus and the nun Baudenivia. Feast: August 13.

Raphael, St.

The name Raphael means "God heals," an apt description of the role Raphael plays in the Old Testament Book of Tobit (the only place he is mentioned in Scripture). God sends him to restore Tobit's sight and to bring about the marriage of his son Tobiah to Sarah and to drive a demon from her (see Tb 3:17). Raphael is also identified as one of the seven archangels who stand before the glory of the Lord (12:15). Because he was Tobiah's traveling companion, pilgrims too have a certain protective kinship with Raphael. Feast (with the archangels Michael and Gabriel): September 29.

Raphaela, St. Mary

(1850-1925. B. at Pedro Abad, Spain; d. at Rome.) Raphaela and her sister Delores joined a religious order in Cordoba. But a misunderstanding with the bishop led to his expelling all the nuns. He allowed sixteen novices to remain, including Raphaela and Delores, but imposed a new rule that the women refused to accept. Feeling they had no other recourse, they fled under cover of night and eventually were welcomed at Madrid.

Here, in 1877, they began the Handmaids of the Sacred Heart of Jesus, devoted to educating children and giving retreats. Raphaela was elected superior and the order grew rapidly, due in large measure to her charity and common sense. "When you are in a panic, mosquitoes look like elephants," she told one fearful nun. She told another to eat more so as not to look as though the nuns were fed "on lizards."

Her sister and others, motivated perhaps by jealousy and overconfidence, felt they could do a better job, made life difficult for the superior, and forced her resignation. She was assigned to their house in Rome, where she lived in obscurity, did domestic chores, and later served as mistress of novices. She endured the humiliation with great courage and charity and was revered for her holiness. "God wants me to submit to all that happens to me as if I saw him there commanding it," she said. She died at the age of seventy-four after several years of ill health. Feast: January 6.

Rasoamanarivo, Bd. Victoria

(1848-1894. B./d. at Antananarivo, Madagascar.) The primary religion of Madagascar, an island off the southeast coast of Africa, centered on ancestor worship. Victoria's family was of the Hova tribe, influential at court and faithful to the traditional religious practices. Protestant missionaries had made headway on Madagascar throughout the nineteenth century, but it wasn't until the arrival of Jesuits and the sisters of the Congregation of St. Joseph of Cluny in 1861 that Catholicism took root. Victoria attended the sisters' school and, against her family's wishes, asked to be baptized in 1863. She soon gained a reputation as an extremely committed Christian, persevering through several outbreaks of persecution.

In 1864 she married the chief minister's son, a heavy drinker and adulterer who treated her so badly that even his father urged her to leave him. She refused and through her influence he accepted baptism before his death in 1887. During the persecution of 1883-86, Victoria courageously rallied the Catholics, visited those in outlying areas, and defended the church at court. She was one of those primarily responsible for the survival of the faith. She died at the age of forty-six after suffering from a variety of illnesses. Feast: August 21.

Rinaldi, Bd. Phillip

(1856-1931. B. at Lu, Italy; d. at Turin.) Rinaldi did his best to dodge a vocation to the priesthood, resisting even quiet encouragement from St. John Bosco, founder of the Salesians. He reluctantly attended a Salesian school but left within a year, worked the family farm, and considered marriage but decided against it. Meanwhile, Bosco stayed in touch with the restless young man and visited the family when Philip was twenty-one. He "answered all my objections [to a religious vocation] and slowly but surely ... won me over," Rinaldi wrote. Bosco must have sensed something of Rinaldi's character and future importance to the order for he personally steered him away from his intention of being a lay brother and quickly advanced him through his studies to early ordination.

For the next fifty years, Rinaldi served in a variety of positions for the Salesians, from assistant to the novice master, to provincial of the Spanish province, prefect general of the order, and, for the last ten years of his life, Rector Major (or head) of the Salesians. He was known for his fatherly spirit— "In him, we felt the love of a father

he authority of a superior."
lf-effacing man who stayed
ground and readily and frequently interrupted his administrative
work when approached for confession:
"I need to feel that I am a priest," he
said. During Rinaldi's tenure as Rector
Major, the Salesians doubled their
membership. He was especially supportive of the work of the Salesian Sisters.
Feast: December 5.

Rita of Cascia, St.

Cheryl

(1381-1457. B. at Roccaporena, Italy;
d. at Casacia.) Rita wanted to be a nun
but married, out of respect for her
parents' wishes. Her husband was
violent and unfaithful and a bad
influence on their two sons. The
marriage endured for eighteen years
until Rita's husband was brought home
dead from wounds sustained in a feud.
It is said that he repented of his life
shortly before his death but this is
uncertain. His sons died shortly after,
also possibly repentant. Eventually,
Rita joined an Augustinian convent at
Cascia where she lived in great holiness,
particularly devoted to the passion of
Christ. A wound appeared in her fore-
head and remained for fifteen years,
as if from a mystical experience of the
crown of thorns. Rita is a patron of
difficult causes and is invoked especially
for marriage problems.
Feast: May 22.

Rodriguez, St. Alphonsus

(c. 1531-1617. B. at Segovia, Spain; d.
on the island of Majorca.) Rodriguez
was a teenager when his father died. To
help make ends meet, he joined his
mother full-time in the family textile
business. When he was twenty-six, he
married Maria Suarez and they had two
children, but soon the business failed
and his wife and daughter died. He
moved with his son to the home of his
two unmarried sisters and there began
to pray and go to confession regularly,
and to attend Mass. His son died after
a few years and Alphonsus, forty years
old, applied to the Jesuits. They rejected
him twice because of his age and limited
education, but the provincial overruled
the second rejection, perhaps seeing in
him a future saint. As a lay brother, he
was sent to the College of Montesion
on Majorca, where he served as door-
keeper for the remaining forty-five years
of his life.

Alphonsus' holiness, deep prayer life,
obedience, and devotion to the
Immaculate Conception were evident
to all. Many consulted him on spiritual
matters. St. Peter Claver placed himself
under his direction while a student at
the college. Alphonsus had a difficult
spiritual life and endured much dryness
in prayer and severe temptations. He
countered these trials through a strict
regimen of prayer and spiritual practices. Gerard Manley Hopkins, the
Jesuit poet, dedicated a poem to

Rodriguez, honoring him for the intense spirituality he lived out in the most ordinary of settings. Feast: October 30.

Rose of Lima, St.

(1586-1617. B./d. at Lima, Peru.) Rose refused to marry and chose, instead, to dedicate herself to God. She helped to support her family when her parents fell on hard times, became a member of the Third Order Dominicans, and lived for years in a tiny hermitage in her parents' garden. Rose ministered to abandoned children and the elderly in an infirmary she set up at her parents' house. She had a reputation as a woman of prayer and penance and experienced visions and mystical phenomena.

Her influence throughout Lima was so great that the church thought it prudent to examine her spirituality. The theologians and doctors who led the investigation declared her experiences to be "impulses of grace." Rose practiced severe and unwise mortifications, unacceptable today but apparently tolerated in the harsh and violent culture of the time. She rubbed lime in her face to disfigure herself, for example, and wore a silver crown of thorns embedded with small spikes. She was revered in her own day and several times was credited with saving the city of Lima through her prayers. She is the patron saint of South America. Feast: August 23.

Rua, Bd. Michael

(1837-1910. B./d. at Turin, Italy.) Rua was St. John Bosco's right-hand man in his work among neglected boys in the slums of Turin. Bosco said of the young priest: "If God said to me, 'Imagine a young man with all the virtues and an ability greater than you could even hope for, then ask me and I will give him to you,' I could still never have imagined a Father Rua." Rua was one of the first to take vows in Bosco's order, the Salesians, and the "second father" of the order. He became its head on the founder's death. A gifted administrator, he was also known for his kindness, particularly to the troubled, and for his intellegence. "If I had six men like Father Rua, I would open a university," a prelate of the day commented.

As head of the order, Rua expanded the society from 64 to 341 houses and from 768 to over 4000 members. He established Salesian missions in twenty-three countries and saw the society through periods of government harassment in various countries, an anti-Salesian media campaign in Italy, and an earthquake in Sicily that killed nine Salesian priests and thirty pupils. Never robust, he died of heart disease, quietly slipping away after a two-month illness. Feast: April 6.

S

Sagheddu, Bd. Maria Gabriella

(1914-1939; B. in Dorgali, Sardinia; d. in Rome, Italy.) According to witnesses, Sagheddu was a stubborn, rebellious child and adolescent although she had a strong sense of duty. "She would say 'no' but go at once," someone said of her. When she was eighteen, she experienced a change of heart when her favorite sister died. She gained control of her temper, began to teach catechism to children, and entered a Trappist convent at Grottaferrata when she was twenty-one.

The abbess there was passionately devoted to Christian unity, and Sagheddu responded strongly to the ecumenical vision she presented. She felt called to offer her life for Christian unity—"I feel urged, even when I don't want to think about it," she told the abbess. Sagheddu dedicated herself to prayer for this cause and centered her meditation on the Gospel of John, particularly chapters 17-20 in which Jesus prays that his followers might be one.

She developed tuberculosis when she was about twenty-two, suffered much pain, and died a year later. At her beatification, Pope John Paul II hailed her "voluntary spiritual martyrdom": "The explicit act of offering her life conformed her even more perfectly to Christ ... who immolated himself so that all might be one." Feast: April 23.

Savio, St. Dominic

(1842-1857. B./d. at San Giovanni di Riva, Italy.) The remarkably good Savio died at the age of fifteen. In his biography of the teenager, St. John Bosco, his teacher and spiritual guide, said: "I saw that the child was truly filled with the Holy Spirit and I marveled at the workings of Divine Grace in one so young."

When Savio was a student boarding at Bosco's school, he started the Sodality of the Immaculate Conception with a band of his schoolmates. Their goal was to encourage frequent use of the sacraments, a disciplined life, and a charitable spirit toward all the boys, particularly those in special need. Savio seemed to have mystical experiences—"my distractions," he called them—and the ability to prophesy. (A vision that he had was used to encourage Pope Pius IX in his work to restore the Catholic Church in England.) Bosco helped Savio integrate his spirituality into his total personality and restrain any tendency to excessive piety. As a result, he was so cheerful and friendly that "everybody liked Dominic," Bosco said. Nevertheless, "his innocence, his love of God, his great longing for heaven, all seemed to combine to produce in his soul a state of almost perpetual ecstasy." Savio, whose health had always been delicate, went home to recover from a lung infection but died there, his parents at his side. Feast: March 9.

Scalabrini, Bd. John Baptist

(1839-1905. B. at Fino Mornasco, Italy; d. at Piacenza.) Scalabrini was only thirty-six when appointed as bishop of Piacenza. One of his first acts was to instruct his secretary to study his—Scalabrini's—failings and call them to his attention. For thirty years, the secretary did just that. This sort of humility, combined with Scalabrini's commitment to the needs of ordinary people, made him an excellent choice for the bishopric in 1876. He had already distinguished himself by his work on behalf of the industrialized poor and his efforts to make religious education accessible to children.

As bishop, he threw himself into pastoral work, visiting all 365 of his parishes five times, often traveling on foot or by mule to remote mountain areas. He championed the worker, reconciled feuding clergy, promoted religious education, and opened an institute for the deaf. During the famine of 1879-80, he sold his horse, pectoral cross, and a chalice from Pope Pius IX to buy food for the needy.

The turbulent political climate and miserable economic outlook of the times forced thousands of impoverished Italians to emigrate. Walking through a train station one day, Scalabrini saw, he said, "...four hundred individuals, poorly dressed ... marked with premature wrinkles drawn by privation ... all united in a single thought, all heading for a common goal. They were migrants."

Worried about their spiritual and economic welfare, he started the Congregation of the Missionaries of St. Charles (Scalabrinians) in 1887 and the Missionary Sisters of St. Charles (1895) to minister to migrants. He visited his missionaries in America in 1901 and spent a day on Ellis Island, watching Italian immigrants as they went through the process of entering the country. Saddened at the mistreatment he witnessed, he made a half-hour report to President Theodore Roosevelt and received his assurance that the abuse at customs would stop. It did. He visited members of his order in Brazil and Argentina in 1904 but died soon after. Shortly before his death, he gave the pope a plan for the care of migrants, which has strongly influenced the church's approach to their needs. Feast: June 1.

Schervier, Bd. Frances

(1819-1876. B./d. in Aachen, Germany.) Schervier identified from an early age with the poor. Her mother died of tuberculosis when Frances was thirteen, and the young girl, placed in charge of the prosperous household, quietly diverted money and goods to the needy.

In 1845, after the death of her father, Frances and four companions began the Sisters of the Poor of St. Francis and almost immediately started helping prostitutes who were trying to leave the streets. The intrepid Frances threw herself into the ministry, once disguising herself as a man and entering a brothel to reclaim a relapsed prostitute. After a few years, the diocese turned over their work to another order that specialized in that ministry. The sisters then confined their assistance primarily to nursing the sick (with a special concern for syphilitic women), helping prisoners, and running soup kitchens. Frances herself often prepared condemned prisoners for death and accompanied them to execution.

In 1858, Frances sent her sisters to Cincinnati and later to Columbus, Ohio, and Hoboken and Jersey City, New Jersey. She visited the United States twice, helping her sisters in Ohio nurse the wounded during the Civil War. Frances' generosity was legendary, even when the order was debt-ridden. "One had to be careful not to mention the wants of others ... with her," a friend said, in order that she not destitute herself in helping them. She was practical—"Let us make sacrifices in a heroic, sensible way," she told one sister—and tenderhearted, bursting into tears each Christmas when she read aloud to her community the words from the Gospel of John, "The Word was made flesh." Feast: December 15.

Scholastica, St.

(D. c. 547 near Monte Casino, Italy.) Scholastica, sister of St. Benedict, was the first Benedictine nun. She founded a convent of nuns at Plombariola, about five miles from Benedict's monastery at Monte Cassino where brother and sister met once a year for spiritual discussion. At what proved to be their last meeting, Scholastica begged her brother to stay overnight to continue their talk. The monastic rule forbade that, but when he refused, she simply bowed her head and prayed. A terrible thunderstorm broke out that prevented his leaving, and when he blamed her she said: "I asked a favor of you and you refused it. I asked it of God and he has granted it." They talked through the night about heaven, and Scholastica died three days later. Benedict buried her in the tomb he had retained for himself. The little we know of her comes from the *Dialogues* of St. Gregory the Great, written about forty-five years after her death. Feast: February 10.

Schwartz, Bd. Anton

(1852-1929. B. in Baden, Austria; d. in Vienna.) In 1875, Schwartz was newly ordained and so poor that he had to borrow vestments and a chalice for his first Mass. He was assigned to Marchegg, east of Vienna, where, for his strictness and pursuit of social justice, fellow Catholics dubbed him the "Pope of Marchegg." In 1879, while serving as chaplain at a hospital in Vienna, he encountered the sufferings of apprentices and workers who worked long hours in dangerous conditions for little money. A dying apprentice told him, "The church has religious institutes for everyone.... We apprentices are the only ones forgotten."

Schwartz decided to found a religious community to serve them and began the Congregation for the Devout Workers of St. Joseph Calasanz in 1889. He and his followers appealed to Christian businessmen to protect their employees, placed apprentices in Catholic businesses, started savings associations for workers and a home for foreign apprentices, and rescued homeless apprentices from the street.

Schwartz denounced the exploitation of workers, joined strikes of bus drivers, carpenters, and servants and also helped tailors and cobblers in their demands against their employers. He initially experienced much opposition within the church but that abated under the protection of the supportive Viennese Cardinal Friedrich Piffl. Schwartz hoped to win estranged workers back to the church and to reevangelize Austria. Feast: September 15.

Seelos, Bd. Francis Xavier

(1819-1867. B. in Fussen, Germany; d. in New Orleans, Louisiana.) Seelos was a theology student at the University of Munich when he read an appeal for priests to serve German immigrants in America. He left for New York in 1843, became a Redemptorist priest in 1845, and went to St. Philomena's in Pittsburgh. The pastor there was the future saint John Neumann ("In every respect ... like a remarkable father to me," Seelos said).

Seelos developed a reputation for his extraordinary gifts in the confessional (his fellow priests noted that once someone went to Seelos for confession they never went to anyone else). He often emphasized the mercy of God saying, in one sermon: "If only all the sinners of the whole wide world were present here ... even those close to despair, I would call out to them: 'The Lord is merciful and gracious, patient and of much compassion.'" In Pittsburgh, he also became known for the remarkable physical healings that took place through his prayers.

Seelos was pastor of several parishes in Maryland, ministered to soldiers and the wounded during the Civil War, and worked briefly in Detroit. He also held several positions in the Redemptorist order. Assigned to St. Mary the Assumption parish in New Orleans in 1866, he died a year later of yellow fever contracted while caring for other victims of the epidemic. The New Orleans newspaper, the *Daily Picayune*, said of Seelos that his "only human weakness was his overflowing sympathy and charity for poor, erring humanity." Feast: October 4.

Serra, Bd. Junipero

(1713-1784. B. in Petra, Majorca, Spain; d. in Carmel, California.) Serra was fifty-six years old in 1769 when he began the most rigorous phase of his missionary career, the evangelization of California's native people. He had been ordained a Franciscan priest in 1737 and taught philosophy at the Franciscan college in Majorca before requesting assignment to the mission fields.

In 1749 he arrived in Mexico. Almost as soon as he began the rugged walk from the coast to Mexico City, an insect bit him on the leg and the sore never healed, flaring up and causing great suffering for the rest of his life. Serra was also asthmatic and in generally poor health, but he served with distinction in Mexico for twenty years. He had good organizational ability coupled with piety and a flair

for getting his point
he wanted to encou
frequent the sacrame
knelt before the enti
made his confession to another priest.

In California, Serra developed the mission system, sites that included a church, living quarters, barracks for soldiers, dining facilities, and work-shops. They were located near Indian villages. He pioneered and administered the system, taught agricultural skills, worked side-by-side with the Indians, and vigorously defended them against government abuse and exploitation. Although the mission system was closely tied to the Spanish colonial venture, within the constraints of the times Serra worked for the genuine spiritual and economic development of the native people. In 1773, he made the grueling trip back to Mexico City to present to the authorities what amounted to a bill of rights on the Indians' behalf.

Serra founded nine missions in California including San Luis Obispo, San Juan Capistrano, and San Carlos Borromeo at Carmel. He is buried in the mission church in Carmel, the site of his headquarters. Feast: August 28.

Seton, St. Elizabeth Ann

(1774-1821. B. at New York City; d. at Emmitsburg, Maryland.) America's first native-born saint, Elizabeth grew up in a wealthy and prominent Episcopalian ly. Her father, a doctor, was New York's first public health officer. Her mother died when she was three. Elizabeth's lonely childhood was exacerbated by her father's absorption in his work and, on his remarrying, by her stepmother's dislike of her. Her happy marriage to William Seton in 1794—they had five children—ended with his death in 1804 from tuberculosis. He died while in Italy with Elizabeth, on a trip meant to restore his health.

Elizabeth became a Catholic on her return to New York, attracted by her experience of the church in Italy. Feeling the sting of anti-Catholic prejudice—common, at the time—she accepted an invitation to open a school in the diocese of Baltimore, Maryland. She moved there with her children and, not long after, started a Catholic school that accepted children of the poor at no charge. Other women joined her in the work and this was the beginning of the Sisters of Charity, the first religious order founded in the United States.

Seton endured painful losses in her later years. Two of her daughters and two sisters-in-law died. "I have lost the little friend of my heart," she said of her fourteen-year-old daughter, Rebecca. Her religious order flourished, not without difficulty, and today six branches of the Sisters of Charity trace their origin to Elizabeth Seton. Feast: January 4.

Siedliska, Bd. Frances

(1842-1902. B. in Roszkowa Wola, Poland; d. in Rome.) Siedliska was born into the Polish nobility, a gifted, intelligent, warm individual with a quick temper and a sharp way of reacting to a situation ("When I wanted something, I really wanted it," she said). She was baptized a Catholic but her parents provided little religious education, a situation remedied by a Capuchin friar, Fr. Leander Lendzian, who prepared her for the sacraments and guided her throughout her life.

Her father attempted to introduce her to society in spite of her inclination to the religious life. Under the strain of the situation, Frances and her mother became seriously ill and her father took them on a tour of several European countries. While walking on the beach at Cannes, Frances told her father that her decision to pursue the religious life was final. "He sobbed," Frances said. "He suffered that his only daughter chose such a life." Reluctantly, he gave his permission to Frances to pursue her vocation.

She started the Congregation of the Holy Family of Nazareth in Rome in 1875, modeling her order on the total surrender of Jesus, Mary, and Joseph to God. In a then revolutionary emphasis on the needs of the individual, she insisted on "freedom of conscience ... regard for the psyche of the sisters, their temperament and their natural disposition." The sisters ministered to neglected and abandoned children, young women, and the poor and worked in education, including catechesis. In 1999, Pope John Paul II canonized eleven sisters of the order who were shot by the Nazis in 1943 (see Stella and Companions). Feast: November 21.

Simon, St.

(first century) Simon the Zealot is listed as an apostle in the synoptic Gospels and Acts. We know nothing else about him. According to tradition, he preached in Persia with St. Jude where both were martyred. Feast: October 28.

Siphong, Bds. Philip and Companions (Martyrs of Thailand)

(D. 1940 at Songkhon, Thailand.) A rise in Thai nationalism in 1940 led to the expulsion of many French missionaries from the country. Their religion was associated with foreign influences. The situation was particularly grave for Catholics in the northeast, where local police tried to force believers to apostatize. Philip Siphong (1907-40) was a teacher in the local parochial school, a catechist, and he and his wife, Maria, had five children. The missionaries, confident of his pastoral ability, entrusted the Catholics to his care when they left

(the villagers called him the "man of oak" for his unshakable faith). On December 16, 1940, the police took him to the woods outside Songkhon and shot him when he refused to renounce his beliefs.

Six others also chose death to apostasy and were shot near the Songkhon cemetery on December 26. Sr. Agnes Phila (b. 1909 at Ban) and Sr. Lucia Khambang (b. 1917 at Viengkuk) were teachers and members of the Institute of the Lovers of the Cross. Agatha Phutta (b. 1881) was a single woman and convert who worked in the mission kitchen. Sixteen-year-old Cecelia Butsi (b. 1924 at Songkhon) helped in the kitchen. At a meeting held in front of the church the day before she died, she publicly identified herself as a Christian in spite of a death threat from the head of the police. Bibiana Khamphai (b. 1925 at Songkhon), fifteen years old, was described as "a girl of blameless life." Maria Phon (b. 1926 at Songkhon) was fourteen when martyred. Pope John Paul II beatified the seven in 1989.

Solano, St. Francis

(1549-1610. B. at Montilla, Spain; d. at Lima, Peru.) Solano, a Franciscan priest, had an unusual devotional practice: he played the lute and sang to the Blessed Mother at her altar, sometimes well into the night. He was a gifted preacher, effectively bringing people to repentance and conversion, and his Franciscan community made him the master of novices. When one of his novices needed correction, Francis gave himself a penance instead. He felt that he was to blame for the shortcomings of his charges.

In 1589, he went to Peru as a missionary. En route, the boat foundered in a storm, and while others crowded the single lifeboat, Solano remained on board to care for the black slaves left behind. After three days, they were rescued. Francis proceeded to Tucuman, in what is now Argentina, to begin twenty years of service to the Indians and colonists in Argentina, Paraguay, and Peru. He learned the languages of the Indians and traveled frequently over difficult terrain to minister to them. He won many to the faith. His friendly manner, humility, music, singing, and powerful preaching combined to make him a most effective missionary. He also served in administrative positions for the Franciscans. Feast: July 14.

Soubiran, Bd. Mary Teresa de

(1835-1889. B. at Castelnaudary, France; d. at Paris.) At the age of nineteen, Mary Teresa joined a community of laywomen living under temporary vows but decided she wanted a more austere, committed life. To that end, she founded the Society of Mary the Helper at Toulouse in 1864.

The sisters started a hostel for young working women, and this ministry became their principal work although they also cared for orphans and taught the children of the poor. Rome approved the congregation in 1868.

In 1871, the sisters elected a Sr. Mary Francis as assistant mother general to Mary Teresa. Mary Francis was domineering and ambitious, traits cloaked by her intelligence and apparently lively faith. She orchestrated a too-rapid expansion of the order, and when a financial crisis developed, blamed Mary Teresa, accusing her of pride and poor religious spirit. Mary Teresa resigned under pressure, and Mary Francis took her place and expelled her from the order. Eventually, Mary Teresa joined the Sisters of Our Lady of Charity in Paris and, according to her spiritual director, heroically banished her first religious family from her mind. She had learned, she said, that God is everything and all else is nothing. She wouldn't have learned this, she wrote, without the "cruel anguish" of the preceding years.

In 1890, the sisters finally deposed Mary Francis, who left the order. The congregation then flourished. When she died in 1921, it came to light that she had been married when she entered the convent, had deserted her husband, and was therefore never canonically a nun. All her actions as mother general were invalid. In effect, Mary Teresa in fact never ceased to be a member of her own congregation. Feast: October 20.

Soubirous, St. Bernadette

(1844-1879. B. at Lourdes, France; d. at Nevers.) Bernadette's poverty-stricken family lived in the basement of the former town jail and subsisted on the income from odd jobs. Bernadette had little education, suffered from asthma, and was an ordinary girl in every respect until February 11, 1858. At that time she received the first of eighteen apparitions of Our Lady at the rock of Massabielle, Lourdes.

The reported visions met with complete disbelief on the part of authorities, but Bernadette won them over with her simplicity, common sense, and intense dislike of the publicity she faced. The primary message from Mary, she said, was a call to do penance for the conversion of sinners and to visit the site of the apparitions on pilgrimage. During one of her visions, a spring began to flow where none had been before. It is in these waters that the sick bathe and where some have been healed.

Following the visions, Bernadette returned to complete obscurity. She entered the Sisters of Notre Dame at Nevers in 1866, where she lived a self-effacing life, refusing to receive any attentions or entertain any requests regarding the apparitions. She chose not to attend the opening of the new basilica at Lourdes in 1876. She compared herself to a broom: "Our Lady used me. They have put me back in my corner. I am happy to stop there." Bernadette suffered tremendously from ill health but endured with patience. Feast: April 16.

Southwell, St. Robert

(1561-1595. B. at Norfolk, England; d. at London.) Southwell was a Jesuit priest and martyr. He was also a popular writer, a contemporary of Shakespeare, and almost certainly read by the bard.

Ordained a priest in Rome in 1584, Southwell left for the dangerous English mission in 1586 (priests, if caught, were executed). He hid at the homes of Catholics, writing and praying by day, ministering by night. Although bookstores freely sold his works, he lived largely in the shadows until betrayed to the notorious interrogator Topcliffe.

Tortured about a dozen times—"each one worse than death," he said—he was then held in the Tower of London for three years until finally condemned to be hanged and drawn and quartered. With sentiment running high against execution of the talented young writer, a large crowd was on hand at the gallows. He threw his handkerchief to a fellow Jesuit in the crowd. He then argued for and won the right to make a short speech, concluding his remarks with the words of St. Paul: "Whether we live or die, we belong to the Lord." The execution began, but the executioner attempted to cut the rope before death in order for the butchering to proceed. Lord Mountjoy pushed him aside. The sheriff then attempted to cut Southwell down, but the crowd shouted its defiance, so that Robert was allowed to die before being disemboweled. When the executioner held up the martyr's head, the crowd remained silent, refusing to give the customary shout of "Traitor!" Feast: February 21.

Stein, St. Edith
(Teresa Benedicta of the Cross)

(1891-1942. B. at Breslau, Germany [now Wroclaw, Poland]; d. at Auschwitz.) In 1942, Dutch Catholic bishops released a pastoral letter denouncing the deportation of Jews to concentration camps. In retaliation, the occupying German forces rounded up Catholic Jews, among them Edith Stein, who was a convert, a renowned philosopher, and a Carmelite nun living at Echt, Holland. She was murdered in a gas chamber at Auschwitz shortly after, along with hundreds of other Catholic Jews. Stein identified closely with her Jewish heritage and had anticipated her fate, seeing it as a sharing in the redemptive suffering of Christ:

"...His cross ... was now being laid on the Jewish people. Most of them did not understand it but those who did ... must accept it willingly in the name of all. I wanted to do that...."

Stein became an atheist when fourteen and turned to philosophy, studying under the phenomenologist Edmund Husserl. He recognized her genius and invited her to be his assistant at the University of Freiburg, where she received her doctorate. Gradually, Stein reevaluated what she called her "rationalist prejudice." Several in her philosophical circle were Christians—Husserl was a convert from Judaism—and, she said, "the world of faith suddenly stretched out before me." In 1921, she read the autobiography of St. Teresa of Avila. "I ... did not stop until I reached the end. As I closed the book, I said, 'That is the truth.'" She was baptized into the Catholic Church on January 1, 1922.

For ten years, she taught philosophy, lectured in Germany and surrounding countries, and wrote a two-volume study of the work of Thomas Aquinas. In 1933, Nazi law barred Jews from teaching and Edith left her position to enter the Discalced Carmelite Order at Cologne. In the face of mounting Nazi terror, she fled to the Echt Carmel in 1939. She was at work on *The Science of the Cross*, a commentary on St. John of the Cross, when arrested. A prisoner at Westerbork, where Stein was briefly held, recalled that she "walked among the prisoners, talking and praying like a saint. She spoke in such a humble and clear way.... A talk with her was like a voyage into another world." Feast: August 9.

Stella of the Most Blessed Sacrament and Ten Companions, Bds. (Sisters of the Congregation of the Holy Family of Nazareth)

(D. near Nowogrodek, Belarus, 1943.) German forces entered the Nowogrodek area in 1941, and in 1942 the Gestapo began a series of terrorist actions against civilians. In July 1943, 120 were arrested and slated for death, many of them fathers of families. The sisters prayed that they might offer their lives in exchange for the prisoners: "Accept [this sacrifice] from us who are free from family obligations and spare those who have wives and children in their care." Shortly after, some of the prisoners were released but most were sent to forced-labor camps in Germany (all survived the war).

On July 31, the sisters were ordered to appear at Gestapo headquarters. They were shot to death the next morning in the woods along with a young boy who happened to witness their execution. The sisters were: Stella, the superior, known for her sensitivity to others' suffering; Imelda, teacher and sacristan; Raymond; Danilla; Canuta, who had planned to marry until a dream directed her to enter the convent; Sergia, who spent time in the United States but returned to her country in spite of the threat of war, saying she was not afraid of martyrdom; Gwidon, known for her cheerfulness and called "a powerhouse of prayer"; Felicita; Heliodora; Canisia, who was impetuous; and Boromea, who was sensitive, struggled with her vocation, and left the convent until, she wrote, "something urged me to return." Feast: August 1.

Stensen, Bd. Niels

(1638-1686. B. at Copenhagen, Denmark; d. at Schwerin, Germany.) Stensen was a medical doctor credited with the discovery of the parotid duct, known since as Stensen's duct, as well as discoveries about glands of the mouth and the anatomy of the tongue, brain, and heart. He studied at the University of Copenhagen, received his degree from the University of Leiden in 1664, and over the next decade continued his anatomical research primarily in Paris and Italy. Renowned as a scientist throughout Europe, he expanded his field of enquiry to include paleontology, geology, and mineralogy, laying the foundation of scientific geology.

Stensen was a devout Lutheran when he saw the annual Corpus Christi procession in an Italian town in 1666. Impressed by the reverence of the crowd as the host was carried past, he asked himself: If "it really is the body of Jesus Christ ... why do I not venerate it as well?" Stensen conducted a thorough study of Catholicism, reading the Bible in Hebrew and Greek as well as Latin, and in 1667 became a Catholic. He served for several years as Royal Anatomist in Copenhagen before deciding to become a priest. This was not an unnatural progression for Stensen, who once said: "This is the true aim of anatomy, to lift up our gaze through the accomplished artistry of the body to grasp the value of the soul ... to teach us to know and love the Creator."

Ordained in 1675, he was first sent as bishop to Hanover and then in 1680, as bishop to Munster. Stensen lived an ascetic life in complete poverty, giving away all he had and even selling his episcopal ring in order to help the poor. He resigned his bishopric in 1683 and moved to Schwerin to do missionary work for which he felt better suited. He became ill in 1686, diagnosed himself as having a blocked kidney stone, and died within a few days. Feast: December 5.

Stephen, St.

(D. c. 35 at Jerusalem.) Stephen is the first martyr of Christian history, most probably a Greek-speaking Jew, and one of the seven deacons chosen to look after the practical needs of the widows in the Christian community. The Acts of the Apostles, chapters six and seven, record all we know about him. Stephen was filled with "faith and the holy Spirit ... grace and power" and worked miracles among the people. When he prevailed in debate over some Jewish opponents, he was accused of blasphemy and arrested. He defended himself against false witnesses by recounting Israel's history and ending with a sharp rebuke: "You stiff-necked people ... you always oppose the holy Spirit.... You received the law as transmitted by angels, but you did not observe it."

Stephen then had a vision of Jesus standing at the right hand of God, and when he described this to his accusers, they dragged him from the city and stoned him to death. Saul, later to become St. Paul, stood by and approved the murder. Feast: December 26.

Stepinac, Bd. Aloysius

(1898-1960. B. d. at Krasic, Croatia) Stepinac became the archbishop of Zagreb in 1937 and led the church in Croatia in its resistance to fascism, national socialism, and communism. When the pro-Nazi Ustasha party took power in 1941, he soon became their most outspoken critic, protesting the persecution and execution of Orthodox

Serbs, Jews, Gypsies, and others.

At public ceremonies, Stepinac carried in his pocket a list of prisoners awaiting execution so that he could intercede for them with authorities in attendance. He condemned Nazi and Ustasha policies relentlessly from his pulpit and in pastoral letters. When the government ordered all Jews to wear the yellow Star of David, he preached: "The church has always condemned and condemns today all violence and injustice which is committed in the name of racial and nationalistic theories." The government then exempted eight priests and nuns of Jewish heritage from the new law. Stepinac rejected the dispensation: "I have ordered [them] to continue wearing this sign of belonging to the people from which Our Savior was born as long as any others will have to do so." He hid Jews under his own roof, rescued the residents of the Lavoslav Schwartz retirement home, and secured passports to smuggle hundreds of Jews out of the country.

After the war, the communist government under Joseph Tito attempted to persuade Stepinac to break with Rome and form a national Catholic church. Stepinac rejected the overture and endured a government-orchestrated media campaign that accused him, among other crimes, of collaborating with the Nazis. He was subjected to a sham trial. Sentenced to sixteen years' hard labor, the authorities released him from prison to house arrest in 1951. Tito would have welcomed his quiet departure from the country, but Stepinac wouldn't leave his flock. Pope Pius XII named him a cardinal in 1953. In 1959, the authorities asked him to testify at the trial of the spiritual director of the diocesan seminary. He refused and died two months later, still under house arrest, his health undermined by the rigors of his imprisonment. Feast: February 10.

T

Taigi, Bd. Anne Mary

(1769-1837. B. at Siena, Italy; d. at Rome.) When Anne's father, a druggist, lost his job, he moved his destitute family to Rome. Both parents became servants and Anne went to work when she was thirteen, first in factories and then as a housemaid. She married Domenico Taigi in 1790 and they had seven children, two of whom died in infancy.

Sometime after her marriage, Anne experienced a deeper conversion through the ministry of her confessor, Fr. Angelo. She continued to be an exemplary wife and mother while devoting herself to prayer and penance. She cared for the poor, supplemented the family income through sewing, and gathered her extended household for prayer in the morning and evening. She developed a reputation for spiritual insight and experienced mystical graces. Many people came to her for guidance.

In the process of her beatification, her husband, ninety-two at the time, provided a loving deposition. He said that often, when he returned home, the house was full of people. But Anne left them to wait upon him "affectionately and attentively. One could see that she did it with all her heart.... She was my comfort and the consolation of all."

Anne endured many spiritual trials and a painful illness before her death. Feast: June 9.

Talbot, Ven. Matthew

(1856-1925. D. at Dublin, Ireland.) Matt, a native of Ireland, was an alcoholic whose first job, at the age of twelve, was in a wine shop. He dropped out of school and drank steadily over the course of sixteen years. One day, when he was twenty-eight and penniless, he waited in vain outside a bar for passing friends to buy him a drink as he did for them when they were broke. Disillusioned when they ignored him, Matt found a priest, went to confession, and took a pledge of sobriety for three months. He renewed it and never touched alcohol again for the remaining forty-one years of his life.

He sustained his commitment to sobriety through penance and prayer—he prayed till late at night, far from his drinking buddies. Two crossed pins in his coatsleeve reminded him to pray without ceasing. He slept for three-and-a-half hours a night, rose at two for prayer, and attended Mass each morning. He gave generously to the missions and the poor from his salary as a storekeeper for a lumber company. Matt remained single, joined the Third Order

Franciscans, and died in Dublin on June 7, 1925, worn out from his austerities. After his death, penitential chains were found wrapped around his body under his clothing.

Tansi, Bd. Cyprian Iwene

(1903-1964. B. at Igboezunu, Nigeria; d. at Leicestershire, England.) Cyprian was born to a farming family of the Ibo tribe of southern Nigeria. Tabansi, his father, died when Cyprian was young. Although the family was pagan, his mother, Ejikweve, sent him to a nearby Christian mission school, where he was baptized in 1912. He began teaching when he was sixteen while continuing his own education.

Cyprian entered the seminary in 1925, where he was well loved and devout but "nearly killed himself fasting," according to a friend. Ordained in 1937, he became pastor of a far-flung region and for the next thirteen years traveled constantly to the mission stations in his care. Huge crowds— sometimes as many as eight hundred people—would arrive for confession and Mass. He was involved in every aspect of his people's lives, working on building projects, treading clay for bricks, and helping men to repair thatch roofs and women to clean floors. Cyprian started the League of Mary in the area, encouraged vocations, and developed marriage preparation centers.

His assistant later said of him that he was a "man for difficult situations ... [with] a mixture of boldness and fearlessness and humility."

In 1950, Cyprian went to the Trappist abbey of Mount St. Bernard in England to receive training for the monastic life. He was then to help establish a monastery in Nigeria. Those plans failed, to his regret, but Cyprian was chosen to help form a monastery in Cameroon. Shortly before his scheduled departure, he died of an aneurysm. Feast: January 20.

Tchang Ta-Pong, Bd. Joseph

(c. 1754-1815. B. at Tou-yun-fou, China; d. at Kouy-yang.) Joseph, a Buddhist who embraced Taoism, became interested in Catholicism through the newly converted son of his business partner. He enrolled as a catechumen in 1798 after first dealing with a practical matter: his second marriage, contracted when he and his first wife were unable to produce an heir. He had a son by his second wife, but Joseph provided for them both and had the marriage annulled, freeing his wife to remarry.

Joseph was baptized in 1800, but his brothers, claiming he had dishonored the family, stirred up a persecution of Catholics in the area and Joseph fled. In spite of the danger, he later returned and carried on an intense ministry, caring for the sick and poor, working as a catechist, and bringing many to the faith. In 1811, fresh persecution broke out and although Joseph escaped, his son, Antony, was captured. He refused to say where his father had gone: "If my father has committed a crime, I take the responsibility for it. Let me bear the punishment you intend to inflict on him." Antony was exiled and died the next year. Joseph again returned home to carry on his ministry in the face of tremendous opposition. Denounced by his brother-in-law, he was imprisoned and executed as required by imperial laws that condemned Catholicism. Feast: March 12.

Tejedor, Sts. Cyril Bertrand and Companions (Martyrs of Asturias)

(D. 1934 at Asturias, Spain.) Eight of these nine martyrs were members of the Brothers of the Christian Schools. The ninth, Fr. Innocencio Arnau, was a Passionist priest and the chaplain for the brothers. All were in their twenties or early thirties with the exception of Cyril and Innocencio, who were in their forties.

Cyril was the superior of the brothers' community at Santander, where his reputation in the classroom and administrative abilities began to draw students from other schools. In 1933 the order reassigned him to head up a school in Turon, Asturias, for the children of miners. He began that assignment by making a thirty-day retreat, abandoning himself to the will of God. The Asturias province was a hotbed of political intrigue and anticlerical sentiment in the years prior to the Spanish Civil War, and the brothers, in particular, irritated town leaders because they defied the ban on teaching religion, escorted the students to Mass, and exercised considerable religious influence on the young.

During an uprising authorities arrested the brothers and their chaplain and, in the middle of the night, took them to a cemetery, lined them up at the edge of a pit, and shot them. The rebel commander was so impressed by the demeanor of the men that he said, "Hardened as I am, I could not help being moved.... I think that while walking and when waiting at the gate, they prayed in a subdued voice." The brothers included: Marciano Jose Lopez; Julian Alfredo Zapico; Victoriano Pio Cano; Benjamin Julian Andres; Augusto Andres Fernandez; Benito de Jesus Saez; Aniceto Adolfo Gutierrez. Feast: October 9.

Tekawitha, Bd. Kateri

(c. 1656-1680; Auriesville, New York; d. at Saulte St. Louis, Canada [near Montreal].) Known as the Lily of the Mohawks, Kateri is the first Native American to be declared Blessed. Her father was a Mohawk chief and her mother, a Christian, was of the Algonquins. Kateri's parents and brother died in a smallpox epidemic when she was four, and the disease left her with a disfigured face and poor eyesight. She was raised by an uncle but refused to marry, to the distress of her family. In 1676, she was baptized by a Jesuit missionary and was immediately persecuted for her new faith. So that she might live in peace, she trekked two hundred miles through the forests to a Christian Indian village in Canada.

Kateri cared for the sick and elderly, attended two Masses daily, and was devoted to the Eucharist and to the crucified Christ. In 1679, she took a vow of chastity. A missionary who knew her wrote: "She had an insatiable thirst for spiritual knowledge, and a great zeal to put into practice all she understood. Her soul was well disposed toward perfection." She died at the age of twenty-four. Feast: April 17.

Teresa of Avila, St.

(1515-1582. B. at Avila, Spain; d. at Alba de Tormes.) Teresa was born to a wealthy, pious family and grew into an attractive, intelligent young woman with the ability, she said, of always being able to please people. She attended a convent school when she was sixteen and there felt both attracted to and repelled by the religious life.

"I asked God not to give me that vocation," she later wrote. She struggled with the decision and her father refused his permission, but in 1536, she secretly entered the local Carmelite Convent of the Incarnation. The relaxed atmosphere there was typical of the times—the nuns lived in relative comfort, received guests, traveled, and retained servants.

Teresa left the Incarnation in 1536 due to serious illness and began to develop a habit of contemplative prayer during her recuperation. When she returned three years later, she fell back into the worldly life of the convent, gave up private prayer, then returned to it after several years and continued to struggle with her spiritual life for nearly fifteen years. "All the things of God gave me great pleasure," she wrote, "but I was held captive by the things of the world." She began to experience interior voices and visions, received good spiritual direction, and by 1555 her slow conversion was complete.

In 1562, she founded the Convent of St. Joseph at Avila, which was small, strict, and poor. With this, she began her famous work of Carmelite reform. Her Discalced Carmelites, so named because they wore no shoes, endured strong opposition from the calced Carmelites and from civil authorities. However, for the next twenty years, Teresa traveled tirelessly throughout Spain, under appalling conditions, establishing reformed convents. She founded a reformed monastery for men and enlisted the aid of St. John of the Cross to continue that work. The Discalced Carmelites were eventually recognized as a distinct order.

One of the great mystics of all time, Teresa combined her intense prayer life with endless travel, great organizational skills, and a sharp business sense. She wrote hundreds of letters, and her books are considered spiritual classics, including *The Way of Perfection, The Interior Castle,* and her autobiography. She had a practical, good-humored approach to life and professed a dislike for "long-faced saints that make both virtue and themselves abhorrent." She was named a Doctor of the Church in 1970 for her work in the area of mystical theology and Christian spirituality. Feast: October 15.

Teresa of Jesus (of the Andes), St. (Juanita Fernandez Solar)

(1900-1929. B. at Santiago, Chile; d. at Los Andes.) Teresa, born to a wealthy mining family, was devout, outgoing, and musically gifted. She was an exceptional athlete, excelling particularly at her favorite sport, horseback riding. Devoted to the Blessed Mother, she said that, as a child, "I heard her voice within me, quite clearly.... I thought that was a perfectly normal thing and it never occurred to me to relate to others

what [she] was telling me." After she received her First Communion at age eleven, she had a similar experience, hearing Jesus' voice within her.

Teresa felt attracted to marriage but decided instead to enter the Carmelite order. She joined the very poor Carmel at Los Andes in 1919, living the same sort of "hidden" life as St. Thérèse of Lisieux, whose writings influenced and inspired her. She fell victim to typhoid fever the following year. She died after being allowed to make her religious profession on her sickbed. Her spiritual diary, along with about seventy letters she wrote from Carmel, reveals her intense, unaffected, joyful spirituality. Feast: April 12.

Thérèse of Lisieux, St.

(1873-1897. B. at Alencon, France; d. at Lisieux.) Thérèse was born to Louis Martin, a watchmaker, and his wife Zélie Guérin, who died of breast cancer when Thérèse was five. Her family was intensely religious—her four surviving siblings all became nuns and her parents, too, had considered the religious life before they met and married. Thérèse entered the Carmelite convent in Lisieux at the age of fifteen, taking the name Thérèse of the Child Jesus and the Holy Face. She died there of tuberculosis nine years later.

Her autobiography, *The Story of a Soul,* was published posthumously and brought her instant fame. The book described Thérèse's "little way," a simple path to holiness based on living out the gospel in the mundane events of daily life. Her sister Celine said that it was "in a multitude of slight, almost microscopic acts" that Thérèse revealed her strength. Her life, ordinary on the surface, was a continual crucifixion of self-will.

During the last year of her life, she suffered tremendous physical pain as well as temptations to despair and unbelief. She endured this final trial with serenity: "My agony may reach the furthest limits, but I am convinced he will never forsake me," she said. "We can never have too much confidence in God."

Her cult spread rapidly upon her death due to the appeal of her little way and to her deathbed promise to send a "shower of roses," answers to prayer, to those who sought her intercession. She is a Doctor of the Church. Feast: October 1.

Thomas, St.

(first century) Thomas, an apostle whose name means "twin," emerges as a distinct and energetic personality in the Gospels. He urged his companions to go with Jesus to Bethany, a dangerous trip due to hostility in Judea toward Jesus: "Let us go along to die with him" (Jn 11:16). When Jesus said,

"You know the way that leads where I go," Thomas interrupted to point out that, since they didn't know where he was going, "how can we know the way?" (Jn 14:5). Thomas was not present for the initial post-resurrection appearance of Jesus to the disciples and refused to believe their report without proof. Jesus appeared again a week later, and Thomas, who was present, responded: "My Lord and my God" (see Jn 20:24-29).

A tradition long viewed skeptically by scholars claims that Thomas evangelized India and was martyred there. The story appears in the apocryphal Acts of Thomas, written in the third or fourth century in support of Gnostic views. Recent archaeological evidence lends credence to this claim, although nothing can be said with certainty of Thomas' career after Pentecost. According to another tradition, he evangelized the Parthians. Feast: July 3.

Thomas Aquinas, St.

(1225-1274. B. at Roccasecca, near Aquino, Italy; d. at Fossanuova.) Thomas entered the newly established Dominican order in 1244 and quickly left, kidnapped by his horrified relatives. His wealthy family hoped to settle him in a more prestigious career than that of a friar, and imprisoned him to think it over. They relented fifteen months later when he refused to change his mind. He rejoined the order, went to Cologne to study with St. Albert the Great, and there his quiet demeanor and powerful (later, corpulent) build earned him the nickname "the Dumb Ox." Albert, who recognized Thomas' genius, said in reference to the nickname that one day his "lowing" would be heard around the world.

He was ordained in about 1250, and from 1252 to his death at the early age of forty-nine, Thomas divided his time between Italy and Paris. He studied, taught, and wrote the immense body of work that has played such an influential role in Catholic theology. The most famous of these are the *Summa contra Gentiles* and *Summa Theologica,* a systematic exposition of theology that underlies much of Catholic thought today. His other works, too numerous to list, include commentaries on the Gospels, the epistles, and several Old Testament books. His love for the Eucharist and deep devotion to the person of Christ are evident not just in his theological works but in his famous hymn "Pange Lingua" ("Tell, my soul, the mystery of the glorious body").

Thomas is famous for his scholarship but not as well known for his equally impressive holiness. Toward the end of his life, however, his piety led him to make a startling decision: He stopped writing his *Summa*

Theologica and left it unfinished. He had had an experience—a revelation he never discussed—while celebrating Mass. As a result, he said, "all that I have written appears to me as so much straw...." Brother Reginald, his confidant and secretary, protested, but was probably not surprised. "His marvelous science was far less due to the power of his genius than to the efficacy of his prayer," Reginald wrote in tribute to the spirit underlying Thomas' work.

Neither Thomas' piety nor intellect isolated him from the small pleasures of life. He was quiet and reserved but a warm and devoted friend. "No possession is joyous without a companion," he said.

On the other hand, he was easily absorbed in thought. One famous incident occurred while at a gathering with King St. Louis of France. While conversation flowed around him, Thomas sat silently. Suddenly, smashing his fist down on the table, he exclaimed, "And *that* settles the Manichean heresy!" The party was transfixed but the king, who valued the theologian's advice and insight, sent his secretary to Thomas' side to record the great man's argument lest it be forgotten.

The pope asked him to attend the Council at Lyon in 1274, but Thomas fell ill—possibly of a stroke—on the way there. He was taken to the nearby

Cistercian abbey of Fossanuova, where he died on March 7. He is a Doctor of the Church. Feast: January 28.

Timothy, St.

(first century) Timothy, companion of Paul on some of his missionary journeys, appears in the Acts of the Apostles and several epistles. He is the named recipient of the two Pauline epistles known as 1 and 2 Timothy.

The son of a Greek father and a Jewish Christian mother, he was most likely a native of Lystra in Galatia. His grandmother, Lois, and mother, Eunice, passed the faith on to him (2 Tm 1:5), but Paul had him circumcised because of his Jewish heritage so that he would be more acceptable to the Jews. Paul called him his "own true child in faith" (1 Tm 1:2) and sent him as his representative on various difficult missions. He entrusted the care of the Christians around Ephesus to Timothy. Eusebius in his *History of the Church* (c. 323) calls Timothy "the first bishop appointed to the see of Ephesus." According to late tradition, he was beaten to death for opposing a pagan festival. Feast: January 26.

Titus, St.

(first century) Titus was a gentile and a companion of Paul who traveled with him to Jerusalem for the council held there in about A.D. 49. He handled dif-ficult assignments for Paul such as delivering his harsh letter to the Corinthians (see 2 Cor 7:5-16). Titus is considered the first bishop of Crete, an assignment rife with problems (see Ti 1:10-16) among a people Paul seemed to hold in low esteem (see Ti 1:12-13). Paul clearly had great confidence in Titus and called him "my own true child in our common faith" in the epistle he addressed to him. Feast: January 26.

Tomasi, St. Joseph Maria

(1649-1713. B. at Alicata, Sicily, Italy; d. at Rome.) Anglicans as well as Catholics revere Tomasi for his liturgical scholarship, which opened up a vast field of research for liturgists. He combined his immense erudition with a simplicity and affection that led the poor to besiege him on the streets and prompted him to teach religion classes to children even after he had been named a cardinal.

Tomasi was ordained in Rome as a member of the Theatine order in 1673 and immediately devoted himself to biblical, patristic, and liturgical studies. He published the *Codices Sacrementorum* (four texts of ancient liturgies), the *Psalterium* (an account of the Roman and Gallican translations of the psalms), and numerous other groundbreaking works. In 1704 the pope appointed him theologian to the Congregation of Discipline of

Regulars, and in that capacity he worked zealously for the reform of all religious orders.

Cardinal Albani chose the saintly priest as his confessor, a move that appeared to have backfired when Tomasi ordered the reluctant cardinal to accept the papacy under pain of mortal sin. As Clement XI, Albani used the same argument to convince Tomasi to accept the cardinalate. Tomasi continued his austerities as a cardinal, was increasingly absorbed in the love of God, and was sometimes found in ecstasy before the Blessed Sacrament. His health, never good, was undermined by his penances and availability to all in need. He died after an illness of several days. Feast: January 2.

To Rot, Bd. Peter

(1912-1945. B./d. at Rakunai, New Britain.) Peter lived and died on the Melanesian island of New Britain, off the northeast coast of Papua New Guinea. His father, the village chief, invited Catholic missionaries to evangelize his people. Peter's family was baptized, and Peter's father, who took to his new faith with great enthusiasm, built a church for the area. Peter trained to be a catechist—lay people were instrumental in evangelizing New Guinea—and worked in his own village. He was in charge of the school, gave religious instruction, led prayer, and

counseled people. In 1936, he married Paula la Varpit; the couple had three children.

The Japanese occupied New Britain during World War II and imprisoned missionaries in concentration camps. Peter, left in charge of the Catholics of his area, zealously carried out his duties, even building a bush church when the occupiers destroyed the village church. The Japanese forbade Christian worship and any religious gatherings and reinstituted polygamy, a practice Peter forcefully opposed. He was arrested for his resistance to polygamy and for his other religious work, subjected to a sham trial, and killed by lethal injection. The Japanese attempted to pass off his death as due to illness, but an eyewitness contradicted them. Peter was immediately hailed as a martyr. Feast: July 17.

Toussaint, Ven. Pierre

(c. 1778-1853. B. in Haiti; d. in New York City.) Toussaint was a slave for the Berard family in Haiti but left with them for New York City during the slave revolts of the 1790s. Soon after their arrival in New York, the Berards lost their property in Haiti's revolution, Monsieur Berard died, and his wife, Marie Elizabeth, was reduced to poverty. Toussaint, trained as a hairdresser, developed a clientele among the richest women of New York and became the sole support of the household. Marie

Elizabeth, who was devoted to the dignified, discreet Toussaint, gave him his freedom in 1807, and in 1811 he married Juliette Gaston, a fellow Haitian.

The Toussaints were childless but adopted a niece (her death at the age of fourteen plunged Toussaint into a lengthy depression). They also cared for abandoned boys, taking them into their home, educating them, and finding them jobs. Pierre gave away a substantial part of his considerable income to the poor, telling a friend who urged him to retire: "I have enough for myself but if I stop working I have not enough for others." Toussaint also cared for the sick, sometimes bringing them to his home and repeatedly, during one yellow fever epidemic, crossing the barricades of a deserted street to visit an abandoned victim.

For sixty years, he attended daily Mass at six in the morning at St. Peter's on Barclay Street. He frequently quoted the Beatitudes and *The Imitation of Christ* and delicately provided spiritual guidance to his wealthy clients, urging them to pray and submit their anxieties to God. He was "...full in the faith of his church," a contemporary said, "liberal, enlightened and always acting from the principle that God is our common Father and mankind our brethren." Toussaint never recovered from the death of Juliette in 1851, and died on June 30, two years later. His last words

were "God is with me" and then, when asked if he wanted anything, "Nothing on earth." He is buried in a crypt behind the main altar at St. Patrick's Cathedral in New York City.

Tsuji, Bd. Thomas

(1571-1627. B. at Sonogi, Kyushu, Japan; d. at Nagasaki.) Tsuji was a Jesuit with a reputation as an effective preacher. He left for Macao when Catholic priests were expelled from Japan during one of the many persecutions that swept the country during the seventeenth century. After four years, Tsuji returned, disguised as a merchant. He ministered in secret but soon felt the strain, particularly as so many of his colleagues went to their deaths. Afraid he would betray the faith if arrested, he asked to be freed from his vows.

The necessary permission took a long time in arriving and by the time it did, Tsuji had changed his mind. The Jesuits were willing to readmit him, and after six years of probation, during which he ministered with great courage, they received him back into the order. Shortly after, he was celebrating Mass at the home of Louis Maki and his son John when soldiers raided the house and arrested the three. Tsuji's family begged him to deny the faith but he refused. Imprisoned for thirteen months, he and the Makis were finally burned at the stake. Feast: September 7 (also, with the Martyrs of Japan, February 6).

Turibius of Mogrovejo, St.

(1538-1606. B. at Mayorga, Spain; d. at Santa Clara, Peru.) Turibius taught law at the University of Salamanca and was chief judge of the Inquisition at Granada. The king appointed him archbishop of Lima, Peru (Spanish colonial territory), in 1580, even though Turibius was still a layman. He was ordained, consecrated as bishop, and arrived in his vast diocese in 1581.

His first visitation took seven years due to the terrain, lack of roads, and sheer size—eighteen thousand square miles—of his diocese. He found the church in disarray, with many clergy living scandalous lives. Large numbers of baptized Indians had no knowledge of their faith. In spite of opposition, Turibius instituted many reforms. He insisted, for example, that all parish priests learn the Indian languages so that they could effectively teach the faith and hear confessions. He also oversaw the production of a catechism in native languages.

For twenty-four years, Turibius worked tirelessly to rebuild the church. He summoned councils and visited and stayed with Indians in areas so remote that "no prelate or visitor had ever come." He went without food and sleep on his difficult journeys, refused to accept gifts, and generously dispensed alms. Turibius became ill and died peacefully on Holy Thursday in Santa Clara while on one of his pastoral journeys. He is the patron saint of Peru. Feast: March 23.

Uganda, Martyrs of, Sts.

(D. 1886 at Namugongo and else-where.) Joseph Mkasa and Charles Lwanga are the best known of the Catholic martyrs who died during the persecution initiated by Mwanga, king of the Baganda.

Joseph Mkasa was the chief steward of the court and the leader of the Catholic community. He rebuked Mwanga for his murder of an Anglican missionary and his companions and for his repeated attempts to force sexual favors from the young pages at his court. In retaliation, Mwanga speared Joseph and then had him beheaded. Charles Lwanga took Joseph's place, continued instructing the Catholics, and kept the boys and young men safe. After a few months, Mwanga rounded up the pages, ordering the execution of all who were Christian. Lwanga was the oldest and Kizito, only thirteen, the youngest. An eyewitness remembered Kizito "laughing and chattering" as the men and boys trekked to the place of execution at Namugongo on Lake Victoria.

Three boys were killed on the way and the rest were imprisoned for a week while forced to build a huge pyre. Charles Lwanga died first by slow fire, and then the rest were wrapped in reed mats and stacked on the pyre. "We have killed many people," one of the executioners said, "but never such as these.... There was not a sigh, not even an angry word. All we heard was a soft murmur on their lips. They prayed until they died."

Other Catholics who died in the general persecution included Matthias Murumba, a judge, Andrew Kaggwa, a chief, and Denis Sebuggwawo, a catechist. Of the group executed at Namugongo, thirteen were Catholics, eleven were Protestants, and seven or eight had Christian sympathies but were unbaptized. Pope Paul VI canonized the Catholic martyrs of Uganda—in all, there were twenty-two, including others killed separately—in 1964. Feast: June 3.

Valencia, Bd. Rafael Guízar

(1878-1938. B. at Cotija, Mexico; d. at Mexico City.) Valencia, ordained a priest in 1901, often said, "I will give my life for the salvation of souls." This was more than a pious comment in the anticlerical atmosphere of revolutionary Mexico. Determined to counter the anti-Catholic propaganda of the revolutionary press, he started a print shop and published the Catholic paper *La Nacion*. Persecution forced him to move to Mexico City, where he disguised himself as a junk dealer and ministered in secret until Mexican courts sentenced him to death in absentia. He fled to the United States and Cuba but returned to Mexico when the immediate threat passed.

Valencia was appointed bishop of Vera Cruz in 1919 and set about evangelizing his diocese, writing a catechism to help in the education of the people, and rebuilding the long-closed seminary. "A bishop can do without a mitre, crosier and ... cathedral ... but never without a seminary because the future of his diocese depends on the seminary," he said. When persecution intensified, the government confiscated the seminary building, but the enterprise continued to operate secretly in Mexico City. The bishop ministered heroically throughout this period, giving away his pectoral cross, ring, clothes, and shoes to the needy. In tribute, he was known as "the bishop of the poor." He carried out these personal deprivations in spite of his own seriously ill health.

He was again forced into exile but stayed in touch with his diocese through correspondence until able to return. He devoted his last years to preaching popular missions, teaching religious education, and caring for the sick. He died on June 6, 1938, and was beatified by Pope John Paul II in 1995. Feast: June 6.

Vaz, Bd. Joseph

(1651-1711. B. at Sencoale, India; d. at Kandy, Sri Lanka.) Vaz was born to Catholics of the Brahmin caste and ordained a priest in 1676. He joined three other priests intent on an ascetic life, and the group modeled itself on the Oratorians, the congregation of St. Philip Neri. They elected Vaz as superior. He resigned after six months in order to pursue his dream to minister to persecuted Catholics in Ceylon (now Sri Lanka). Under Dutch control, that country proscribed Catholicism.

Joseph and a family servant, John, dressed as poor laborers and went barefoot. So disguised, they were able to slip into Sri Lanka, where they slept in the open, begged for food, and nearly died of dysentery. Joseph succeeded in identifying Catholic families by wearing a rosary around his neck as he begged. After two years, the Dutch intensified their anti-Catholic measures and Joseph escaped into the interior to the Buddhist kingdom of Kandy. He won the respect of the Buddhists and was allowed to bring Oratorian priests into the kingdom to minister to Catholics there.

Joseph ate sparingly, slept on the ground, and was revered as a holy man by Buddhists and Catholics alike. He is mentioned in a Buddhist chronicle now held at the British Museum for his heroic work among the sick during a smallpox epidemic. He restored Catholicism to Sri Lanka and died after ministering there for twenty-five years. Feast: January 16.

Venard, St. Theophane

(1829-1861. B. near Poitiers; d. at Hanoi, Vietnam.) Venard was a French missionary to Vietnam, revered by St. Thérèse of Lisieux who sought to imitate him by volunteering (unsuccessfully) for the missions.

He entered the Society for Foreign Missions in Paris and was ordained in 1852. In 1854, he arrived in Tonkin, Vietnam, during an outbreak of persecution. There was still an active missionary presence there, but over the next two-and-a-half years Venard suffered from asthma, typhoid, and tuberculosis and was unable to minister effectively. During his recovery, further persecution forced him to flee to Hoang-Nguyen, where he served as district head of missions. When persecution reached there, he went into hiding. "How would you like to be with us?" he wrote to a friend. "Three [missionaries] ... lying side-by-side, day and night, in a space of about two yards square. The only light we have comes through three little holes.... These are punched through the mud wall." In spite of these conditions, he translated the New Testament into Vietnamese.

The authorities captured him in 1860 and placed him in a wooden cage, where he remained until his execution. Taken to Hanoi for interrogation, he refused to trample on a cross, and after two months was beheaded for his Christian faith. Letters he wrote after his arrest detail the kind treatment he received from his captors, who evidently regretted what the law compelled them to do. He met his death with composure: "We are all flowers planted on this earth, which God picks in his time, some earlier, some later."
Feast: February 2.

Versiglia, Bd. Aloysius (1873-1930. B. in Oliva Gessi, Italy; d. near Lin Kong How, China.) **Caravario, Bd. Callistus** (1903-1930. B. at Cuorgne, Italy; d. near Lin Kong How, China.) Versiglia was a devout and good-natured child who wanted to be a veterinarian, not a priest as others predicted. However, he attended St. John Bosco's school in Turin, was attracted there to the missionary life, and entered the Salesian order. He led the first Salesian mission to China, arriving in Macao in 1906. Versiglia opened an orphanage and persevered through civil wars, pirate attacks, an outbreak of plague, and misunderstanding from within his own order. He was named bishop of the Shiu Chow region in 1920.

Caravario was a particularly mature and enthusiastic seminarian whose example encouraged other boys to enter the Salesians. He joined the mission in China in 1924, was ordained there in 1929, and in 1930 accompanied Bishop Versiglia on a pastoral visit to Linchow. Others in the group, which was traveling by boat, included several laymen and three young women, one of whom was returning home to tell her parents she was entering the convent.

Pirates attacked the boat, demanded money, and attempted to seize the women. When the priests came to their rescue, the pirates savagely beat them.

All were captured and herded into a bamboo thicket. The priests quietly made their final confessions to one another, and then the bishop, seeing the women seated at a distance, winked and raised his eyes to heaven to give them courage. The pirates led the bishop and Caravario, deeper into the woods, saying they were going to kill them because they belonged to a hated foreign religion. The bishop asked them to spare Caravario but the pirates shot them both as they knelt in prayer. Government soldiers rescued the women several days later. Feast: February 25.

Veuster, Bd. Damien de: *see Damien.*

Vianney, St. John (1786-1859. B. at Dardilly, France; d. at Ars.) Vianney's family, impoverished farmers, remained loyal to the church during the French Revolution. When Vianney turned twenty, he began to study for the priesthood. He had had little formal education up to this point, however, and proved a poor student, due to his inability to master Latin. A summons to military service interrupted his schooling, but he deserted the army through a series of apparent misadventures, hid for fourteen months, and was pardoned during Napoleon's general amnesty of 1810. He returned to his studies and, in spite of his dismal academic performance, was ordained in 1815 because he was "a model of goodness."

In 1818, John was assigned parish priest of Ars, a depressing backwater of about 250 people. He remained there for forty-one years, exercising a remarkable ministry that eventually drew thousands of pilgrims a month to Ars in search of spiritual direction. At first, he met with resistance from his parishioners, but he personally visited each one, started religion classes for the children, insisted on Sunday observance, closed the taverns, preached simply but forcefully against sin, and practiced severe penance. Through unremitting toil and personal holiness, he gradually transformed the village. As his reputation spread, he spent sixteen hours a day in the confessional to accommodate the throng of penitents, often displaying supernatural knowledge of people's inner lives.

Worn out by the demands and seeking a more contemplative life, John ran away from the village three times, but each time his parishioners persuaded him to return. He was made an honorary canon but sold the robes of office and gave the money to the poor. He resisted all other honors saying, "What if, when death comes and I present myself with these baubles, God were to say to me: 'Begone! You've had your reward.'?" Vianney, who is also known by his title, the Curé of Ars, died at the age of seventy-three. He is the patron saint of parish priests. Feast: August 4.

Vicuna, Bd. Laura

(1891-1904. B. at Santiago, Chile; d. at Junin, Argentine.) Laura's father, a soldier, died when Laura was three, and her mother, Mercedes, moved with her children to the frontier town of Las Lajas. Here, Mercedes became the mistress of Manuel Mora, a rancher.

When Laura was eight, she attended the Salesian mission school as a boarder. Home on vacations, she became the target of Mora's sexual advances, which she successfully resisted. Her mother intervened on her behalf but Mora, when drunk, persisted. Angered by Laura's resistance, he refused to pay her tuition at school, but the sisters took her in for free, noting her piety and courage.

In 1902, Laura, with the permission of her confessor, offered her life to God for her mother's conversion. About a year later, she became ill and returned to the ranch, where Mora threatened her once again. When she fled with her mother, he followed and demanded that the family return with him. Laura attempted to run from Mora, but he caught her and whipped and kicked her. When bystanders intervened, he threw her down and ran away. Laura died

about ten days later. Shortly after, her mother returned to the faith.
Feast: January 22.

Vincent de Paul, St.

(c. 1580-1660. B. at Pouy, France; d. at Paris.) Vincent was ordained a priest at the age of twenty, young even by the relaxed standards of the day. He was not a particularly impressive cleric, running up debts and trying to make his way in society. After about ten years, he apparently experienced a conversion that led him to renounce ambition and wholeheartedly embrace his vocation.

From 1613 to 1625 he served as tutor to the children of Philip de Gondi, Count of Joigny. In this and other ministry, he combined an apostolate among the well-to-do with an intense devotion to the poor and oppressed. He was the chaplain to galley slaves and served neglected country people, abandoned children, and victims of war. To all in need he responded with generosity. He organized the laity into parish confraternities to help him in this work.

In 1625 Vincent founded the Congregation of the Mission (the Vincentians), an order of priests dedicated to the training of the clergy and to missionary work, especially in country districts. "There is nothing so grand as a good priest," he said, and his work helped to transform the badly deteriorated French priesthood. He actively opposed the flourishing Jansenist heresy with its harsh and rigorous view of God and humanity. In 1633, he founded the Sisters of Charity with St. Louise de Marillac.

Vincent was legendary in his own lifetime, drawing all he met into the orbit of his love and charisma. This was so even though he had, he said, "a caustic temper," and had to keep in check his "black and boiling moods." Two hundred years after de Paul's death, Bd. Frederick Ozanam founded the St. Vincent de Paul Society, naming the charitable organization in his honor.
Feast: September 27.

Walburga, St.

(D. 779. B. at Wessex, England; d. at Heidenheim, Germany.) Walburga was a nun in England and the niece of St. Boniface, the great missionary to Germany. When Boniface called for nuns to establish a convent there, she went with others to Tauberbischofsheim in 750. She studied and practiced medicine for two years and then joined her brother, St. Winnibald, at his double monastery at Heidenheim. He governed the monks and she the nuns until his death in 761. She then ruled both men and women. Her memory thrives today primarily due to a fluid with curative properties that flows from the rock where her relics are enshrined. To the present time, healings are ascribed to what has become known as St. Walburga's oil. Feast: February 25.

Ybarra de Villalonga, Bd. Raphaela

(1843-1900. B. d. at Bilbao, Spain) Raphaela was born to a wealthy industrial family and married at eighteen. She and her husband had seven children and in 1875 adopted the five children of her recently deceased sister. Ten years later, with her husband's consent, Raphaela took vows of poverty, chastity, and obedience and gradually developed a broader apostolic ministry. She started a food kitchen where she served about seventy young people every day, and opened a shelter for young women, a center for unmarried mothers, and another for young working women. She also founded an orphanage for girls and began a congregation, the Institute of the Guardian Angels, to care for them.

Her husband died in 1898, and when a daughter-in-law also died, she put aside her plans to enter her own congregation in order to care for her six grandchildren. She died of stomach cancer in 1900, having provided practical, compassionate care for thousands while maintaining an intense spiritual life. Feast: February 23.

Youville, St. Marie Marguerite d'

(1701-1771; B. at Varennes, Canada; d. at Montreal.) At twenty-nine, Marguerite was a widow with two children, no means of support, and an enormous debt left by her husband. In eight years of marriage, she had endured the deaths of four of her children, life with an antagonistic mother-in-law, and an unhappy union with the shiftless Francois. His illegal business—trading liquor for furs offered by Native Americans—also left the family with a bad reputation. Sustained by profound faith in God as a loving Father, Marguerite nursed her husband through his final illness, opened a store, paid off her debts, and began to assist the poor. She also raised her two sons, who both became priests.

Marguerite volunteered at Montreal's hospital for the needy. She bathed the sick, cleaned their rooms, and mended their clothes. She also begged on behalf of the poor, raised money to pay for the burial of executed criminals, and lived with the taunts of those who despised her late husband and, by extension, Marguerite. In 1737, three women joined her in her work, and this is regarded as the birth of the Sisters of Charity of Montreal, known as the Grey Nuns. Marguerite's life was one of constant trial—the sisters' first house burned down, they were evicted from another, and their hospital later burned—but she had a remarkable confidence in God: "God has a way of comforting those who depend on him no matter what happens." Feast: December 23.

Z

Zita, St.

(1218-1278. B. in Monte Sagrati, Italy; d. in Lucca). Zita is the primary patron saint of domestic servants. She joined the household staff of Pagano de Fatinelli in Lucca at the age of twelve and served there the remaining forty-eight years of her life. Initially, her fellow servants regarded her hard work, piety, almsgiving, and disdain for coarse conversation as a reproach to their own ways. They managed to stir up her employers against her, but eventually she won the entire household over through her patience and humility. She took care of the Fatinelli children, became housekeeper, and was the only person who could deal with her master's terrible temper.

In her later years the family relieved her of her domestic duties, and she spent the rest of her life visiting the sick, the poor, and prisoners, especially those condemned to death. For these, she spent hours in prayer. She was one of the most popular saints of medieval Europe. Feast: April 27.

Calendar of Feast Days

January

1. Odilo
2. Basil; Del Bufalo; Tomasi
4. Seton
5. Neumann
6. Bessette; Raphaela
12. Bourgeoys; Kitbamrung; Pucci
14. Macrina
16. Vaz
17. Anthony of Egypt
20. Tansi
22. Pallotti; Vicuna
24. Francis de Sales
26. Kozal; Paula; Timothy; Titus
27. Matulaitis-Matulewicz
28. Thomas Aquinas
31. Bosco; Marcella

February

1. Brigid
2. Lestonnac; Libermann; Venard
4. Britto
6. Miki
7. Mary of Providence
8. Bakhita
9. Cordero Munoz
10. Scholastica; Stepinac
18. Angelico
21. Southwell
22. Margaret of Cortona
23. Polycarp; Ybarra
25. Versiglia/Caravario; Walburga
27. Line; Possenti

March

3. Drexel; Philip
7. Perpetua/Felicity
8. John of God;
9. Frances of Rome; Savio
10. Milleret
12. Maximilian; Orione; Tchang Ta-Pong
15. Marillac
17. Patrick
19. Callo; Joseph
21. Nicholas of Flue
22. Owen
23. Oriol; Turibius of Mogrovejo
25. Clitherow; Januszewski
30. Kafka

April

1. Apor
2. Calungsod
4. Benedict the Moor
6. Morosini; Rua
8. Billiart
12. Moscati; Teresa of Jesus
13. Margaret of Metola
15. Bus; Damien
16. Labre; Soubirous (Bernadette)
17. Tekawitha
18. Mary of the Incarnation
19. Bernard the Penitent
23. Sagheddu
24. Menni; Pelletier
25. Mark
26. Radbert
27. Zita

28. Molla
29. Catherine of Siena
30. Cottolengo; Guyart; Kowalska

May

1. Laziosi; Pampuri
2. Athanasius; James the Less
3. Philip
9. Pachomius
11. Girolamo
13. Fournet
14. Mandic; Mazzarello
16. Bobola; Brendan
18. Felix of Cantalice; Potaman
19. Ivo of Brittany
22. Rita of Cascia
25. Bede; MacKillop
26. Neri
27. Augustine of Canterbury;
    Julius the Veteran
28. Pole
30. Diego; Joan of Arc

June

1. Scalabrini
2. Blandina
3. John XXIII; Uganda (martyrs of)
5. Boniface
6. Valencia
9. Anchieta; Taigi
12. Cebula; Leszczewicz/Kaszyra
13. Anthony of Padua
21. Gonzaga
22. More
23. Cafasso
26. Escrivá

28. Irenaeus of Lyons
29. Paul; Peter

July

1. Plunkett
3. Thomas
4. Elizabeth of Portugal; Frassati
6. Goretti
9. Giuliani
11. Benedict
13. Barbieri
14. Camillus; Solano
15. Javouhey
17. Compiegne (martyrs of); To Rot
22. Mary Magdalen; Prat y Prat
24. Guadalajara (martyrs of)
25. James the Great
26. Andrew (of Vietnam); Brandsma
31. Ignatius of Loyola

August

1. Eymard; Liguori; Stella and
   Companions
2. Malla
4. Vianney (Curé of Ars)
8. Dominic
9. Stein
10. Lawrence
11. Clare; Favre
13. Benildua; Gapp; Neururer;
    Radegund
14. Kolbe
15. Alipius; Bakanja
18. Helen
20. Bernard of Clairvaux
21. Rasoamanarivo

23. Rose of Lima
24. Bartholomew
25. Calasanz; Louis IX
26. Mary of Jesus Crucified
27. Barberi; Monica
28. Augustine of Hippo;
    Mas y de Vedruna; Serra
29. Mary of the Cross

September

3. Gregory the Great
7. Tsuji
8. Ozanam
9. Claver
11. Perboyre
13. Chrysostom
15. Catherine of Genoa; Schwartz
17. Bellarmine
18. Joseph of Cupertino
20. Imbert; Kim Hyo-im;
    Kim Hyo-ju; Kim Tae-gon
21. Matthew
23. Pius of Pietrelcina (Padre Pio)
27. Vincent de Paul
28. Lioba
29. Gabriel; Michael; Raphael
30. Jerome

October

1. Thérèse of Lisieux
3. Guerin
4. Francis of Assisi; Seelos
9. Tejedor
15. Teresa of Avila
16. Alacoque
17. Ignatius of Antioch

18. Luke
19. Brébeuf; Chabanel; Daniel;
    Garnier; Goupil; Jogues; Lalande;
    Lalemant
20. Boscardin; Soubiran
22. Giaccardo
24. Guanella
25. Owen
27. Ferrini
28. Jude; Simon
30. Rodriguez

November

1. Mayer
3. Martin de Porres
5. Lichtenberg
8. Elizabeth of the Trinity
11. Bossilkov; Martin of Tours
13. Pietrantoni
15. Albert the Great; Kalinowski
16. Margaret of Scotland
17. Elizabeth of Hungary;
    Gonzales (martyrs of Paraguay);
    Hilda of Whitby
18. Duchesne; Odo; Pro
21. Siedliska
23. Clement of Rome
28. Labouré
30. Andrew

December

1. Campion; Nengapeta
3. Francis Xavier
5. Rinaldi; Stensen
6. Nicholas
7. Ambrose

13. Grassi
14. Buonaccorsi; John of the Cross
15. Schervier
17. Olympias
22. Cabrini
23. Youville
24. Cerioli; Makhlouf
26. Stephen
27. Fabiola; John
29. Becket

Newly beatified individuals (feast days not yet available):
Al-Hardini; Biernacka; Cantarero; David; Diez y Bustos de Molina; Frackowiak; Kowalski; Leisner; Lewoniuk and Companions; Liguda; Marto; Mzyk; Siphong and Companions

Bibliography

Alacoque, Margaret Mary. *The Autobiography of St. Margaret Mary.* Sisters of the Visitation, trans. Rockford, Ill.: Tan, 1986.

St. Anthony's Guild. *The Anthonian.* Patterson, N. J.: St. Anthony's Guild, 1972, vol 47, 2nd, 3rd quarter.

Attwater, Donald, with Catherine Rachel John. *The Penguin Dictionary of Saints.* New York: Penguin, 1965.

Augustine. *St. Augustine: Confessions.* R.S. Pine-Coffin, trans. Hardmonsworth, England: Penguin, 1961.

Ball, Ann. *Faces of Holiness.* Huntington, Ind. Our Sunday Visitor, 1998.

___. *Modern Saints: Their Lives and Faces, vols. 1 & 2.* Rockford, Ill.: Tan, 1983 and 1990.

Benedict, St. *The Rule of St. Benedict.* Translated by Anthony Meisel and M.L. del Mastro. New York: Doubleday, 1975.

Bernoville, Gaetan. *Saint Mary Euphrasia Pelletier.* Westminster, Md.: Newman, 1959.

Bosco, John. *Life of Blessed Dominic Savio.* Roderic Bright, ed. Paterson, N.J.: Salesiania, 1950.

Bunson, Matthew, et al. *John Paul II's Book of Saints.* Huntington, Ind.: Our Sunday Visitor, 1999.

Burns, Paul, revised by. *Butler's Lives of the Saints, January.* Collegeville, Minn.: Liturgical Press, 1995.

___. Butler's Lives of the Saints, February. Collegeville, Minn.: Liturgical Press, 1998.

Camillus, Father. *St. Gabriel, Passionist.* New York: Catholic Book, 1956.

Caraman, Philip, ed. *Saints and Ourselves: Personal Portraits of Favorite Saints by 24 Outstanding Catholics.* New York: Doubleday, 1958.

___. *Saints and Ourselves: A Selection of Saints Lives.* © Philip Caraman, 1958.

Collesei, Gabriella. *Thecla: A Prophetic Woman.* Boston: St. Paul, 1994.

Connolly, Francis X. *Wisdom of the Saints.* New York: Pocket Books, 1963.

Cross, F.L., and E.A. Livingstone, eds. *Oxford Dictionary of the Christian Church.* Oxford, England: Oxford Univ. Press, 1983.

Cumming, John, revised by. *Butler's Lives of the Saints, August.* Collegeville: Minn.: Liturgical Press, 1998.

Curtayne, Alice. *The Trial of Oliver Plunkett.* New York: Sheed and Ward, 1953.

Delaney, John J. *Dictionary of Saints.* New York: Doubleday, 1980.

DeNevi, Don and Noel F. Moholy. *Junipero Serra.* San Francisco: Harper and Row, 1985.

Doyle, Peter, revised by. *Butler's Lives of the Saints, April.* Collegeville, Minn.: Liturgical Press, 1999.

___. *Butler's Lives of the Saints, July.* Collegeville, Minn.: Liturgical Press, 2000.

___. *Butler's Lives of the Saints, October.* Collegeville, Minn. Liturgical Press, 1996.

Elliott, Lawrence. *I Will Be Called John.* New York: Reader's Digest Press, 1973.

Englebert, Omer. *Catherine Labouré and the Modern Apparitions of Our Lady.* Alaistair Guinan, trans. New York: Kenedy, 1959.

Eusebius. *The History of the Church.* Translated by G.A. Williamson. Baltimore, Md.: Penguin, 1965.

Farmer, David Hugh, revised by. *Butler's Lives of the Saints, May.* Collegeville, Minn.: Liturgical Press, 1996.

___. *The Oxford Dictionary of Saints.* Oxford, England: Oxford Univ. Press, 1992.

Felici, Icilio. *Father to the Immigrants.* New York: Kenedy, 1955.

Fornasari, Eugenio. *Blessed Timothy Giaccardo.* Translated by K.D. Whitehead. New York: Alba House, 1991.

Foucauld, Charles de. *Spiritual Autobiography of Charles de Foucauld.* Edited by Jean-Francois Six. New York: Kenedy, 1964.

Gaynor, John S. *The Life of St. Vincent Pallotti.* United States: Pallottine Fathers, 1962.

Gerard, John. *The Autobiography of a Hunted Priest.* Translated by Philip Caraman. New York: Doubleday, 1955.

Gorska, M. Teresa and M. Noela Wojtatowicz. *Blessed Martyrs of Nowogrodek: Sr. M. Stella and Companions.* Translated by M. Rita Kathryn Sperka. Chicago: Sisters of the Holy Family of Nazareth, 2000.

Guerin, Mother Theodore. *Journals and Letters.* St.-Mary-of-the-Woods, Ind.: Sisters of Providence, 1937.

Gumbley, Walter. *Parish Priests Among the Saints.* Freeport, New York: Books for Libraries Press, 1947.

Hamell, Patrick J. *Handbook of Patrology.* New York: Alba House, 1968.

Hanley, Boniface. *No Strangers to Violence, No Strangers to Love.* Notre Dame, Ind.: Ave Maria, 1983.

___. *Ten Christians.* Notre Dame, Ind.: Ave Maria, 1979.

___. *With Minds of Their Own.* Notre Dame, Ind.: Ave Maria, 1991.

___. *The Anthonian.* Paterson, N.J.: St. Anthony's Guild. Vol. 49, 1st quarter (1975); vol. 50, 1st, 2nd quarter (1976); vol. 58, 1st quarter (1984); vol. 61, 1st, 3rd, 4th quarter (1987).

John of the Cross. *John of the Cross: Selected Writings.* Edited by Kieran Kavanaugh. New York: Paulist, 1987.

Johnston, Francis. *The Wonder of Guadalupe.* Rockford, Ill.: Tan, 1981.

Jones, Kathleen, revised by. *Butler's Lives of the Saints, June.* Collegeville, Minn.: Liturgical Press, 1997.

Kelly, J.N.D. *Oxford Dictionary of Popes.* Oxford, England: Oxford Univ. Press, 1986.

Kittler, Glenn. *The Woman God Loved: The Life of Blessed Anne-Marie Javouhey.* New York: Hanover House, 1959.

LaChance, Stephen. "Marian Martyrs." Thirteenth of the Month Club, Oct. 1999.

Largent, Father. *St. Jerome.* Translated by Hester Davenport. New York: Benziger, 1913.

Lapomarda, Vincent A. "Five Heroic Catholics of the Holocaust," Annals of St. Anthony's Shrine, 1987. Reprinted on web site: www.holycross.edu under Hiatt Holocaust Collection.

Likoudis, Paul. *Saints and the Struggle for a Christian Society.* Buffalo, New York: Gallagher, 1986.

Luce, Clare Booth, ed. *Saints for Now.* New York: Sheed and Ward, 1952.

MacBride, Alfred. *Saints Are People.* Dubuque, Ia. Brown, 1981.

Maynard, Theodore. *Through My Gift: The Life of Frances Schervier.* New York: Kenedy, 1951.

Michalenko, Sophia. *Mercy My Mission: Life of Sister Faustina H. Kowalska.* Stockbridge, Mass.: Marian, 1995.

Milcent, Paul. *Jeanne Jugan: Humble So As to Love More.* Translated by Alan Neame. London: Darton, Longman, Todd, 1980.

Mitchell, Penny Blaker. *Mother Theodore Guerin: A Woman for Our Time.* St. Mary-of-the-Woods, Ind.: Sisters of Providence, 1998.

Molinari, Paul. *Bl. Rupert Mayer.* Dublin: Irish Messenger Publications, 1988.

Murphy, Francis J. *Pere Jacques: Resplendent in Victory.* Washington, D.C.: ICS Publications, 1998.

Murville, M.N.L. Couve de. *Slave from Haiti: a Saint for New York? The Life of Pierre Toussaint.* London: CTS Publications, 1995.

O'Brien, Anthony H. *Archbishop Stepinac: The Man and His Case.* Westminister, Md.: Newman Bookshop, 1947.

O'Brien, Felicity. *Saints in the Making.* Dublin: Veritas, 1988.

O'Driscoll, David. *Martyr of Service and Charity: A Life of Baron Vilmos Apor.* London: Incorporated Catholic Truth Society, 1993.

Palsson, Erik Kennet. *Niels Stensen: Scientist and Saint.* Translated by M.N.L. Couve de Murville. Dublin: Veritas, 1988.

Pascucci, Philip J. *A Spiritual Father: A Brief Account of the Life of Bd. Philip Rinaldi.* New Rochelle, New York: Salesian Missions, 1998.

Praskiewicz, Szczepan. *St. Raphael Kalinowski: An Introduction to His Life and Spirituality.* Translated by Thomas Coonan, et al. Washington, D.C.: ICS Publications, 1998.

Prestige, G.L. *Fathers and Heretics.* London: S.P.C.K., 1940.

Rodrigues, Teresa, Revised by. *Butler's Lives of the Saints, March.* Collegeville, Minn.: Liturgical Press, 1999.

Ruffin, C. Bernard. *Padre Pio: The True Story*. Huntington, Ind.: Our Sunday Visitor, 1991.

Sawyer, Hannah Lee. *Memoir of Pierre Toussaint*. Sunbury, Penn.: Western Hemisphere Cultural Soc., 1992.

Sheed, F.J., ed. *Saints Are Not Sad*. New York: Sheed and Ward, 1949.

Sheridan, John V. *Saints in Time of Turmoil*. New York: Paulist, 1977.

Staniforth, Maxwell, trans. *Early Christian Writings: The Apostolic Fathers*. Baltimore, Md.: Penguin, 1968.

Strzalkowska, Frances. *Blessed Mary of Jesus the Good Shepherd: Frances Siedliska*. Translated by S.M. Jolanta Basiewicz et al. Rome: Romagrafik Printers, 1989.

Teresia de Spiritu Sancto. *Edith Stein*. New York: Sheed and Ward, 1952.

Thomas, Sarah Fawcett, revised by. *Butler's Lives of the Saints, September*. Collegeville, Minn.: Liturgical Press, 2000.

___. *Butler's Lives of the Saints, November*. Collegeville, Minn.: Liturgical Press, 1997.

Thurston, Herbert J. and Donald Attwater, ed. *Butler's Lives of the Saints, vols. 1, 2, 3, 4*. Allen, Tex.: Thomas More, 1956.

Trochu, Francis. *The Curé d'Ars: St. John Vianney*. London: Burns, Oates & Washbourne, 1927.

Van Kaam, Adrian. *A Light to the Gentiles: The Life Story of Venerable Francis Libermann*. Milwaukee, Wis.: Bruce, 1959.

Walsh, James. *A Modern Martyr: A Biography of Blessed Theophane Venard*. New York: McMullen, 1952.

Ward, Maisie. *Saints Who Made History: The First Five Centuries*. New York: Sheed and Ward, 1959.

Waugh, Evelyn. *Edmund Campion.* Oxford, England: Oxford Univ. Press, 1980.

Webb, J.F., trans. *Lives of the Saints.* Baltimore, Md.: Penguin, 1965.

White, Dorothy, trans. *Pope John XXIII: Journal of a Soul.* New York: New American Library, 1965.

Wynne, John J. *Jesuit Martyrs of North America.* Auriesville, New York: Ossernenon Press, 1925.

Internet Sites

www.ewtn.net   Saints, including recently beatified/canonized

www.beafriar.com   Franciscan Capuchin saints

www.oblates.org/center   Saints Francis de Sales and Jane de Chantal

www.seelos.org   Bd. Francis Seelos

www.svd-ca.com/   Society of the Divine Word, saints/martyrs

www.bettnet.com/Frassati/

www.katolrkus.hu/hun-saints/apor_en.html

General Index

A guide to occupations, ministries, countries of ministry/origin and notable personal circumstances

Addiction: Alipius; Talbot

African Heritage: Alipius; Anthony of Egypt; Athanasius; Augustine; Bakanja; Bakhita; Benedict the Moor; Monica; Nengapeta; Perpetua and Felicity; Potamon; Tansi; Uganda, Martyrs of.

Americas

North (including missionaries to): Bourgeoys; Brébeuf; Cabrini; Casey; Chabanel; Daniel; Day; Drexel; Duchesne; Garnier; Geurin; Guyart; Jogues; Lalande; Lalemant; Neumann; Seelos; Serra; Seton; Tekawitha; Toussaint

South: (including missionaries to): Anchieta; Gonzales; Namuncura; Porres; Rose of Lima; Teresa of Jesus of the Andes; Turibius; Vicuna

Mexico: Diego; Pro; Valencia;

Art: Angelico

Australia: MacKillop

Carpentry: Joseph; Owen

China (including missionaries to): Perboyre; Tchang Ta-Pong; Versiglia and Caravario

Criminal/Anti-Social Behavior: Bernard the Penitent; Buonaccorsi; Laziosi

Communists, Persecution under: Bossilkov; Stepinac

Depression, Failure or Spiritual Dryness: Catherine of Genoa; Chabanel; Chantal; Libermann; Liguori; Rodriguez; Thérèse of Lisiuex

Doctors (see Medical Work)

Doctrinal Controversy/Doctrinal Development: Albert the Great; Ambrose; Athanasius; Augustine; Basil; Bellarmine; Ignatius of Antioch; Martin of Tours; Thomas Aquinas

Eastern Rite: Al-Hardini; Lewoniuk; Makhlouf; Mary of Jesus Crucified

Ecumenism: Apor; Favre; John XXIII; Sagheddu

Eucharist, Devotion to/Doctrinal Development: Eymard; Radbert

Exiles: Chrysostom; Kalinowski

Family Life

Difficult: Alacoque; Boscardin; Catherine of Genoa; Margaret of Cortona; Rita of Cascia

Grandmother, Influence of: Macrina the Elder

Step-father, Influence of: Oriol

Gypsy: Malla

Hairdresser: Toussaint

Haitian Heritage: Toussaint

Healing Ministry: Bessette; Casey; Seelos

Homeless: Labre; Day (ministry to)

Incapacity, Mental/Physical: Albert the Great; Mas y de Vedruna; Orione

Lay Apostolate: Escriva de Balaguer; Frances de Sales; John XXIII; Pallotti; To Rot

Law: Alipius; Ferrini; Ivo of Brittany; Ligouri; Turibius

Lightening, Struck by: Grassi

Marian Apparitions: Alacoque; Diego; Labouré; Marto; Soubirous

Married: Catherine of Genoa; Cerioli; Chantal; Clitherow; Elizabeth of Hungary; Elizabeth of Portugal; Fabiola; Frances of Rome; Guyart; Helen; Joseph; Lestonnac; Louis IX; Margaret of Scotland; Marillac; Mary; Mary of the Incarnation; Mas y de Vedruna; Monica; More; Nicholas of Flue; Ozanam; Paula; Radegund; Rasoamanarivo; Rita of Cascia; Seton; Taigi; To Rot; Ybarra de Villalonga; Youville

Martyrs

Africa: Nengapeta; Uganda, Martyrs of

China: Perboyre; Tachang Ta Pong; Versiglia and Caravario

Communists, Under: Bossilkov

Early Church: Andrew (apostle); Blandina; Ignatius of Antioch; James the Great; Lawrence; Matthew; Paul; **Perpetua/Felicity and Companions;** Peter; Polycarp; Potamon; Stephen; Thomas; Timothy

Elderly: Boniface; Polycarp; Pole

England (Reformation): Campion; Clitherow; Line; More; Owen; Plunkett (Irish archbishop); Pole; Southwell

France (Revolution): Compiegne, Martyrs of

India: Britto

Japan: Miki; Tsuji

Korea: Imbert; Kim Hyo-Im; Kim Tae-gon

Mexico: Pro

North America: Brébeuf; Chabanel; Daniel; Garnier; Goupil; Jogues; Lalande; Lalemant

Phillipines (martyred at Guam): Calungsod

Poland: Britto (also, **Martyrs/World War II**)

South America: Gonzales

Spanish Civil War: Cantarero; David; Guadalajara, Martyrs of; Prat y Prat; Tejedor

Thailand: Kitbamrung; Siphong and Companions

Vietnam: Andrew; Venard

World War II (by nationality): Apor (Hungarian); Biernacka (Polish); Brandsma (Dutch); Callo (French); Cebula (Polish); Frackowiak (Polish); Gapp (German); Jacques of Jesus (French); Januszewski (Polish); Kafka (Austrian); Kolbe (Polish); Kowalski (Polish); Kozal (Polish); Leisner (German); Leszczewicz and Kaszyra (Polish); Lichtenberg

(German); Liguda (Polish); Mayer (German); Mzyk (Polish); Neururer (German); Stein (German); Stella and Companions (Died at Belarus); To Rot (New Guinean)

Virtue, for: Goretti; Morosini; Nengapeta

Medical Work: Camillus of Lellis; Cantarero; Cottolengo; Guanella; John of God; Jugan; Molla; Moscati; Pampuri; Pietrantoni; Stensen; Veuster; Schervier; Youville

Mexican Heritage: Diego; Pro; Valencia

Migrants: Scalabrini

Military: Camillus; Foucauld: Ignatius of Loyola; Julius the Veteran; Maximilian; Martin of Tours

Mystics: Catherine of Genoa; Catherine of Siena; Elizabeth of the Trinity; Giuliani; John of the Cross; Joseph of Cupertino; Kowalska; Pius of Pietrelcina (Padre Pio); Rose of Lima; Teresa of Avila

Nurses (see Medical Work)

Parish Priests: Oriol; Pucci; Vianney (Curé of Ars)

Persecution by Church or Fellow Religious: Calasanz; John of the Cross; Jugan; Lestonnac; Libermann; Liguori; Menni; Milleret; Pallotti; Raphaela; Soubiran

Preaching, Noted for: Ambrose; Anthony of Padua; Bossilkov; Chrysostom; Del Bufalo; Girolamo; Ligouri

Prisoners, Ministry to: Cafasso; Catherine of Siena; Schervier; Zita

Prostitutes, Ministry to: Pelletier; Schervier

Religious Education: Barbieri; Benildus; Bus; Gapp; Scalabrini; Valencia

Scholarship: Albert the Great; Anthony of Padua; Augustine; Bede; Bellarmine; Bernard of Clairvaux; Cordero-Munoz; Ferrini; Jerome; Thomas Aquinas; Tomasi

Servants: Zita

Slaves: Bakhita; Benedict the Moor; Claver (ministry to); Toussaint

Social Justice: Apor; Basil; Bosco; Cottolengo; Day; Guanella; Jacques of Jesus; Jaricot; Orione; Ozanam; Pallotti; Schwartz

Sri Lanka: Vaz

Teachers: Augustine; Benildus; Calasanz; Chabanel; Cordero-Munoz; Diez Y Bustos de Molinas; Ferrini; Ozanam

Teenagers (see Young Saints)

Vocation, Resistant to: Fournet; Rinaldi; Teresa of Avila

Young Saints/Candidates for **Canonization:** Frassati; Gonzaga; Joan of Arc; Marto; Namancura; Nengapeta; Perpetua and Felicity; Possenti; Sagheddu; Savio; Vicuna

Uniat (in communion with Rome): Al-Hardini; Lewoniuk; Makhlouf; Mary of Jesus Crucified